PROBLEMS AND SOLUTIONS IN THEORETICAL STATISTICS

PROBLEMS AND SOLUTIONS IN THEORETICAL STATISTICS

D.R. COX
Department of Mathematics,
Imperial College, London

D.V. HINKLEY
School of Statistics, University of Minnesota

LONDON   NEW YORK
CHAPMAN AND HALL

First published 1978
by Chapman and Hall Ltd
11 New Fetter Lane, London EC4P 4EE

Reprinted 1980, 1986

Published in the USA by
Chapman and Hall
29 West 35th Street, New York NY 10001

Printed in Great Britain at the
University Press, Cambridge

ISBN 0 412 15370 X

CONTENTS

Preface   page   vii

Chapter 1. Introduction
            Summary   1

Chapter 2. Some general concepts
            Summary   2
            Problems and solutions   3

Chapter 3. Pure significance tests
            Summary   19
            Problems and solutions   20

Chapter 4. Significance tests: simple null hypotheses
            Summary   35
            Problems and solutions   36

Chapter 5. Significance tests: composite null hypotheses
            Summary   53
            Problems and solutions   54

Chapter 6. Distribution-free and randomization tests
            Summary   67
            Problems and solutions   68

Chapter 7. Interval estimation
            Summary   82
            Problems and solutions   84

Chapter 8. Point estimation
            Summary   95
            Problems and solutions   97

Chapter 9. Asymptotic theory
            Summary   117
            Problems and solutions   119

Chapter 10.   Bayesian methods
              Summary   148
              Problems and solutions   149

Chapter 11.   Decision theory
              Summary   164
              Problems and solutions   165

References   176

Author Index   185

Subject Index   187

PREFACE

In our book *Theoretical Statistics* we gave about 150 *Further results and exercises* mostly intended to illustrate material of intrinsic interest that it was not possible to cover in the main text. In many cases the statements were based quite directly on recent papers.

The present book gives outline solutions and discussion of these problems. To make the book selfcontained we have preceded each set of problems by a brief summary of the main general ideas required. The collection of these summaries provides a rapid review of the theory of statistics. The book contains a substantial amount of general material not previously available in book form.

The detailed solution of special problems is a vital part of the study of any mathematical subject and we hope therefore that teachers and students of statistics especially at graduate level will find the problems and outline solutions helpful. In addition we hope that research workers in statistics interested in special problems will find the book an effective review of some useful theoretical ideas including the associated elementary mathematical techniques.

While the numbering and arrangement of the problems is the same as in *Theoretical Statistics*, we have rewritten a number of the problems, partly in order to make them selfcontained and partly for clarification and correction.

D.R. Cox
London

D.V. Hinkley
Twin Cities

June 1977

1 INTRODUCTION

Summary

The overwhelming majority of the formal theory of statistics is concerned with situations in which a probability model is given for a data vector y, representing it as the observed value of a random vector Y having unknown probability density $f_Y(y)$. This is often known except for a finite dimensional vector θ of unknown parameters; we then write $f_Y(y; \theta)$. By contrast a major aspect of applied statistical work is the choice of a suitable model.

The theory of statistics deals with the general ideas that are useful for answering questions about the unknown density. The book is based on an implicitly eclectic attitude, namely that a variety of approaches are required, depending on the nature of the specification. In fact the more detailed is the specification, the more clear-cut are the solutions and the less is the need for rather *ad hoc* criteria.

Chapter 2 deals with some general notions such as likelihood and sufficiency. The subsequent chapters deal with procedures in broadly increasing level of specification, starting in Chapter 3 with pure significance tests in which only a null hypothesis is specified, and ending in Chapter 11 with decision problems, in which a prior probability distribution for the unknown parameters is available, together with a list of possible decisions and an associated utility function.

As far as possible a standard notation is used. For the probability of an event A, we write $\mathrm{pr}(A)$; expectation, variance and covariance are denoted by $E(X)$, var (X) and cov (X, Y). The normal distribution of mean μ and variance σ^2 is written $N(\mu, \sigma^2)$ and the p-dimensional multivariate normal distribution of mean vector μ and covariance matrix Σ is written $MN_p(\mu, \Sigma)$. Sums of squares and mean squares connected with the linear model are written SS and MS respectively. We denote the standardized normal integral by $\Phi(.)$ and numerical constants by an asterisk; in particular k_α^*, defined by $\Phi(k_\alpha^*) = 1 - \alpha$, is the upper α point of the standardized normal distribution.

Abbreviations are kept to a minimum, although we do use the following quite frequently: i.i.d., independent and identically distributed; l.r., likelihood ratio; m.l., maximum likelihood; p.d.f., probability density function.

2 SOME GENERAL CONCEPTS

Summary

Suppose that a vector of observations y is represented by a random variable Y having a probability density function (p.d.f.) $f_Y(y; \theta)$ depending on a parameter θ. Then the likelihood lik $(\theta; y)$ is defined as $f_Y(y; \theta)$ and is considered for fixed y as a function of θ. When Y is a vector of independent components the log likelihood $l(\theta; y) = \log$ lik $(\theta; y)$ is a sum of contributions.

A statistic is a function $T = t(Y)$, in general a vector; the corresponding observed value is $t = t(y)$. A statistic S is sufficient for the above family of distributions if the conditional density of Y given $S = s$ does not depend on θ. Sometimes sufficiency is best proved by calculating the conditional density explicitly, but more commonly the Neyman factorization theorem is used: a necessary and sufficient condition that S is sufficient for θ is that there exist functions $m_1(s, \theta)$ and $m_2(y)$ such that for all θ

$$\text{lik } (\theta; y) = m_1(s, \theta) m_2(y). \tag{1}$$

So long as the model is assumed to be correct, there are compelling reasons for expecting the conclusions about θ to involve the data only through s; the additional information obtained from y corresponds to sampling a fixed distribution independent of θ. For assessing the adequacy of the model, the full observations y may be compared with the conditional distribution of Y given $S = s$.

We nearly always work with the minimal sufficient statistic, a function of all other sufficient statistics and providing the most concise summary of the data given the model. The minimal sufficient statistic can be obtained by assigning the same value to two sample points y and z if, and only if, they give proportional likelihood functions, $f_Y(y; \theta)/f_Y(z; \theta) = h(y, z)$ for all θ.

A sufficient statistic S is complete if, and only if, $E\{k(S); \theta\} = 0$ for all θ implies $k(s) = 0$, except for a set of values of s of probability zero; this property is mathematically important in some uniqueness considerations. Completeness implies minimal sufficiency.

An important special form arises when $Y_1, \ldots, Y_n$, the components of Y, are independent, Y_j having p.d.f.

$$\exp\{a(\theta)b_j(y_j) + c_j(\theta) + d_j(y_j)\}. \tag{2}$$

Then $\Sigma b_j(Y_j)$ is sufficient. A particular case is when the Y_j are identically distributed. Many standard distributions are special cases. (2) is the simplest example of the exponential family of distributions. A more general form, covering in particular vector parameters, has for Y_j the density

$$\exp\left\{\sum_{k=1}^{m} a_k(\theta)b_{jk}(y_j) + c_j(\theta) + d_j(y_j)\right\}. \tag{3}$$

If $m = q$, the dimensions of θ, (3) is the most general form of distribution for which the dimensions of the minimal sufficient statistic and the parameter are the same, subject to the range of the distribution not involving θ.

When parameter ϕ and single observation z are chosen so that (2) becomes

$$\exp\{-\phi z + c\dagger(\phi) + d\dagger(z)\} \tag{4}$$

the observation and parameter are said to be in natural form.

If $m > q$ there is the possibility that some components of the minimal sufficient statistic have fixed distributions not depending on θ; such component statistics are called ancillary. There are convincing reasons for making inferences conditionally on the observed value of any ancillary statistics.

The main broad approaches to using observations to study θ are:

(i) sampling theory, in which interpretation refers to probability behaviour under hypothetical repetitions;

(ii) pure likelihood theory, in which lik $(\theta; y)$ is used directly;

(iii) various forms of Bayesian theory, in which θ is regarded as corresponding to a random variable Θ having a known prior p.d.f. $f_\Theta(\theta)$ and in which interpretation depends on finding via Bayes's theorem the posterior distribution, namely the conditional p.d.f. of Θ given $Y = y$:

$$f_{\Theta|Y}(\theta|y) \propto f_\Theta(\theta)f_{Y|\Theta}(y|\theta);$$

(iv) decision theory in which in addition a list of possible actions to be taken is available and the consequences of a particular action can be measured for each θ.

Problems

2.1. Verify the factorization (1) of the likelihood for the particular normal-theory linear model representing linear regression through the origin. Obtain also from first principles the factorization for the two-way cross-classification, i.e. for random variables $Y_{jk}(j = 1, \ldots, m_1; k = 1, \ldots, m_2)$ with

$$E(Y_{jk}) = \mu + \alpha_j + \beta_k, \quad \Sigma\alpha_j = \Sigma\beta_k = 0.$$

Show that if the model is supplemented by a term $\gamma \alpha_j \beta_k$, where γ is unknown, no reduction of dimensionality by sufficiency is achieved.

Solution

The neatest starting point for investigating sufficiency is usually the log likelihood. If $Y_1, \ldots, Y_n$ are independently normally distributed with variance σ^2 and with $E(Y_j) = \beta x_j$, the log likelihood is, except for a constant,

$$-n \log \sigma - \Sigma(y_j - \beta x_j)^2/(2\sigma^2) = -n \log \sigma - \{\Sigma(y_j - \hat{\beta} x_j)^2 + (\hat{\beta} - \beta)^2 \Sigma x_j^2\}/(2\sigma^2),$$

where $\hat{\beta} = \Sigma x_j y_j/\Sigma x_j^2$. Thus the data enter only through $\hat{\beta}$ and $\text{ss}_{\text{res}} = \Sigma(y_j - \hat{\beta} x_j)^2$, the residual sum of squares, proving the required sufficiency, from a special case of the Neyman factorization theorem, equation (1) of the Summary. If σ^2 is known, the sufficient statistic reduces further to just $\hat{\beta}$.

For the two-way cross-classification we have, similarly, the log likelihood

$$-m_1 m_2 \log \sigma - \Sigma\Sigma(y_{jk} - \mu - \alpha_j - \beta_k)^2/(2\sigma^2)$$
$$= -m_1 m_2 \log \sigma - \Sigma\Sigma\{(y_{jk} - \bar{y}_{j.} - \bar{y}_{.k} + \bar{y}_{..})$$
$$+ (\bar{y}_{j.} - \bar{y}_{..} - \alpha_j) + (\bar{y}_{.k} - \bar{y}_{..} - \beta_k) + (\bar{y}_{..} - \mu)\}^2/(2\sigma^2)$$

in the standard notation in which, for example, $\bar{y}_{j.} = \Sigma_k y_{jk}/m_2$. On squaring the expression in curly brackets, as a sum of four components, cross-product terms vanish, so that the log likelihood is a function of $\Sigma\Sigma(y_{jk} - \bar{y}_{j.} - \bar{y}_{.k} + \bar{y}_{..})^2$, the row × column interaction sum of squares, and the row and column means.

If an extra term $\gamma \alpha_j \beta_k$ is added to the model no such factorization is possible, and hence the minimal sufficient statistic is the full data array. A careful proof proceeds by supposing that for two different arrays $\{y_{jk}\}$ and $\{z_{jk}\}$, the difference of the log likelihoods is independent of the parameters, and obtaining a contradiction.

For discussion of the relevance of γ in examining interactions, see Scheffé (1959, p. 129) and Mandel (1971).

[*Theoretical Statistics*, Sections 2.1, 2.2(ii); Rao, Section 4e; Silvey, p. 58]*

2.2. Suppose that random variables follow the first-order autoregressive process

$$Y_r = \mu + \rho(Y_{r-1} - \mu) + \varepsilon_r,$$

---

*References to *Theoretical Statistics*, Lehmann, Lindley, Rao and Silvey, which occur throughout the text, are given in greater detail at the beginning of the list of references, p. 176.

where $\varepsilon_1, \ldots, \varepsilon_n$ are i.i.d. in $N(0, \sigma_\varepsilon^2)$ and $|\rho| < 1$. Write down the likelihood for data $y_1, \ldots, y_n$ in the cases where the initial value y_0 is
  (i) a given constant;
  (ii) the value of a random variable with the p.d.f. $N\{\mu, \sigma_\varepsilon^2/(1 - \rho^2)\}$, independent of $\varepsilon_1, \ldots, \varepsilon_n$;
  (iii) assumed equal to y_n.
Find the minimal sufficient statistic for the parameter $(\mu, \rho, \sigma_\varepsilon^2)$ in each case and show in particular that in cases (i) and (ii) the statistic $(\Sigma Y_j, \Sigma Y_{j-1} Y_j, \Sigma Y_j^2)$ has to be supplemented by end corrections.

Solution

The likelihood for a time series or stochastic process is usually best obtained by calculating the conditional probabilities in sequence, i.e. by writing

$$f_{Y_0, \ldots, Y_n}(y_0, \ldots, y_n) = f_{Y_0}(y_0) \prod_{j=1}^{n} f_{Y_j | Y^{(j-1)}}(y_j | y^{(j-1)}), \tag{1}$$

where $Y^{(j)} = (Y_0, \ldots, Y_j)$. For Markov processes, of which the normal-theory first-order autoregressive process is a special case,

$$f_{Y_j | Y^{(j-1)}}(y_j | y^{(j-1)}) = f_{Y_j | Y_{j-1}}(y_j | y_{j-1}).$$

Thus, in this special problem, the contribution to the log likelihood from the jth observation $(j = 1, \ldots, n)$ is

$$-\log \sigma_\varepsilon - \{(y_j - \mu) - \rho(y_{j-1} - \mu)\}^2/(2\sigma_\varepsilon^2).$$

The contribution from y_0 is ignored in cases (i) and (iii), except that in the latter case we write $y_0 = y_n$, whereas in case (ii) the initial factor for $j = 0$ in (1) is the indicated normal density.
  Thus in the first case the log likelihood is

$$-n \log \sigma_\varepsilon - \left\{ \sum_{j=1}^{n} y_j^2 + \rho^2 \sum_{j=0}^{n-1} y_j^2 - 2\mu \left(\sum_{j=1}^{n} y_j + \rho^2 \sum_{j=0}^{n-1} y_j - \rho \sum_{j=0}^{n-1} y_j - \rho \sum_{j=1}^{n} y_j \right) \right.$$
$$\left. - 2\rho \sum_{j=1}^{n} y_j y_{j-1} + n\mu^2 (1 - \rho)^2 \right\}/(2\sigma_\varepsilon^2).$$

Therefore the minimal sufficient statistic is $\Sigma Y_j, \Sigma Y_j^2, \Sigma Y_j Y_{j-1}$ summed over $j = 1, \ldots, n$, supplemented by Y_n, and by the fixed constant y_0. In the 'circular' case (iii), $y_n = y_0$,

$$\sum_{j=1}^{n} y_j^r = \sum_{j=0}^{n-1} y_j^r$$

and no 'end corrections' are needed.

In case (ii) the log likelihood is supplemented by an additional term from the density of Y_0. The sufficient statistic is the same as in case (i).

The distinction between the various initial conditions is unimportant when a single long series is analysed, but when information is pooled from a number of independent short sections use of (ii), when justified, adds an appreciable amount of information. A similar point applies to more general time series models. The circular case is rarely appropriate in applications.

[*Theoretical Statistics*, Sections 2.1, 2.2 (ii); Bartlett, 1966, Section 8.3]

2.3. In a simple queueing system customers arrive in a Poisson process of rate α. There is a single server and the distribution of service-time is exponential with parameter β, i.e. given that there is a customer present the probability of a service completion in the time interval $(t, t + \Delta t)$ is $\beta \Delta t + o(\Delta t)$ independently of the system's past history. Prove that, provided there is at least one customer present, the time between successive 'events', i.e. arrivals or service completions, is exponentially distributed with parameter $\alpha + \beta$, and that the probability that the event is an arrival is $\alpha/(\alpha + \beta)$ independently of the corresponding time intervals. The system is observed for a fixed time t, starting from a given arbitrary state. By building up the likelihood from (a) the intervals between events in the busy state, (b) the types of these events, (c) the intervals spent in the empty state, (d) the duration of any incomplete interval at the end of the period of observation, show that the likelihood is

$$\alpha^{n_a} \beta^{n_b} e^{-\alpha t} e^{-\beta(t - t_0)},$$

where n_a and n_b are the numbers of arrivals and service completions and t_0 is the time for which no customers are present.

Solution

A general point illustrated by the example is that a stochastic process can often be formulated in distinct although equivalent ways and that calculation of the likelihood may be appreciably simplified by a choice of formulation.

Let A and S be times to the next arrival and to the next service completion, starting from an arbitrary event. Let T be the time between successive events, customers being assumed present. Then $T = \min(A, S)$ and

$$\mathrm{pr}\,(T \geqslant t) = \mathrm{pr}\,(A \geqslant t \text{ and } S \geqslant t) = e^{-\alpha t}\, e^{-\beta t},$$

so that T has an exponential distribution of parameter $\alpha + \beta$. Further

$$\mathrm{pr}\,(\text{next event arrival} \,|\, t \leqslant T < t + \delta)$$
$$\sim \mathrm{pr}\,(t \leqslant A < t + \delta, S \geqslant t + \delta \,|\, t \leqslant T < t + \delta)$$

$$= \text{pr}(t \leqslant A < t + \delta, S \geqslant t + \delta)/\text{pr}(t \leqslant T < t + \delta)$$
$$= \alpha/(\alpha + \beta) + o(1),$$

independently of t.

The contributions to the likelihood from the times are (i) $(\alpha + \beta) \, e^{-(\alpha + \beta)x}$ from each time interval, x, in the busy state ending in an 'event';

(ii) $\alpha e^{-\alpha x}$ from each time interval in the empty state ending in an event;

(iii) $e^{-(\alpha + \beta)x}$ from the interval from the last event up to the end of the period of observation, if customers are present;

(iv) $e^{-\alpha x}$ from the latter interval if the system is empty.

In addition there is a factor $\alpha/(\alpha + \beta)$ from each inter-event interval ending in an arrival and a factor $\beta/(\alpha + \beta)$ for each such interval ending in a service completion.

The required form follows immediately on combining these factors.

[*Theoretical Statistics*, Section 2.1; Billingsley, 1961b; Cox, 1964a]

2.4. In the one-way random effects model of analysis of variance, random variables Y_{jk} $(j = 1, \ldots, m; k = 1, \ldots, r)$ have the form

$$Y_{jk} = \mu + \eta_j + \varepsilon_{jk},$$

where the η_j's and the ε_{jk}'s are independently normally distributed with zero means and variances respectively σ_b^2 and σ_w^2. The unknown parameter is thus $(\mu, \sigma_b^2, \sigma_w^2)$. Show that the minimal sufficient statistic is $\{ \bar{Y}_{..},$ $\Sigma(\bar{Y}_{j.} - \bar{Y}_{..})^2, \Sigma\Sigma(Y_{jk} - \bar{Y}_{j.})^2 \}$, where $\bar{Y}_{j.} = \Sigma Y_{jk}/r$ and $\bar{Y}_{..} = \Sigma \bar{Y}_{j.}/m$. What is the minimal sufficient statistic if it is given that $\mu = 0$? Generalize the results to cover the case where each Y_{jk} is a $p \times 1$ multivariate normal vector.

Solution

One approach to the likelihood for the random effects model is to work first conditionally on $\eta_1, \ldots, \eta_m$. A more direct argument is that the vectors $Y_j = (Y_{j1}, \ldots, Y_{jr})^\mathrm{T}$ are independently multivariate normal with mean $(\mu, \ldots, \mu)^\mathrm{T} = \mu \mathbf{1}$ and covariance matrix

$$\Sigma = \sigma_w^2 \mathbf{I} + \sigma_b^2 \mathbf{J} = \sigma_w^2 \mathbf{I} + \sigma_b^2 \, \mathbf{1}\mathbf{1}^\mathrm{T},$$

where $\mathbf{I}$ is the $r \times r$ identity matrix and $\mathbf{J}$ is the $r \times r$ matrix all of whose elements are one. It is easily shown that

$$\Sigma^{-1} = \sigma_w^{-2} \{ \mathbf{I} - \sigma_b^2 \mathbf{J}/(\sigma_w^2 + r\sigma_b^2) \}.$$

The log likelihood is

$$-\tfrac{1}{2}m\log|\Sigma| - \tfrac{1}{2}\sum_{j=1}^{m}(y_j - \mu 1)^{\mathrm{T}}\Sigma^{-1}(y_j - \mu 1)$$

$$= -\tfrac{1}{2}m\log|\Sigma| - (2\sigma_w^2)^{-1}\{\Sigma y_j^{\mathrm{T}}y_j - 2\mu 1^{\mathrm{T}}\Sigma y_j + m\mu^2 1^{\mathrm{T}}1$$
$$- \lambda(\Sigma y_j^{\mathrm{T}}\mathbf{J}y_j - 2\mu 1^{\mathrm{T}}\mathbf{J}\Sigma y_j + \mu^2 1^{\mathrm{T}}\mathbf{J}1)\},$$

where $\lambda = \sigma_b^2/(\sigma_w^2 + r\sigma_b^2)$. Because $\mathbf{J} = 11^{\mathrm{T}}$ the expression in curly brackets becomes

$$\Sigma\Sigma y_{jk}^2 - 2\mu rm\bar{y}_{..} + rm\mu^2 - \lambda(r\Sigma\bar{y}_{j.}^2 - 2\mu rm\bar{y}_{..} + r^2\mu^2),$$

from which the sufficiency follows, essentially because of the exponential family form. Completeness implies minimal sufficiency.

If $\mu = 0$, the minimal sufficient statistic becomes $\{\Sigma\Sigma Y_{jk}^2, \Sigma\Sigma(Y_{jk} - \bar{Y}_{j.})^2\}$. In the general multivariate case the statistic is

$$\{\bar{Y}_{..}, \Sigma(\bar{Y}_{j.} - \bar{Y}_{..})(\bar{Y}_{j.} - \bar{Y}_{..})^{\mathrm{T}}, \Sigma\Sigma(Y_{jk} - \bar{Y}_{j.})(Y_{jk} - \bar{Y}_{j.})^{\mathrm{T}}\},$$

i.e. the overall mean and the matrices of between and within groups sums of products, and is minimal sufficient for $(\mu, \Sigma_b, \Sigma_w)$.

Similar results hold generally for balanced normal-theory random effects models.

[*Theoretical Statistics*, Section 2.2; Rao, Sections 4f, 4j]

2.5. Independent binary random variables $Y_1,\ldots, Y_n$ are such that the probability of the value one depends on an explanatory variable x, which takes corresponding values $x_1,\ldots, x_n$. Show that for the model

$$\rho_j = \log\left\{\frac{\mathrm{pr}(Y_j = 1)}{\mathrm{pr}(Y_j = 0)}\right\} = \gamma + \beta x_j,$$

the minimal sufficient statistic is $(\Sigma Y_j, \Sigma x_j Y_j)$; the quantity ρ_j is called the logistic transform. Generalize to the case where the $n \times 1$ vector ρ is given by the linear model $\rho = \mathbf{x}\beta$ with $\mathbf{x}$ a known $n \times q$ matrix of rank q and β a $q \times 1$ vector of unknown parameters.

Solution

The contribution to the likelihood from the jth observation can be written concisely $\exp(\gamma y_j + \beta x_j y_j)/\{1 + \exp(\gamma + \beta x_j)\}$. Hence, on multiplication, it follows that the likelihood involves the data only via $(\Sigma y_j, \Sigma x_j y_j)$. For the general linear logistic model, the minimal sufficient statistic is $\mathbf{x}^{\mathrm{T}} Y$.

[*Theoretical Statistics*, Section 2.2; Cox, 1970]

2.6.* The random variables $Y_1,..., Y_n$ are i.i.d. with probability density equal to $2/(3\theta)$ on $0 \leqslant y \leqslant \frac{1}{2}\theta$, and equal to $4/(3\theta)$ on $\frac{1}{2}\theta < y \leqslant \theta$. Prove that the minimal sufficient statistic consists of those order statistics above $\frac{1}{2}Y_{(n)}$.

Solution

Denote the order statistics by $y_{(1)} \leqslant ... \leqslant y_{(n)}$ and let hv $(x) = 1$ $(x \geqslant 0)$, $hv(x) = 0 (x < 0)$. One concise way of writing the likelihood is

$$\left(\frac{4}{3\theta}\right)^n \prod_{s=1}^n \{hv(\theta - y_{(s)}) - \tfrac{1}{2}hv(\tfrac{1}{2}\theta - y_{(s)})\}.$$

This is zero if $\theta < y_{(n)}$ and it follows that all $y_{(s)} < \frac{1}{2}y_{(n)}$ contribute to the product an amount not depending on their actual value. Further any $y_{(s)} > \frac{1}{2}y_{(n)}$ contributes for some θ a factor 1 and for others a factor $\frac{1}{2}$, depending on whether $\theta \leqslant 2y_{(s)}$. More formally, the ratio of the likelihoods for two different sample points y and z is independent of θ if and only if $y_{(n)} = z_{(n)}$ and all other order statistics greater than one-half the maximum are identical. Thus the minimal sufficient statistic is the set of order statistics greater than $\frac{1}{2}y_{(n)}$ and this defines in particular the number, r, of such values.

Note incidentally that the distribution of R does not involve θ, as is obvious because of invariance under scale transformations. Thus R is ancillary.

[*Theoretical Statistics*, Section 2.2]

2.7. Suppose that Y_1 and Y_2 are independent random vectors with a distribution depending on the same parameter θ, and that S_1 and S_2 are corresponding minimal sufficient statistics. Show that for the combined random vector $Y = (Y_1, Y_2)$, $S = (S_1, S_2)$ is sufficient, although not necessarily minimal sufficient. Use the Gaussian first-order autoregressive process as an explicit example to show that the result does not hold in general for dependent random variables. Suggest an extended definition of sufficiency which is such that when dependent data sets are merged, the sufficient statistic for the extended set can always be recovered and illustrate the definition on the Gaussian first-order autoregressive process.

Solution

For independent vectors Y_1 and Y_2, we have the combined likelihood

*Amended version.

$$f_{Y_1, Y_2}(y_1, y_2; \theta) = f_{Y_1}(y_1; \theta) f_{Y_2}(y_2; \theta)$$
$$= f_{Y_1|S_1}(y_1|s_1) f_{Y_2|S_2}(y_2|s_2) f_{S_1}(s_1; \theta) f_{S_2}(s_2; \theta)$$
$$= m_2(y_1, y_2) m_1(s_1, s_2; \theta),$$

proving sufficiency. If Y_1 and Y_2 have the same exponential family distribution, then S_1 and S_2 can be chosen so that $S_1 + S_2$ is minimal sufficient.

The practical interpretation is that if the separate sets of data are reduced to their minimal sufficient statistics, no further information is required when the data sets are merged.

For a case with dependent variables, take the autoregressive process

$$X_{j+1} = \theta X_j + \varepsilon_{j+1} \ (j = 1, 2, \ldots),$$

where the ε_j are i.i.d. $N(0,1)$. Let $Y_1 = (X_1, \ldots, X_n)$, $Y_2 = (X_{n+1}, \ldots, X_{n+r})$ with X_1 given its stationary $N\{0, 1/(1 - \theta^2)\}$ distribution. Then, as in Problem 2.2, we find

$$S_1 = s(Y_1) = \left(X_1^2, \sum_{j=2}^{n-1} X_j^2, \sum_{j=1}^{n-1} X_j X_{j+1}, X_n^2 \right),$$
$$S_2 = s(Y_2) = \left(X_{n+1}^2, \sum_{j=n+2}^{n+r-1} X_j^2, \sum_{j=n+1}^{n+r-1} X_j X_{j+1}, X_{n+r}^2 \right).$$

But (S_1, S_2) is not capable of yielding

$$s(Y_1, Y_2) = \left(X_1^2, \sum_{j=2}^{n+r-1} X_j^2, \sum_{j=1}^{n+r-1} X_j X_{j+1}, X_{n+r}^2 \right).$$

without the sign of the product $X_n X_{n+1}$. In this particular case one needs to replace $S_1 = s(X_1, \ldots, X_n)$ by

$$S_1' = (X_1, \Sigma X_j^2, \Sigma X_j X_{j+1}, X_n)$$

in order to get the reduction property when Y_1 is combined with any other data set from the same realization of the process. A sufficient property in general is that $S = s(X_1, \ldots, X_n)$ should be sufficient and that for any vector $Y = (X_{j_1}, \ldots, X_{j_m})$ distinct from $X_1, \ldots, X_n$ the conditional distribution of Y given S should be the same as the conditional distribution of Y given $X_1, \ldots, X_n$. This is true for S_1' above in the first-order autoregressive model, since conditional distributions given $X_1, \ldots, X_n$ depend only on X_1 and X_n.

[*Theoretical Statistics*, Section 2.2; Fisher, 1925; Bahadur, 1954; Lauritzen, 1974]

2.9*. A population consists of an unknown number θ of individuals. An

*Amended version. Problem 2.8 omitted.

individual is drawn at random, is marked and returned to the population. A second individual is drawn at random. If it is the marked individual, this is noted; if not, the individual is marked. The individual is then returned to the population. At the mth step, an individual is drawn at random. It is noted whether the individual is marked. If not, it is marked. The individual is then returned to the population. This continues for n steps; the observation consists of a binary sequence indicating, for each step, whether the individual is or is not marked. Show that the likelihood is proportional to $(\theta - 1)\ldots$ $(\theta - n + r + 1)/\theta^{n-1}$, where r is the number of times that the individual drawn is already marked, and hence that R is a sufficient statistic. Prove that the same conclusion holds

(a) if the number n is chosen by an arbitrary data-dependent sequential stopping rule;

(b) if for each marked individual selected, a record is available of the particular previous trials on which it was observed;

(c) if at the mth step, not one but k_m individuals are drawn at random from the population.

List the assumptions made in this analysis and comment on their reasonableness in investigating biological populations.

Solution

The experiment yields a sequence $(Y_1,\ldots, Y_n)$ where $Y_j = 0$ if the drawn individual is marked and $Y_j = 1$ otherwise; clearly $Y_1 = 1$. If M_j is the number of marked individuals immediately after the jth drawing, then $M_j = Y_1 + \ldots + Y_j$ and

$$\mathrm{pr}\,(Y_j = 0 | Y_1,\ldots, Y_{j-1};\theta) = \mathrm{pr}\,(Y_j = 0 | M_{j-1};\theta) = m_{j-1}/\theta\,(j = 1,\ldots,n),$$

where, of course, $M_0 = 0$. The likelihood is then

$$\mathrm{lik}\,(\theta;y_1,\ldots,y_n) = \prod_{j=1}^{n} (m_{j-1}/\theta)^{1-y_j}(1 - m_{j-1}/\theta)^{y_j}. \tag{1}$$

Since r is the number of times the drawn individual has been marked, $m_n = n - r$ and there are $n - r$ 1's in $(Y_1,\ldots, Y_n)$. Therefore the sequence $(m_1,\ldots, m_{n-1})$ runs through the values $(1,2,\ldots,n - r - 1)$, and the term $(\theta - k)$ only appears once in the likelihood, i.e. at the drawing where $y = 1$ and m increases to $k + 1$; the term $(\theta - m_n)$ does not appear since there are no 1's in the sequence after $m = m_n$. Hence

$$\mathrm{lik}\,(\theta;y_1,\ldots,y_n) \propto \theta^{-n}\theta(\theta - 1)\ldots(\theta - n + r + 1).$$

In case (a), refer to Example 2.34 of *Theoretical Statistics*.

In case (b), the likelihood (1) is multiplied by constant terms $m_1^{-1},\ldots,m_n^{-1}$, since the conditional probability of a *particular* marked individual being drawn at stage j is assumed to be m_{j-1}^{-1}.

In case (c) the terms occur in bunches, rather than singly, and the likelihood is unaltered. Note the extreme case $k_m = n$, when $R = 0$ and no information is obtained.

The primary assumptions are of the closure of the population (no birth, death, immigration and emigration), of equal catchability, both as between different individuals in the population and as to the absence of an effect of previous capture on subsequent events, and of independence for different individuals. With suitably extensive data, the first assumption can be relaxed, but the second assumption remains a major one.

[*Theoretical Statistics*, Section 2.2; Goodman, 1953; Cormack, 1968; Seber, 1973]

2.10. The random variables $Y_1, \ldots, Y_n$ obey a second-order linear model, i.e. they are uncorrelated and have constant variance and $E(Y) = \mathbf{x}\beta$, where $\mathbf{x}$ is $n \times q_x$, $q_x < n$ and of full rank. The vector statistic S is called *linearly sufficient* for β if any statistic uncorrelated with S has expectation independent of β. Comment on the relation of this definition with ordinary sufficiency and show that $(\mathbf{x}^T\mathbf{x})^{-1}\mathbf{x}^T Y$ is linearly sufficient.

Solution

If T is an arbitrary statistic uncorrelated with S, then

$$0 = \text{cov}(T,S) = E(TS) - E(T)E(S)$$
$$= E\{E(TS|S) - E(T)S\}$$
$$= E[S\{E(T|S) - E(T)\}].$$

Now if S is complete and sufficient, this implies that $E(T) = E(T|S)$ and is thus independent of β. That is, complete sufficiency implies linear sufficiency.

In the normal-theory linear model with known variance, $S = (\mathbf{x}^T\mathbf{x})^{-1}\mathbf{x}^T Y$ is complete and sufficient and the result follows. The spirit of the definition does not require normality and in fact a direct proof requiring neither normality nor that the variance is known follows because cov$(T,S) = 0$ implies $T = c^T Y$, with $c^T = d^T \{\mathbf{I} - \mathbf{x}(\mathbf{x}^T\mathbf{x})^{-1}\mathbf{x}^T\}$, for some d. Then

$$E(T) = d^T\{\mathbf{x}\beta - \mathbf{x}(\mathbf{x}^T\mathbf{x})^{-1}\mathbf{x}^T\mathbf{x}\beta\} = 0.$$

These ideas lead fairly directly to a proof of Gauss's theorem that in the second-order linear model the least squares estimates have maximum variance among all linear unbiased estimates, or equivalently among all linear estimates with bounded mean square error; for general ideas on point estimation, see Chapter 8.

[*Theoretical Statistics*, Section 2.2; Barnard, 1963; Rao, Sections 4a, b]

2.11. Suppose that $Y_1, \ldots, Y_n$ are i.i.d. with probability density $f(y;\theta)$ and that $S = s(Y)$ is a one-dimensional sufficient statistic for θ for all values of n. If θ_1 and θ_2 are any two fixed values of θ, show, starting with the factorization (1), that for any θ

$$\frac{\partial}{\partial y_j} \log\left\{\frac{f(y_j;\theta)}{f(y_j;\theta_1)}\right\} \Big/ \frac{\partial}{\partial y_j} \log\left\{\frac{f(y_j;\theta_2)}{f(y_j;\theta_1)}\right\}$$

is independent of y_j and hence is a function of θ alone. Since θ_1 and θ_2 are fixed, deduce from this that $f(x;\theta)$ has the exponential family form (2).

Solution

This is based on Pitman (1936). Let

$$\text{lik}(\theta;y) = f_Y(y;\theta) = f_{Y_1,\ldots,Y_n|S}(y_1,\ldots,y_n|s)f_S(s;\theta).$$

Therefore

$$\frac{\partial}{\partial y_j} \log\left\{\frac{\text{lik}(\theta;y)}{\text{lik}(\theta_1;y)}\right\} = \frac{\partial}{\partial y_j} \log\left\{\frac{f(y_j;\theta)}{f(y_j;\theta_1)}\right\}$$

$$= \frac{\partial}{\partial y_j} \log\left\{\frac{f_S(s;\theta)}{f_S(s;\theta_1)}\right\} = \frac{\partial s}{\partial y_j}\frac{d}{ds} \log\left\{\frac{f_S(s;\theta)}{f_S(s;\theta_1)}\right\},$$

assuming differentiability. The ratio in the statement of the Problem eliminates $\partial s/\partial y_j$ and leaves a function of s, which is symmetric in $(y_1,\ldots,y_n)$. But since the ratio does not depend on $y_k (k \neq j)$ it cannot depend on y_j. (For precise versions of these conclusions, and comment on the case of the uniform distribution on $[0,\theta]$, see Pitman (1936) or Koopman (1936).) If the given ratio is $a(\theta)$, we have on integration that

$$\log\left\{\frac{f(y_j;\theta)}{f(y_j;\theta_1)}\right\} = a(\theta)\log\left\{\frac{f(y_j;\theta_2)}{f(y_j;\theta_1)}\right\} + c(\theta),$$

so that the standard exponential family form is obtained with $b(y_j) = \log\{f(y_j;\theta_2)/f(y_j;\theta_1)\}, d(y_j) = -\log f(y_j;\theta_1)$.

[*Theoretical Statistics*, Section 2.2 (vi)]

2.12. Check the form of the natural parameter for the Poisson distribution (log mean), binomial distribution (log odds), exponential distribution (reciprocal of mean), gamma distribution with index known (reciprocal of mean), negative binomial distribution with index known (log probability), normal distribution with both parameters unknown (mean divided by variance and reciprocal of variance) and multivariate normal distribution of zero mean and unknown covariance matrix (inverse of covariance matrix). Discuss in each case the extent to which it is sensible to use the natural parameter for interpretation, e.g. in the comparison of different sets of data. Relevant considerations include directness of physical meaning and range of possible values.

Solution

The simplest form of the one-parameter exponential family is (4) of the Summary. In the multiparameter case the first term is replaced by a sum. Table 1 shows the main special cases: conventional notation has been used.

A technical property of the natural parameter is that comparison of two samples and more generally analysis of linear models is theoretically simple when the difference is a difference of natural parameters or the linear model is expressed in terms of the natural parameter; Problem 2.5 is an illustration. Such a scale for the parameter is physically appealing for the Poisson and binomial distributions, but rather less so for the other examples. Thus $\log \sigma$

Table 1

Distribution	Density	Natural parameter
Poisson	$\exp(y \log \mu - \mu - \log y!)$	$\log \mu$
Binomial	$\exp\left\{ y \log\left(\dfrac{\theta}{1-\theta}\right) + n \log(1-\theta) + \log\binom{n}{y}\right\}$	$\log\{\theta/(1-\theta)\}$
Exponential	$\exp(-y/\mu - \log \mu)$	$1/\mu$
Gamma (index known)	$\exp\{-k_0 y/\mu + k_0 \log(k_0/\mu) + (k_0 - 1)\log \mu - \log \Gamma(k)\}$	$1/\mu$
Negative binomial (index known)	$\exp\left\{ y \log \theta + k_0 \log(1-\theta) + \log\binom{k_0 + y - 1}{k_0 - 1}\right\}$	$\log \theta$
Normal	$\exp\left\{ -\dfrac{y^2}{2\sigma^2} + \dfrac{y\mu}{\sigma^2} - \dfrac{\mu^2}{2\sigma^2} - \tfrac{1}{2}\log(2\pi)\right\}$	$\dfrac{1}{\sigma^2}, \dfrac{\mu}{\sigma^2}$
Multivariate p dim. normal (zero mean)	$\exp\{-\tfrac{1}{2}y^{\mathrm{T}}\Sigma^{-1}y - \tfrac{1}{2}\log|\Sigma| - \tfrac{1}{2}p \log(2\pi)\}$	elements of Σ^{-1}

is usually a more natural function in terms of which to compare dispersions of normal distributions than $1/\sigma^2$. For the exponential distribution $1/\mu$ does have the interpretation as a rate but again multiplicative models for rates, or means, will often be sensible. Because the parameter space for $1/\mu$ is (at most) the positive half line linear models in terms of $1/\mu$ are meaningful only for restricted ranges of parameter values and this can raise difficulties both of fitting and of interpretation. For both Poisson and binomial distributions, the natural parameter can take any real value.

Nelder and Wedderburn (1972) have introduced the important idea of a generalized linear model in which some function of the natural parameter follows a linear model.

[*Theoretical Statistics*, Section 2.2(vi); Lehmann, pp. 50 et seq.]

2.13. Prove that when the exponential family density is taken in its natural form

$$f_Z(z;\phi) = \exp\{ -z\phi + c\dagger(\phi) + d\dagger(z)\},$$

the cumulant generating function of Z is $c\dagger(\phi) - c\dagger(\phi - t)$; use, for this, the condition that the total integral of the density is one. Hence express the cumulants of Z for small ϕ in terms of those for $\phi = 0$; compare with a non-degenerate case for which the exact cumulants are known.

Solution

If $\qquad\qquad f_Z(z;\phi) = \exp\{ -z\phi + c\dagger(\phi) + d\dagger(z)\}$
then

$$E(e^{tZ};\phi) = \exp\{c\dagger(\phi) - c\dagger(\phi - t)\} \int \exp\{ -(\phi - t)z + c\dagger(\phi - t) + d\dagger(z)\}\,dz,$$

with a similar expression in the discrete case, and the integral is one. The cumulant generating function is thus

$$\begin{aligned} K(t;\phi) &= \log E(e^{tZ};\phi)\\ &= c\dagger(\phi) - c\dagger(\phi - t)\\ &= K(t - \phi;0) - K(-\phi;0). \end{aligned}$$

Thus the rth cumulant of Z when the parameter value is ϕ is $\kappa_r(\phi) = [\partial^r K(t;\phi)/\partial t^r]_{t=0}$, so that

$$\kappa_r(\phi) = [\partial^r K(u;0)/\partial u^r]_{u=-\phi}$$

$$= \sum_{s=0}^{\infty} (-\phi)^s \kappa_{r+s}/s!,$$

by Taylor's theorem, where $\kappa_t = \kappa_t(0)$.

A simple example is $N(\mu, \sigma_0^2)$, with σ_0^2 known, where $Z = -Y$ and $\phi = \mu/\sigma_0^2$. Here

$$\kappa_1(\phi) = \kappa_1(0) - \phi\kappa_2(0) = 0 - (\mu/\sigma_0^2)\sigma_0^2,$$

an exact result from two terms of the series expansion.

[*Theoretical Statistics*, Section 2.2 (vi)]

2.14. The random variables $Y_1, \ldots, Y_n$ are i.i.d. in the density $\tau^{-1}h\{(y-\mu)/\tau\}$. Find a transformation $Z_1, \ldots, Z_n$ of the order statistics $Y_{(1)}, \ldots, Y_{(n)}$ such that $Z_3, \ldots, Z_n$ are invariant under location and scale changes. Hence find the ancillary part of the minimal sufficient statistic.

Solution

Location-scale transformation takes $Y_{(j)} \to aY_{(j)} + b$ for some a, b; an invariant statistic takes the same value for all a, b. The differences $Y_{(j+1)} - Y_{(j)}$ transform to $a(Y_{(j+1)} - Y_{(j)})$, and a is eliminated by taking ratios. Thus

$$\frac{(Y_{(3)} - Y_{(2)})}{(Y_{(2)} - Y_{(1)})}, \ldots, \frac{(Y_{(n)} - Y_{(n-1)})}{(Y_{(2)} - Y_{(1)})}$$

are invariant, and may be taken as $Z_3, \ldots, Z_n$. Then one can take $Z_1 = Y_{(1)}$, $Z_2 = Y_{(2)} - Y_{(1)}$, which completes a $1-1$ transformation of the minimal sufficient statistic $(Y_{(1)}, \ldots, Y_{(n)})$; it is easy to check that the Jacobian is non-singular. Of course there are many equivalent forms.

The statistic $(Z_3, \ldots, Z_n)$ is ancillary, as can be deduced from a general theorem of Basu (1955). To see this directly, suppose $Y_j = \mu + \tau Y_j'$, the variable $(Z_3, \ldots, Z_n)$ derived from $(Y_{(1)}, \ldots, Y_{(n)})$ being identical to $(Z_3', \ldots, Z_n')$. But the joint density of $(Z_3', \ldots, Z_n')$ is an integral of $\Pi h(y_j')$ and hence does not depend on (μ, τ).

There are theoretically important implications for inference about scale and location parameters.

[*Theoretical Statistics*, Section 2.2(vi); Fisher, 1934]

2.16* A finite population of m individuals labelled $1, \ldots, m$ is such that for each individual there is a binary property θ. Denote the values $\theta_1, \ldots, \theta_m$;

*Problem 2.15 omitted.

these are not probabilities, but rather unknown constants, each either zero or one. From the finite population a random sample of size n is drawn without replacement; this yields in order individuals with numbers $i_1, \ldots, i_n$ and the corresponding θ's are then observed. This gives observations $y_1, \ldots, y_n$, where $y_j = \theta_{i_j}$. Show that the likelihood is

$$\begin{cases} (m-n)!/m! & (\theta_{i_j} = y_j; j = 1, \ldots, n), \\ 0 & \text{otherwise,} \end{cases}$$

and that therefore this does not depend on the values of the unobserved θ's. Show further that essentially the same likelihood function is obtained for any sampling scheme, provided that it is defined independently of θ.

Discuss the implications of this for the various approaches to statistical inference. Does it mean that (a) it is impossible to learn anything about the unobserved θ's; (b) the interpretation of a sample survey should not depend on the sampling scheme; (c) at least in this context, the likelihood principle is inapplicable?

Solution

It is important that $i_1, \ldots, i_n$ are observed. The data are then $(i_1, \ldots, i_n; y_1 = \theta_{i_1}, \ldots, y_n = \theta_{i_n})$. All samples of size n are equally likely under random sampling, the number of distinct samples being $m!/(m-n)!$, disregarding the order of selection. Thus

$$\mathrm{pr}(I_1 = i_1, \ldots, I_n = i_n, y_1, \ldots, y_n; \theta) = \begin{cases} \mathrm{pr}(I_1 = i_1, \ldots, I_n = i_n)(y_j = \theta_{i_j}; j = 1, \ldots, n), \\ 0 \qquad\qquad\qquad\qquad\qquad\qquad\qquad \text{otherwise} \end{cases}$$

and hence

$$\mathrm{lik}\,(\theta; i_1, \ldots, i_n; y_1, \ldots, y_n) = \begin{cases} (m-n)!/m! & (\theta_{i_j} = y_j; j = 1, \ldots, n), \\ 0 & \text{otherwise}; \end{cases}$$

this is not the same as $\mathrm{lik}\,(\theta; y_1, \ldots, y_n)$, which *does* depend on θ through $\Sigma\theta_j$.

The same kind of result will hold if $\mathrm{pr}(I_j = i_j; j = 1, \ldots, n)$ does not depend on θ.

The answers to (a)–(c) involve consideration of facts such as

(i) $E(\Sigma Y_j/n; \theta) = \Sigma\theta_j/m$, $\mathrm{var}(\Sigma Y_j/n; \theta) = O(1/n)$,

(ii) $\displaystyle\sum_{j=1}^{m} \theta_j = \sum_{s \neq \{i_j\}} \theta_s + \sum_{j=1}^{n} y_j;$

(iii) $\mathrm{lik}\,(\theta; y_1, \ldots, y_n) = \mathrm{pr}\!\left(Y_1 = y_1, \ldots, Y_n = y_n; \tau = \displaystyle\sum_{j=1}^{m} \theta_j\right) \propto \binom{\tau}{\Sigma y_j}\binom{m - \tau}{n - \Sigma y_j},$

because the property is binary.

[*Theoretical Statistics*, Sections 2.2, 2.4(viii); Godambe and Thompson, 1971; Royall, 1976]

2.17. For the model $f_Y(y;\theta)$, the statistic S is called *Bayesian sufficient* if, whatever the prior distribution of θ, the posterior distribution involves the data only through s. Show that Bayesian sufficiency is equivalent to 'ordinary' sufficiency.

Solution

Bayesian sufficiency requires by Bayes's theorem that

$$f_{\Theta|Y}(\theta\,|\,y) = f_{Y|\Theta}(y\,|\,\theta)f_{\Theta}(\theta)/f_Y(y)$$
$$= g(s,\theta),$$

say, for $s = s(y)$. This implies that

$$f_{Y|\Theta}(y|\theta) = \frac{g(s,\theta)}{f_{\Theta}(\theta)}f_Y(y),$$

the required factorization for ordinary sufficiency. The converse is proved similarly.

[*Theoretical Statistics*, Sections 2.2, 2.4(ix), p. 368; Lindley, p. 21; Raiffa and Schlaifer, 1961]

3 PURE SIGNIFICANCE TESTS

Summary

A null hypothesis H_0 is explicitly formulated concerning the probability distribution of a random variable Y. The hypothesis is called simple if it completely specifies the distribution, and composite otherwise. Qualitative information is assumed available about the type of departure from H_0 which it is required to detect. A test of consistency with H_0 developed for this rather ill-defined situation is called a pure test of significance.

Such a test is developed by defining a test statistic $T = t(Y)$ with the properties that:

(i) the larger is the value of t, the stronger is the evidence of departure from H_0 in the direction under test;

(ii) if H_0 is true, the distribution of T is known, at least approximately.
For given observations y, we calculate $t = t_{obs} = t(y)$, and the level of significance p_{obs} is then given by $p_{obs} = \text{pr}\,(T \geqslant t_{obs}; H_0)$. This has a hypothetical interpretation in terms of the probability of rejecting H_0 when true, were the data under analysis to be regarded as just decisive against H_0. The random variable P corresponding to p is uniformly distributed under H_0 in the continuous case, and will tend to be smaller under departures from H_0 of the type measured by t.

When H_0 is composite, the distribution of T should be exactly or approximately the same for all simple hypotheses forming H_0. This can often be achieved by calculating the distribution conditional on the sufficient statistic for the nuisance parameter defining H_0. Otherwise, T may sometimes be chosen to be invariant under the data transformations which generate the various simple hypotheses forming H_0.

If m tests are applied to the same null hypothesis and the most significant of the m statistics taken, an allowance for selection is needed. We are in effect using $Q = \min(P_1, \ldots, P_m)$ as a test statistic, small values being significant. The true level of significance corresponding to q_{obs} is bounded above by mq_{obs}.

Pure significance tests, while useful, are of limited importance, particularly because they give no direct idea of the magnitude of possible departure from H_0.

Problems

3.1. Consider random variables $Y_1,\ldots,Y_n$ representing directions round a circle, i.e. angles between 0 and 2π. The null hypothesis is that the random variables are independently uniformly distributed. Show that a suitable test statistic for detecting clustering around 0 is $\Sigma \cos Y_j$ and that it can be interpreted as the abscissa of a random walk in the plane with steps of unit length. Suggest test statistics when clustering may be around 0 and π, and also when clustering may be around an unknown direction. For both cases, obtain a normal approximation to the distribution under the null hypothesis of a uniform distribution of angles around the circle.

Solution

A vector of unit length making an angle Y_j with the axis of coordinates has components $(\cos Y_j, \sin Y_j)$. Thus the resultant of n such vectors has components $(\Sigma \cos Y_j, \Sigma \sin Y_j)$. If the vectors tend to cluster around the zero angle, the component $T = \Sigma \cos Y_j$ will tend to be large. The distribution of T under the null hypothesis has a simple normal approximation based on moments $E(\cos Y_j) = 0$, $\mathrm{var}(\cos Y_j) = \frac{1}{2}$. Thus T is approximately $N(0, \frac{1}{2}n)$.

If the vectors cluster around $y = 0$ or $y = \pi$, then we can either (a) work with $Y_j' = 2Y_j$, so that clustering is around $y = 0 = 2\pi$, leading to the test statistic $\Sigma \cos(2Y_j)$ with the same null distribution as T, or (b) modify $\cos Y_j$ to $|\cos Y_j|$ or $\cos^2 Y_j$, the latter choice leading back to the statistic in (a).

If clustering is around an unknown direction, then the test statistic should be invariant under rotation of axes. Clustering will tend to make the resultant vector long, so that the squared length of the resultant, $T' = (\Sigma \cos Y_j)^2 + (\Sigma \sin Y_j)^2$, is a sensible test statistic; T' is invariant. Under the null hypothesis $\Sigma \cos Y_j$ and $\Sigma \sin Y_j$ are uncorrelated, both having mean zero and variance $\frac{1}{2}n$. Thus, by the bivariate central limit theorem, $2T'/n$ is asymptotically distributed as a chi-squared variable with two degrees of freedom, i.e. is exponential with mean two.

There is an extensive literature on this and similar more complex situations concerned with the analysis of directional data (Mardia, 1972; Pearson and Hartley, 1972, Tables 56–64).

[*Theoretical Statistics*, Sections 3.2, 3.3]

3.2. Suggest a test statistic for the null hypothesis that binary data come from a two-state Markov chain with given transition matrix, the departure of interest being that transitions occur more often than the given matrix would suggest.

Solution

Mostly for reasons connected with sufficiency, it is sensible to consider first test statistics that are functions of the transition counts m_{rs}, the number of one-step transitions from r to s $(r, s = 0, 1)$. Now if the given transition probability matrix is

$$\begin{bmatrix} \alpha_0 & 1 - \alpha_0 \\ 1 - \beta_0 & \beta_0 \end{bmatrix},$$

where α_0 and β_0 are known, the departure of the type being tested is evidenced by $m_{00}/(m_{00} + m_{01}) < \alpha_0$ and $m_{11}/(m_{10} + m_{11}) < \beta_0$.

Simple test statistics are weighted combinations of the discrepancies $m_{00} - \alpha_0(m_{00} + m_{01})$ and $m_{11} - \beta_0(m_{10} + m_{11})$, the simplest being the sum of these. In principle the exact distribution under the null hypothesis can be found by enumeration of all distinct binary sequences. A normal approximation can be based on results reviewed by Billingsley (1961a).

[*Theoretical Statistics*, Section 3.2]

3.3. An *absolute test of significance* of a simple null hypothesis is a pure significance test in which the test statistic at an observational point y is a strictly decreasing function of the p.d.f. at y under the null hypothesis. That is, the significance level is the probability under the null hypothesis of obtaining data with a probability density as small as, or smaller than, that of the data actually obtained. Discuss critically whether this is a useful idea; in particular show that for continuous random variables the test is affected by non-linear transformations of the data and that for discrete data the grouping together of points in the sample space could have a major effect on the level of significance.

Solution

So far as we know, the first example of an absolute test of significance is the chi-squared goodness of fit test as introduced by K. Pearson (1900). In order to test agreement of multinomial data with a specified set of probabilities he imagined the sample points as ordered by their null hypothesis probabilities. Then the chi-squared statistic was introduced as an approximate ordering device; see Problem 3.4. Similar examples occur, at least implicitly, in connection with contingency tables.

There are essentially three difficulties with absolute tests:

(i) For continuous random variables, the ranking of sample points on the basis of the corresponding probability density values can be changed in any way by suitable monotone transformation. Therefore criteria are necessary to define a unique form of Y, or continuous distributions must be excluded.

(ii) For discrete random variables, the ranking of sample points can be changed by 'splitting' sample points or by grouping sample points together. Therefore some requirement is necessary, such as that points with entirely equivalent interpretations are to be grouped together. The preliminary reduction to sufficient statistics is essential here.

(iii) Very often the probabilities under H_0 vary smoothly with the value of a natural test statistic, so that the absolute test is reasonable from the pure test point of view. However, the probabilities may vary irregularly. An extreme example is that of Spearman's rank correlation coefficient (Kendall, 1962), where the absolute test of the independence hypothesis is not sensible.

There is also the rather more philosophical question: Do we regard H_0 with suspicion just because the sample point is unlikely, or do we also need the idea that there is some plausible explanation of the data which make the data more likely?

[*Theoretical Statistics*, Section 3.2; Martin-Löf, 1974; Sverdrup, 1975]

3.4. Suppose that there are m possible outcomes to each trial and the data consist of n independent trials under the same conditions. Show that if the numbers of trials of the various types are given by random variables $(Y_1, \ldots, Y_m)$ then

$$\mathrm{pr}(Y_1 = y_1, \ldots, Y_m = y_m) = n! \Pi(p_j^{y_j}/y_j!),$$

where $(p_1, \ldots, p_m)$ are the probabilities of the individual outcomes. Show that for large n the log of this probability is, in the relevant range $y_j - np_j = O(\sqrt{n})$, a linear function of

$$\Sigma(y_j - np_j)^2/(np_j).$$

Hence show that for large n the absolute test of significance of the null hypothesis which specifies the p_j's completely is equivalent to the test based on the chi-squared goodness of fit statistic.

Solution

In the standard multinomial formula for $\mathrm{pr}(Y = y)$ we write $y_j = np_j +$

$z_j\sqrt{(np_j)}$ for $j = 1, \ldots, m$, and then examine the log probability as $n \to \infty$ with z_j fixed, constrained by $\Sigma z_j\sqrt{p_j} = 0$. Thus

$$\log \mathrm{pr}(Y = y) = \log n! + \Sigma\{np_j + z_j\sqrt{(np_j)}\} \log p_j - \Sigma \log\{np_j + z_j\sqrt{(np_j)}\}!$$
$$= \mathrm{const} - \tfrac{1}{2}\Sigma z_j^2 + o(1),$$

as $n \to \infty$, on expansion by Stirling's Theorem. Therefore the asymptotic distribution of the random variables Z_j representing z_j is the unit spherical normal distribution $MN_m(0, \mathbf{I})$ conditioned by $\Sigma Z_j\sqrt{p_j} = 0$.

There are two principal consequences of this result for testing the null hypothesis that the probabilities are indeed $p_1, \ldots, p_m$. The first is that the ranking of sample points in order of decreasing $\mathrm{pr}(Y = y)$ is asymptotically the same as that of increasing Σz_j^2, the classical chi-squared test statistic. Thus the chi-squared test is an approximation to an absolute test, as discussed in Problem 3.3. The second consequence is that the null distribution of the Z_j is asymptotically that of m i.i.d. $N(0, 1)$ variables with the one linear constraint $\Sigma Z_j\sqrt{p_j} = 0$, so that ΣZ_j^2 is asymptotically chi-squared with degrees of freedom $m - 1$.

[*Theoretical Statistics*, Section 3.2; Rao, Section 6b; Silvey, p. 120]

3.5. Show that for continuous distributions the null hypothesis distributions of the Kolmogorov and Cramér-von Mises statistics do not depend on the particular null distribution G(.) tested. Prove that the latter statistic can be written in the form

$$\frac{1}{12n^2} + \frac{1}{n}\Sigma\left\{G(Y_{(j)}) - \frac{2j-1}{2n}\right\}^2.$$

Solution

Transformations that are strictly monotone on the support of $G(y)$, which preserve distinct data points, leave invariant any functional of the sample distribution function $\tilde{F}_n(y)$ and $G(y)$, and in particular integrals of the form

$$\int a\{G(y), \tilde{F}_n(y)\}\, dG(y) + \int b\{G(y), \tilde{F}_n(y)\}\, d\tilde{F}_n(y).$$

Both the Kolmogorov and Cramér-von Mises statistics are of this form, so that their sample values and hence null hypothesis distributions are invariant under such transformations. We therefore transform y to $G(y)$, so that the null hypothesis distribution to be tested becomes uniform on $(0, 1)$. The Cramér-von Mises statistic becomes

$$\int_0^1 [\tilde{F}_n\{G^{-1}(y)\} - y]^2 dy = \sum_{j=1}^{n+1} \int_{G(y_{(j-1)})}^{G(y_{(j)})} \left(\frac{j-1}{n} - y\right)^2 dy,$$

where $G(y_{(0)}) = 0, G(y_{(n+1)}) = 1$, which reduces to the form stated.

In considering the exact null hypothesis distributions of such statistics it is, of course, very convenient to take $G(y)$ to be uniform.

[Durbin, 1973; Rao, Section 6f; Silvey, p. 140]

3.6. For binary data the null hypothesis is that the data are generated by a two-state Markov chain, the transition matrix being unknown. Suggest some types of departure that it might be of interest to test, indicating an appropriate test statistic in each case.

Solution

The main types of departure from a simple Markov chain model are that:

(a) transitions may depend on supplementary observations that may be available for each trial;

(b) there may be non-stationarity, e.g. time trends or periodic fluctuations;

(c) there may be dependence of transition probabilities on more than, or other than, the current state occupied.

A quite general family of test statistics can be formulated as follows. Associate with each transition $Y_j \rightarrow Y_{j+1}$ an explanatory variable z_j; in (b) above we might have $z_j = j$ or $\cos(\omega_0 j)$, and in (c) we might have $z_j = Y_{j-1}$. We can then form groups of z's corresponding to the four types of transitions, i.e. $0 \rightarrow 0, 0 \rightarrow 1, 1 \rightarrow 0, 1 \rightarrow 1$, and let the group means be $\bar{z}_{rs}(r, s = 0, 1)$. Plausible test statistics include $(\bar{z}_{01} - \bar{z}_{00})^2 + (\bar{z}_{10} - \bar{z}_{11})^2$ and $n_0(\bar{z}_{01} - \bar{z}_{00})^2 + n_1(\bar{z}_{01} - \bar{z}_{11})^2$, where state i is occupied n_i times $(i = 0, 1)$.

While it is possible to suggest such *ad hoc* test statistics, this is the kind of relatively complicated situation in which it is likely to be more fruitful to consider the more formal approach of subsequent chapters in which alternative probability models are explicitly formulated. This has been done for (c) above (Anderson and Goodman, 1957).

[*Theoretical Statistics*, Section 3.3]

3.7. Prove by geometrical considerations that if $Y_1, \ldots, Y_n$ are independently and identically normally distributed the random variables corresponding to the standardized skewness and kurtosis have distributions that are independent of the estimated mean and variance and which do not depend on the mean and variance of the distribution.

Solution

Make an initial orthogonal transformation to new variables $\bar{Y}\sqrt{n}$ and $Z_1, \ldots, Z_{n-1}$, and then transform to spherical polar co-ordinates

$$Z_1 = R \cos \Theta_1, Z_2 = R \sin \Theta_1 \cos \Theta_2, \ldots, Z_{n-1} = R \sin \Theta_1 \ldots \sin \Theta_{n-2}.$$

Then $R^2 = \Sigma(Y_i - \bar{Y})^2$ and it follows from the spherical normal distribution of $Z_1, \ldots, Z_{n-1}$ that R is distributed independently of the angular co-ordinates. Finally, the skewness and kurtosis estimates are, by dimensional arguments, functions only of the angular co-ordinates.

3.8. List and classify some test statistics for the null hypothesis of normality, based on i.i.d. random variables. Examine for each test statistic the possibility of a generalization to test multivariate normality.

Comment for the multivariate tests on:

(a) the ease with which the distribution under the null hypothesis can be found or approximated;

(b) the ease with which the statistic itself can be computed even in a large number of dimensions;

(c) the extent to which the statistic is sensitive to departures from multivariate normality that leave the marginal distributions exactly or nearly normal;

(d) the types of departure from the null hypothesis for which each test is particularly sensitive.

Solution

Classification of test statistics for goodness of fit to a univariate normal distribution with unknown mean and variance is rather arbitrary, because all are functions of the order statistics, or equivalently the sample distribution function. However a convenient grouping is as follows:

(a) measures of agreement of grouped observed frequencies with fitted normal frequencies, such as the chi-squared statistic

$$\Sigma \frac{(\text{obs. freq.} - \text{fitted freq.})^2}{\text{fitted freq.}};$$

(b) measures of distance between sample distribution function and fitted theoretical distribution function $\Phi\{(y - \tilde{\mu})/\tilde{\sigma})\}$, where $\tilde{\mu}$ and $\tilde{\sigma}$ are estimates of μ and σ such as $\bar{y}$. and $\sqrt{\text{MS}}$;

(c) measures of agreement of simple general data properties, such as standardized third and fourth cumulants, with their theoretical values;

(d) measures of linearity of a plot of ordered sample values versus expected normal order statistics, particularly the squared correlation coefficient derived from such a plot (Shapiro and Wilk, 1965).

In principle the distributions of these statistics under H_0 are to be determined conditionally on the sufficient statistics $\bar{Y}$ and MS, but in practice large-sample approximations seem to be necessary. Shapiro *et al.* (1968) have made an extensive simulation study of the sensitivity of these tests, their conclusions tending to favour (d).

An important general consideration is the extent to which the test result helps to indicate the type of departure from H_0, if any. From this point of view it is preferable to use the most significant of a few statistics measuring distinct types of departure. Certainly with all the tests inspection of graphs is an essential complement (Problem 3.12). To discuss the practical role of tests of distributional form would raise basic issues about the relation between models and real situations.

All of the above tests can be adapted to test certain aspects of multivariate normality. The types of departure from multivariate normality are so many that it will be wise to try to specify explicitly that aspect of the multivariate normal distribution thought to be of key importance.

One general approach is to test marginal distributions, either on the original axes or on principal component axes, and to find the null distribution of some suitable composite statistic, such as the most significant of the marginal test statistics. The major problem here is to find the null hypothesis distribution of the selected statistic.

A second approach is to consider statistics which are not directly formed from combinations of univariate statistics. Method (a) above is impracticable unless the dimensionality is very small. Method (b) does not seem to have been investigated. Method (c) has been considered by Mardia (1971). The most fruitful approach for graphical analysis is probably method (d). A simple procedure (Healy, 1968; Cox, 1968) is to compute $d_j = (y_j - \tilde{\mu})^{\mathrm{T}}\tilde{\Sigma}^{-1}(y_j - \tilde{\mu})$ for each data point, where $\tilde{\mu}$ and $\tilde{\Sigma}$ are estimates of the mean vector and covariance matrix, and to plot the ordered d_j against expected order statistics for the chi-squared distribution with p degrees of freedom. Direct analogues of the measures in method (d) can be defined, but nothing seems to be known about null hypothesis distributions.

[*Theoretical Statistics*, Section 3.3; Andrews *et al.*, 1971, 1973; Gnanadesikan, 1977]

3.9. Suggest a plot of ordered values useful for testing consistency with the density $\tau^{-1}g(y/\tau)(y \geqslant 0)$, for unknown τ. What would be the interpretation of a straight line not through the origin? Suggest a test statistic for such an effect and show how to find its exact null hypothesis distribution when $G(.)$ is exponential.

Solution

It follows from the expression for the density of the rth largest observation $Y_{(nr)}$ that $E(Y_{(nr)}) = \tau g_{nr}$, where

$$g_{nr} = \frac{n!}{(r-1)!(n-r)!} \int x\{G(x)\}^{r-1}\{1 - G(x)\}^{n-r}g(x)dx.$$

Thus a plot of $Y_{(nr)}$ versus g_{nr} should be approximately linear if the form of g is correct. Note that the slope of the plot will estimate τ; the initial slope can be used when suspiciously large observations are present (Wilk *et al.*, 1963).

A straight line plot through the point $(\alpha, 0)$ suggests that the density is $\tau^{-1}g\{(y-\alpha)/\tau\}(y \geqslant \alpha)$, i.e. that the distribution is displaced from the origin. It is natural to test this effect with $Y_{(n1)}$, and in the exponential case a test independent of τ can be obtained by conditioning on the sufficient statistic $Y_1 + \ldots + Y_n$; see Problem 5.5. To obtain the conditional distribution under the null hypothesis $H_0 : \alpha = 0$, we use the fact that for exponentially distributed Y_j,

$$Y_{(nr)} = \frac{W_1}{n} + \ldots + \frac{W_r}{n-r+1} \qquad (r = 1, \ldots, n),$$

where $W_1, \ldots, W_n$ are i.i.d. exponential variables with mean τ. Thus the required distribution of $Y_{(n1)}$ conditional on $Y_1 + \ldots + Y_n = s$ is that of W_1/n conditional on $W_1 + \ldots + W_n = s$, which in turn is that of the smallest of $n-1$ uniform random variables on $(0, s/n)$. Therefore

$$\text{pr}(Y_{(n1)} \geqslant y_{(n1)} | \Sigma Y_j = s; H_0) = (1 - ny_{(n1)}/s)^{n-1};$$

we concentrate on the upper tail of the distribution in assessing significance because a negative value of $y_{(n1)}$ is certain disproof of H_0.

[*Theoretical Statistics*, Section 3.3; Sukhatme, 1936]

3.10. Show that for a gamma distribution of unknown mean and index, the first three cumulants are such that $\kappa_3\kappa_1 = 2\kappa_2^2$. Hence suggest a test statistic for examining consistency of data with the gamma family. Assess methods that might be used to determine the distribution of the statistic under the null hypothesis.

Solution

For the probability density $\alpha(\alpha y)^{\beta-1}e^{-\alpha y}/\Gamma(\beta)$ the cumulant generating function $\log E\{\exp(sY)\}$ is $\beta\log(1-s/\alpha)$. Thus, by expansion,

$$\kappa_1 = \beta/\alpha, \quad \kappa_2 = \beta/\alpha^2, \quad \kappa_3 = 2\beta/\alpha^3,$$

and the relation $\kappa_3\kappa_1 = 2\kappa_2^2$ follows. It can be written

$$\gamma_1 = \kappa_3/\kappa_2^{3/2} = 2\kappa_2^{1/2}\kappa_1^{-1} = 2\gamma_0,$$

where γ_0 is the coefficient of variation, or standard deviation divided by mean. For the log normal distribution $\gamma_1 = 3\gamma_0 + \gamma_0^3$, while for the Weibull distribution a quite different relation holds. Thus, with several sets of data, a plot of estimates $\tilde{\gamma}_1$ versus $\tilde{\gamma}_0$ will indicate which, if any, of the main two-parameter families of distributions on $(0, \infty)$ is adequate. This is analogous to the plot of $\tilde{\gamma}_2$ versus $\tilde{\gamma}_1$, useful for families defined on $(-\infty, \infty)$ (Pearson and Hartley, 1970, p. 87).

There are difficulties in converting the above results into a significance test. A first step is to consider $\tilde{\gamma}_1 - 2\tilde{\gamma}_0$ or $\log(\frac{1}{2}\tilde{\gamma}_1/\tilde{\gamma}_0)$, which both have means approximately zero under the null hypothesis. The sampling moments of the sample estimates of cumulants are known up to a high order (Kendall and Stuart, 1967–9, Chapter 12), so that approximate standard errors can be estimated for the above statistics, and normal approximations used. Simulation methods would probably be useful in obtaining more refined null hypothesis distributions.

A quite different approach is to eliminate the null hypothesis nuisance parameters α and β from the distribution by conditioning on the sufficient statistic $(\Sigma Y_j, \Sigma \log Y_j)$. One possibility is then to consider the statistic ΣY_j^2 conditionally on $\Sigma Y_j = s_1, \Sigma \log Y_j = s_2$. However it seems difficult to work with the exact conditional distribution, and again large sample approximations seem necessary.

A final general comment is that useful statements about distributional form can usually be made only after examining several similar sets of data obtained under somewhat different conditions.

[*Theoretical Statistics*, Section 3.3]

3.11. Show how exact index of dispersion tests can be developed for the binomial and geometric distributions, and for the general one-parameter exponential family distribution. Explain why, under suitable circumstances to be stated, the chi-squared distribution will be a good approximation to the null hypothesis distribution in the first case, not in the second and not in general in the third.

Solution

Consider discrete random variables following a single parameter exponential family distribution in the natural form

$$f_Z(z;\varphi) = \exp\{-z\varphi + c\dagger(\varphi) + d\dagger(z)\}.$$

For n observations that are i.i.d. with this distribution under H_0, their joint probability is

$$\exp\{-\varphi\Sigma z_j + nc\dagger(\varphi)\}\exp\{\Sigma d\dagger(z_j)\}.$$

The sufficient statistic for the nuisance parameter φ is $S = \Sigma Z_j$, and conditionally on $S = s$ we have

$$\text{pr}\{Z_j = z_j, j = 1,\ldots,n | S = s; H_0\} = \frac{\exp\{\Sigma d\dagger(z_j)\}}{\displaystyle\sum_{z_k:\Sigma z_k = s} \exp\{\Sigma d\dagger(z_k)\}}. \qquad (1)$$

Now take any test statistic measuring dispersion, in particular $\Sigma(Z_j - \bar{Z})^2$. Its exact distribution under H_0 is in principle determined by (1).

By Problem 2.13, $\text{var}(Z) = -c\dagger''(\varphi) = v(\varphi)$, say, and $E(Z) = c\dagger'(\varphi) = b(\varphi)$, say. Thus $v\{b^{-1}(S/n)\}$ is an estimate of $v(\varphi)$, and we may use this theoretical value to standardize the direct estimate of $\text{var}(Z)$, giving the index of dispersion statistic

$$\Sigma(Z_j - \bar{Z})^2/v\{b^{-1}(S/n)\}. \qquad (2)$$

Approximately we can consider (2) as the corrected sum of squares of n i.i.d. random variables with unit variance under H_0; provided the Z_j's are approximately normal we can expect the chi-squared distribution with $n-1$ degrees of freedom to be a good approximation. If the Z_j are Poisson with large mean, or binomial with large mean, then the Z_j are indeed approximately normal and the chi-squared approximation holds. If, however, the Z_j are geometric, the dispersion of (2) is easily seen to be far greater than that for the chi-squared distribution with $n-1$ degrees of freedom, essentially because, for geometrically distributed observations, the fourth moment is very high compared with the square of the variance, and the distribution of the sample variance therefore much more dispersed than under normal theory.

[*Theoretical Statistics*, Section 3.3]

3.12. The following desirable features have been suggested for graphical methods of analysis:

(a) conformity with a simple model should be shown by a straight line plot, or, where the random part of the variability is of direct interest, by a completely random scatter;

(b) points plotted should be subject to independent errors;

(c) points should be of equal precision;

(d) non-linear transformations should be such as to emphasize ranges of values of particular interest.

Discuss various graphical methods for examining agreement with a normal distribution in the light of these requirements.

Solution

Graphical methods are important both in the preliminary analysis of data and in the final presentation of conclusions. It is, however, difficult to give a systematic discussion. Two initial general principles are first, that systematic relations are usually best put in linear form. Secondly, where evidence of departure from a random structure is being examined, and a linear plot cannot be produced, a plot anticipated to be completely random should be used. These are the two patterns, departures from which are relatively easily detected by eye. This forms (a).

If points are plotted with appreciably correlated errors, superficially systematic departures from the 'true' model are to be expected and have to be allowed for in interpretation. Similarly if points plotted are of unequal precision this has to be allowed for in interpretation; sometimes this can be done by including the standard error of each point, for example by varying the physical size of plotted points in an appropriate way. This covers (b) and (c). The final point (d) is essentially that if there is a scale of practical importance then this should be reflected in the plotting method. Unfortunately the requirements (a)–(d) are often conflicting to some extent.

Among many possible graphical techniques for testing normality are:

(i) to plot ordered sample values against expected order statistics for the $N(0, 1)$ distribution (see Problem 3.8), or some approximation thereto such as $\Phi^{-1}\{(r - 3/8)/(n + 1/4)\}$ (*Theoretical Statistics*, Appendix 2);

(ii) to fit the theoretical cumulative distribution function (c.d.f.) $\Phi\{(y - \tilde{\mu})/\tilde{\sigma}\}$, where $\tilde{\mu}$ and $\tilde{\sigma}$ are estimates of μ and σ, and to plot the fitted curve and sample c.d.f. together;

(iii) to use (ii), but to plot the differences, theoretical c.d.f. $-$ sample c.d.f., at a suitable grid of points, possibly scaling the differences by their estimated standard errors;

(iv) to plot the logarithm of histogram ordinate versus $(y - \tilde{\mu})^2$;

(v) to plot the fitted normal density $\tilde{\sigma}^{-1}\varphi\{(y-\tilde{\mu})/\tilde{\sigma}\}$ and the sample histogram on the same graph;

(vi) to plot differences obtained from (v), possibly in some standardized form either (α) dividing a difference by the square root of fitted frequency or (β) working with differences of square root frequencies;

(vii) to transform sample values by $\Phi^{-1}\{(y_j-\tilde{\mu})/\tilde{\sigma}\}$ into approximately uniform variates and then to apply methods connected with the uniform distribution.

No once-and-for-all choice between these is possible, although method (i) is probably best for general use. Comparisons of fitted curves are probably best made in terms of standardized differences. Whatever method is used, some idea of the effects of typical departures from normality is necessary. To this end it is useful to produce some plots of artificial data of the kind that may be encountered.

[*Theoretical Statistics*, Section 3.4; Cox, 1978]

3.13. In five trials, the first four give zero and the last a one. The null hypothesis is that these are Bernoulli trials with the probability of a one equal to $\frac{1}{2}$ and it is required to test for a preponderance of zeroes. Prove that if the number of trials is fixed, so that the number of ones has a binomial distribution, the significance level is 3/16, whereas if trials continued until the first one, so that the number of trials has a geometric distribution, the significance level is 1/16. Discuss this in the light of the strong likelihood principle, according to which the likelihood is to be used directly, noting that in the formulation in which only the null hypothesis is explicitly formulated there is no opportunity for contradiction to arise.

Solution

If the number of trials is fixed, we have a random variable Y' counting the number of zeroes for which

$$\mathrm{pr}(Y'=r;H_0)=2^{-5}5!/\{r!(5-r)!\}.$$

Thus, in testing for a preponderance of zeroes, the significance level is

$$\mathrm{pr}(Y'=4;H_0)+\mathrm{pr}(Y'=5;H_0)=3/16.$$

If trials continue until the first success, the number of trials Y'' is a random variable having the distribution $\mathrm{pr}(Y''=r;H_0)=2^{-r}$. The significance level is then

$$\sum_{r=5}^{\infty}\mathrm{pr}(Y''=r;H_0)=1/16.$$

The likelihood can only be used when more than one distribution is explicitly defined, so that in the present situation, where only one distribution is explicitly formulated, a likelihood function is not defined. Therefore no comparison with a likelihood principle is possible. To introduce a likelihood function we require at least one other probability model, one possibility being to suppose that the trials are independent with probability θ of a one. Then if the stopping rule is either of those indicated, or indeed any where the probability of terminating trials depends only on results of preceding trials, the likelihood for the given sample is $(1 - \theta)^4 \theta$. Then the strong likelihood principle indicates drawing the same conclusion in the two cases. If, however, we consider just one model in addition to H_0, namely that zero is certain to occur in trials 1,...,4 and one is certain to occur in trial 5, the position is entirely different, so that the particular choice of supplementary model is crucial.

Acceptance of the strong likelihood principle would mean that Chapters 4–9 of this book could be largely disregarded. Our attitude to this is that (a) it would indeed be convenient if specification of the stopping rule were unnecessary; (b) the arguments outlined for deducing the strong likelihood principle from more primitive requirements are not compelling (*Theoretical Statistics*, p. 41; Kalbfleisch, 1975), nor are the arguments for a purely Bayesian approach (Chapter 10); (c) the strong likelihood principle as such does not indicate general likelihood methods, and these are lacking.

[*Theoretical Statistics*, Sections 2.3, 2.4, 3.4(ii)]

3.14.* It is proposed that for testing a hypothesis H_0, when no explicit alternatives are available, one can decide between various statistics as to which is most appropriate solely on the basis of their sampling distributions when H_0 is true. The general proposition is then reduced to the limited proposition that if two statistics have the same sampling distribution under H_0, then they are equally effective for testing H_0. To be specific, consider the hypothesis H_0 that given observations $y_1, \ldots, y_n$ are represented by i.i.d. $N(0, \sigma^2)$ random variables $Y_1, \ldots, Y_n$, for which the Student t statistic $T = \sqrt{n} \bar{Y} / \{\Sigma(\bar{Y}_j - \bar{Y}.)^2/(n-1)\}^{1/2}$ is thought suitable. Refute the above proposal by considering the statistic

$$T' = \frac{(n-1)^{1/2} \Sigma a_j Y_j}{\{\Sigma Y_j^2 - (\Sigma a_j Y_j)^2\}^{1/2}},$$

where $a_j = y_j / \{\Sigma y_k^2\}^{1/2} (j = 1, \ldots, n)$.

*Amended version.

Solution

This is related to the discussion of absolute tests of significance in Problem 3.3. As noted there, if absolute tests are to be applied to continuous data, then some criterion for choosing the scale of measurement is needed. The present example illustrates the slightly different point that many statistics which can be constructed from i.i.d. $N(0, \sigma^2)$ random variables have the Student t distribution.

For fixed a_j an orthogonal transformation can be made to new variables $U_1, \dots, U_n$ such that

$$T' = \frac{U_1}{\left\{ \sum_{j=2}^{n} U_j^2/(n-1) \right\}^{1/2}},$$

so that T' has the same Student t distribution as T. Note, however, that $T' = \infty$ if $Y = y$. In other words, every sample is uniquely extreme in some respect! Of course the form of T is chosen *a priori* to reflect probable departures from the null hypothesis, and not because of its distribution under that hypothesis.

[*Theoretical Statistics*, Section 3.4(ii); Neyman, 1952]

3.15. Suppose that in selecting the most significant of a number of dependent test statistics the joint distributions of pairs of statistics are known. Show how the inclusion-exclusion formula can be used to complement the upper bound mentioned in the summary by a lower bound for the significance level, adjusted for selection.

Solution

We identify B_j with the event $P_j \leqslant q_{\text{obs}}$ and use the inequalities (Feller, 1968, Section iv.5)

$$\Sigma \operatorname{pr}(B_j) - \sum_{j>k} \operatorname{pr}(B_j \cap B_k) \leqslant \operatorname{pr}(B_1 \cup \dots \cup B_m) \leqslant \Sigma \operatorname{pr}(B_j).$$

The right-hand side gives the general Bonferroni upper bound $m q_{\text{obs}}$, but no such simple general expression can be given for the lower bound, since this depends on the particular forms for the joint distributions of (P_j, P_k). When test statistics are independent the exact significance level is $1 - (1 - q_{\text{obs}})^m$, the lower bound being $m q_{\text{obs}} - \frac{1}{2} m(m-1) q_{\text{obs}}^2$.

[*Theoretical Statistics*, Section 3.4 (iii)]

3.16. Suppose that m independent sets of data of size $n_1, \ldots, n_m$ are tested for compatibility with H_0 with a particular type of alternative in mind, and that the results of the significance tests are summarized by the significance probabilities $P_1, \ldots, P_m$. Investigate the relative merits of the summary statistics

$$T_1 = -2\Sigma \log P_j, \qquad T_2 = \max(P_j),$$
$$T_3 = \min(P_j), \qquad T_4 = \Sigma n_j P_j / \Sigma n_j,$$

bearing in mind the following possibilities: (i) H_0 is expected to be incorrect for at most one set of data; (ii) H_0 is expected to be correct for all or none of the data sets; and any others potentially appropriate.

Solution

There is no difficulty in principle in finding the null hypothesis distributions of all the suggested statistics, and similar ones, since then $P_1, \ldots, P_m$ are independently uniformly distributed on $(0, 1)$. For example, $-\log P_j$ is exponentially distributed with unit mean so that T_1 has the chi-squared distribution with $2m$ degrees of freedom.

Some considerations relevant to discussion of the significance test statistics are:

(i) interpretation is indirect because the statistics are unrelated to an estimation problem;

(ii) if it is required to detect several moderately small departures from H_0, weighting of the test statistics as in T_4 is desirable, but specification of precise weights requires a more detailed specification of the problem;

(iii) the statistics T_1 and T_3 are appropriate when H_0 is likely to fail only for one of the data sets and then to fail appreciably, whereas T_4 is sensible when any failure of H_0 is likely to affect all the sets.

These statistics, especially T_1, have a long history. Apparently T_1 corresponds to a special case of a procedure suggested by Fisher, the general procedure being first to define X_j as the upper P_j quantile of the chi-squared distribution with r_j degrees of freedom, and then to compute the overall significance as the upper tail probability corresponding to ΣX_j in the chi-squared distribution with Σr_j degrees of freedom.

Detailed investigation of the suggested tests would require the ideas of power and efficiency introduced in Chapter 4. A general result on asymptotic power is given by Littell and Folks (1971).

[*Theoretical Statistics*, Section 3.4(iii)]

4 SIGNIFICANCE TESTS: SIMPLE NULL HYPOTHESES

Summary

In Chapter 3 we supposed that only the null hypothesis H_0 is explicitly formulated. In the present chapter it is assumed that H_0 is simple, assigning density $f_0(y)$, and that in addition one or more alternative hypotheses, H_A, are available representing the directions of departures from H_0 that it is desired to detect. That is, it is required to assess whether there is evidence of inconsistency of the data with H_0, departures in the directions of H_A being of special interest.

First, suppose that H_A is simple assigning density $f_A(y)$. Then an optimal significance test is defined as follows. Denote by w_α the set of possible observations to be regarded as significantly inconsistent with H_0 at level at least α. The physical significance of α requires w_α to be of size α, i.e. pr $(Y \in w_\alpha; H_0) = \alpha$, and w_α is called a critical region of size α. Optimality is achieved by maximizing the power pr$(Y \in w_\alpha; H_A)$.

A key result is that for continuously distributed random variables the optimal test is obtained from likelihood ratio critical regions of the form $\mathrm{lr}_{A0}(y) = f_A(y)/f_0(y) \geqslant c_\alpha$ for appropriate c_α. This is the Neyman-Pearson lemma. In the discrete case this result is restricted to exactly achievable α.

In most applications there is more than one alternative. Thus we may have a single-parameter family of models with $H_0: \theta = \theta_0$ and, for example, $H_A: \theta > \theta_0$ (one-sided alternatives) or $H_A: \theta \neq \theta_0$ (two-sided alternatives). If the same w_α is optimal for all simple alternatives making up H_A, then the test and critical region are called uniformly most powerful. This property is achieved for one-sided tests connected with the natural parameter of a one-parameter exponential family.

The power function of a general test is defined as pr $(Y \in w_\alpha; H_A)$ considered for fixed α as a function of the parameter indexing H_A.

For the general reasons mentioned in Chapter 2 probability calculation of size is in principle to be done conditionally on suitable ancillary statistic.

Two-sided tests are normally best regarded as a combination of two one-sided tests, but are sometimes studied by requiring that the power function be a minimum at H_0, the test then being called unbiased.

Very often no uniformly most powerful test exists, and then one convenient approach is to maximize power for alternatives close to H_0. When the distribution is specified by a scalar parameter θ, the null hypothesis being $\theta = \theta_0$, expansion of the log likelihood ratio gives

$$\log f_Y(y;\theta_0 + \delta) - \log f_Y(y;\theta_0) = u_.(y;\theta_0)\delta + o(\delta),$$

where $u_.(y;\theta_0) = [\partial \log f_Y(y;\theta)/\partial\theta]_{\theta=\theta_0}$. Thus in testing against one-sided local alternatives, critical regions are determined by $u_.(y;\theta_0)$, such that positive and negative values respectively are significant for $\delta > 0$ and $\delta < 0$.

The statistic $u_.(Y;\theta_0) = U_.(\theta_0)$ is called the efficient score, and its main properties are:

(a) $E\{U_.(\theta_0);\theta_0\} = 0$;

(b) var $\{U_.(\theta_0);\theta_0\} = i_.(\theta_0) = E\{-\partial^2 \log f_Y(Y;\theta)/\partial\theta^2;\theta\}$, called the Fisher information;

(c) $E\{U_.(\theta_0 + \delta);\theta_0\} = i_.(\theta_0)\delta + o(\delta)$;

(d) when Y is formed from independent components, $U_.$ and $i_.$ are sums of contributions from those components, and study of the distribution of $U_.$ is simplified;

(e) if θ is transformed to $\varphi = \varphi(\theta)$, then the efficient score and information calculated from the new parameter are

$$\frac{d\theta_0}{d\varphi_0} U_.(\theta_0), \qquad \left(\frac{d\theta_0}{d\varphi_0}\right)^2 i_.(\theta_0).$$

When the parameter θ is a vector, the efficient score and Fisher information generalize to a vector and a matrix.

For multidimensional alternatives H_A, some compromise is needed because achievement of high power in different directions in the parameter space will require different test statistics. One possibility is to take a suitable quadratic form in the components of the efficient score vector, e.g.

$$\{U_.(\theta_0)\}^T\{i_.(\theta_0)\}^{-1}\{U_.(\theta_0)\}.$$

Problems

4.1. Formulate the choice of the best critical region of size α for testing H_0: $\theta = \theta_0$ versus $H_A : \theta = \theta_A$ as a problem in the calculus of variations subject to a constraint. Apply the Euler equation to obtain the Neyman-Pearson lemma.

Solution

Following the method of Lagrange multipliers we maximize unconditionally

$$\int_w \{f_A(y) - kf_0(y)\} dy. \tag{1}$$

Let z be a co-ordinate specifying the boundary between w and its complement and consider a distortion of the boundary so that the new boundary is distant from z along the normal to w by amount $\varepsilon\varphi(z)$. Then the change in (1) is

$$\varepsilon\int \varphi(z)\{f_A(z) - kf_0(z)\} dz + O(\varepsilon^2), \tag{2}$$

where the integral is a surface integral. But for a stationary value of (1) the integral in (2) must vanish and it can do so for arbitrary $\varphi(z)$ only if on the boundary $f_A(z) = kf_0(z)$.

Note that this proof shows only that a stationary value is obtained. The longer but more elementary proof usually given, in fact a special case of that of Problem 4.2, proves that a maximum is indeed achieved.

[*Theoretical Statistics*, Section 4.3; Lehmann, Section 3.2; Rao, Section 7a; Silvey, p. 98]

4.2. The general non-randomized form of the Neyman-Pearson lemma is as follows. If $k_1(y), \dots, k_{m+1}(y)$ are integrable functions over the sample space, not necessarily probability densities, then the region w which maximizes

$$\int_w k_{m+1}(y) dy,$$

subject to the constraints

$$\int_w k_j(y) dy = a_j \ (j = 1, \dots, m),$$

is defined by $\{y : k_{m+1}(y) \geqslant c_1 k_1(y) + \dots + c_m k_m(y)\}$, provided that such constants $c_1, \dots, c_m$ exist. Prove this and use the result to obtain the forms of the critical regions of the locally most powerful one- and two-sided tests for a one-dimensional parameter.

Solution

Let w' be the optimal region and w'' any other region, both satisfying

$$\int_w k_j(y) dy = a_j \quad (j = 1, \dots, m).$$

Denoting the complement of w by $\bar{w}$, we have

$$w' = (w' \cap \bar{w}'') \cup (w' \cap w'') \text{ and } w'' = (w'' \cap \bar{w}') \cup (w' \cap w''),$$

so that for $j = 1, \dots, m$

$$\int_{w' \cap \bar{w}''} k_j(y)dy = \int_{\bar{w}' \cap w''} k_j(y)dy$$

$$= a_j - \int_{w' \cap w''} k_j(y)dy.$$

Now assuming that

$$k_{m+1}(y) \geqslant \sum_{j=1}^{m} c_j k_j(y)$$

in w' and vice versa in $\bar{w}'$, we have

$$\int_{w' \cap \bar{w}''} k_{m+1}(y)dy \geqslant \sum c_j \int_{w' \cap \bar{w}''} k_j(y)dy = \sum c_j \int_{\bar{w}' \cap w''} k_j(y)dy \geqslant \int_{\bar{w}' \cap w''} k_{m+1}(y)dy.$$

Addition of $\int_{w' \cap w''} k_{m+1}(y)dy$ to both sides of the inequality proves the result, because w'' is arbitrary.

The definition of a locally most powerful test is equivalent to requiring a critical region w_α such that

$$\int_{w_\alpha} f(y;\theta_0)dy = \alpha \text{ and } \frac{d}{d\theta_0} \int_{w_\alpha} f(y;\theta_0)dy \text{ is a maximum.}$$

Under regularity conditions we can interchange differentiation and integration, and, noting that $\partial f(y;\theta_0)/\partial \theta_0 = u(y;\theta_0)f(y;\theta_0)$, we obtain the criterion

$$\text{maximize} \int_{w_\alpha} u(y;\theta_0)f(y;\theta_0)dy.$$

Applying the general result with $k_1(y) = f(y;\theta_0)$, $a_1 = \alpha$ and $k_2(y) = u(y;\theta_0)f(y;\theta_0)$, we find that the optimal critical region is $w_\alpha = \{y : u(y;\theta_0) \geqslant c_1\}$.

For the two-sided test we require that the power function has a local minimum at θ_0, with maximum curvature. That is, under regularity conditions,

$$\int_{w_\alpha} f(y;\theta_0)dy = \alpha, \int_{w_\alpha} \{\partial f(y;\theta_0)/\partial \theta_0\}dy = 0, \int_{w_\alpha} \{\partial^2 f(y;\theta_0)/\partial \theta_0^2\} = \text{max.}$$

The general result now applies to give the optimal region

$$w_\alpha = \{y : \partial^2 f(y;\theta_0)/\partial\theta_0^2 \geqslant c_1 f(y;\theta_0) + c_2 \partial f(y;\theta_0)/\partial\theta_0\}$$
$$= \{y : \partial u_\cdot(y;\theta_0)/\partial\theta_0 + u_\cdot^2(y;\theta_0) \geqslant c_1 + c_2 u_\cdot(y;\theta_0)\}.$$

[*Theoretical Statistics*, Sections 4.3, 4.7; Lehmann, Section 3.6; Neyman and Pearson, 1933, 1936, 1967; Rao, Section 7a]

4.3. To compare two simple hypotheses H_0 and H_1, observations are taken one at a time. After each observation the likelihood ratio is computed from all observations currently available; after, say, m observations denote this by $\mathrm{lr}_{10}(y_1,\ldots,y_m) = \mathrm{lr}_{10}(y^{(m)})$. Positive constants a and b are chosen, $a < 1 < b$ and

   (i) if $a < \mathrm{lr}_{10}(y^{(m)}) < b$, a further observation is taken;
   (ii) if $a \geqslant \mathrm{lr}_{10}(y^{(m)})$, no further observations are taken and H_0 is preferred to H_1;
   (iii) if $b \leqslant \mathrm{lr}_{10}(y^{(m)})$, no further observations are taken and H_1 is preferred to H_0.

Denote by d_i the conclusion that H_i is preferred ($i = 0, 1$).

By writing $\mathrm{lr}_{10}(y^{(m)}) = f_1(y^{(m)})/f_0(y^{(m)})$ and summing over all terminal points in the infinite-dimensional sample space, show that

$$a\,\mathrm{pr}(d_0;H_0) \geqslant \mathrm{pr}(d_0;H_1), \quad b\,\mathrm{pr}(d_1;H_0) \leqslant \mathrm{pr}(d_1;H_1).$$

If, further, it can be assumed that the procedure terminates with probability one, show that $a \geqslant \beta/(1-\alpha)$ and $b \leqslant (1-\beta)/\alpha$, where α and β are the 'probabilities of error'.

Under what circumstances will we have $a \simeq \beta/(1-\alpha)$, $b \simeq (1-\beta)/\alpha$? Prove that if the observations are i.i.d., then the procedure terminates with probability one. Examine the form that the procedure takes for one exponential family problem, and show the relation with random walks.

Discuss critically the limitations on the practical usefulness of this formulation.

Solution

Let $w_j^{(m)}$ be the region in the sample space of $y^{(m)} = (y_1,\ldots,y_m)$ leading to preference of H_j at step m. Then

$$\mathrm{pr}(d_0;H_j) = \sum_m \int_{w_0^m} f_j(y^{(m)})dy^{(m)} \quad (j = 1, 2).$$

At every point in $w_0^{(m)}$, $f_1(y^{(m)}) \leqslant a f_0(y^{(m)})$, so that term-by-term comparison of the two series shows that

$$a \operatorname{pr}(d_0 ; H_0) \geqslant \operatorname{pr}(d_0 ; H_1)$$

and similarly

$$b \operatorname{pr}(d_1 ; H_0) \leqslant \operatorname{pr}(d_1 ; H_1).$$

If the procedure is certain to terminate, $\operatorname{pr}(d_0 ; H_0) + \operatorname{pr}(d_1 ; H_0) = 1$, so that $\operatorname{pr}(d_0 ; H_0) = 1 - \alpha$ and $\operatorname{pr}(d_1 ; H_1) = 1 - \beta$. Thus $a \geqslant \beta/(1 - \alpha)$ and $b \leqslant (1 - \beta)/\alpha$.

The inequalities become approximate equalities if the procedure terminates very close to a decision boundary. It is reasonable to assume this when H_0 and H_1 are quite close together, when large values of m will usually be required, the likelihood ratio correspondingly changing in small steps.

If the component observations are i.i.d., we continue sampling beyond stage m if sampling continues to stage m and then

$$\log a < \sum_{j=1}^{m} v_j < \log b, \tag{1}$$

where $v_j = \log\{f_1(y_j)/f_0(y_j)\}$. Thus the probability that sampling continues beyond stage m is less than

$$\operatorname{pr}\left(\log a < \sum_{j=1}^{m} V_j < \log b\right),$$

which by the central limit theorem tends to zero as $m \to \infty$. The condition (1) shows that the process can be represented as a random walk with two absorbing barriers parallel to the 'time' axis.

If the observations are i.i.d. with exponential family distribution in natural form $\exp\{-z\varphi + c\dagger(\varphi) + d\dagger(z)\}, H_0$ and H_1 corresponding to $\varphi = \varphi_0$ and $\varphi = \varphi_1 < \varphi_0$, then

$$v_j = (\varphi_0 - \varphi_1)z_j + c\dagger(\varphi_1) - c\dagger(\varphi_0).$$

Thus (1) may be expressed

$$\frac{\log a}{\varphi_0 - \varphi_1} - m\{c\dagger(\varphi_1) - c\dagger(\varphi_0)\} \leqslant \sum_{j=1}^{m} z_j \leqslant \frac{\log b}{\varphi_0 - \varphi_1} - m\{c\dagger(\varphi_1) - c\dagger(\varphi_0)\},$$

corresponding to two parallel linear absorbing barriers when Σz_j is plotted against m.

While there is an extensive literature developing the above ideas, there are at least two serious limitations. One is that the discussion is based on two simple hypotheses rather than a continuous range of possibilities. The second is that the sequential schemes are 'open', i.e. there is no definite upper bound to the number of observations required. For details of more practicable sequential schemes, see Wetherill (1975).

[*Theoretical Statistics*, Section 4.3; Lehmann, Section 3.10, 3.11; Rao, Section 7c; Silvey, Chapter 8; Wald, 1947]

4.4. In the comparison of two simple hypotheses H_0 and H_1 the observed likelihood ratio is lr_{obs}. The sampling scheme is unknown; for example, it might be that of Problem 4.3 or it might use a fixed number of observations. Adapt the argument of Problem 4.3 to show that the significance level for testing H_0, i.e. $\mathrm{pr}\{lr_{10}(Y) \geqslant lr_{obs}; H_0\}$, is less than or equal to $1/lr_{obs}$.

Solution

Let C_m be the set of sample points $y^{(m)} = (y_1, \ldots, y_m)$ for which sampling stops after m observations and the likelihood ratio is at least lr_{obs}. Then

$$\mathrm{pr}\{lr_{10}(Y) \geqslant lr_{obs}; H_1\} = \sum \int_{C_m} f_1(y^{(m)}) dy^{(m)}$$

$$\mathrm{pr}\{lr_{10}(Y) \geqslant lr_{obs}; H_0\} = \sum \int_{C_m} f_0(y^{(m)}) dy^{(m)}.$$

Term-by-term comparison of the series, using the definition of C_m, gives

$$lr_{obs}\,\mathrm{pr}\{lr_{10}(Y) \geqslant lr_{obs}; H_0\} \leqslant \mathrm{pr}\{lr_{10}(Y) \geqslant lr_{obs}; H_1\} \leqslant 1,$$

from which the required result follows.

Typically the significance probability will be much less than $1/lr_{obs}$.

[*Theoretical Statistics*, Section 4.3; Barnard, 1947; Efron, 1971]

4.5. Suppose that $Y_1, \ldots, Y_n$ are i.i.d. in a normal distribution of unknown mean μ and known coefficient of variation γ_0, so that the variance is $\gamma_0^2 \mu^2$. Obtain the likelihood ratio statistic for testing $\mu = \mu_0$ against the alternative $\mu = \mu_A$, $\mu_A > \mu_0$, and find the distribution of the statistic under the null hypothesis. Discuss how to compare this test with those using only (a) $\Sigma(Y_j - \mu_0)$ and (b) $\Sigma(Y_j - \mu_0)^2$.

Solution

The likelihood ratio critical region is based on large values of the random variable $T = \Sigma V_j$, where $V_j = (\mu_0^{-1} + \mu_A^{-1})Y_j^2 - 2Y_j$. The moment generating function of T is easily obtained directly. Alternatively, writing $Y_j = \mu_0 + Z_j\gamma_0\mu_0, Z_j$ has the $N(0, 1)$ distribution under H_0 and T is a linear function of

$$T' = \Sigma(Z_j + K_0)^2,$$

where $K_0 = \mu_0/\{\gamma_0(\mu_A + \mu_0)\}$. Thus the distribution of T' under H_0 is non-central chi-squared with n degrees of freedom and non-centrality parameter nK_0^2. Under alternative hypotheses Z_j is still normally distributed, so that T' is again proportional to a non-central chi-squared variable. Hence both exact significance limits and power function can be found from tables of non-central chi-squared.

The statistic T' is a function of sample mean and variance which combines information in the most appropriate way. The statistic $\Sigma(Y_j - \mu_0)$ has the distribution $N(0, n\gamma_0^2\mu_0^2)$ under H_0 and its exact level α power for alternative $N(\mu, \gamma_0\mu)$ is

$$1 - \Phi\left\{k_\alpha^* \frac{\mu_0}{\mu} - \frac{\sqrt{n}(\mu - \mu_0)}{\gamma_0\mu}\right\}.$$

The test based on $\Sigma(Y_j - \mu_0)^2$ uses the central chi-squared distribution under H_0 and has power function depending on the non-central chi-squared distribution.

In fact in principle the tests should be combined conditionally on the ancillary statistic $\Sigma Y_j/(\Sigma Y_j^2)^{\frac{1}{2}}$ (Hinkley, 1977).

[*Theoretical Statistics*, Section 4.4]

4.6. Let Y_1 be a binary random variable, with $E(Y_1) = \mathrm{pr}(Y_1 = 1) = \theta$. Consider $H_0 : \theta = \varepsilon$, $H_A : \theta = 1 - \varepsilon$, with ε small. The 'obvious' critical region consists of the single point $y_1 = 1$. What are the size and power?

Now let Y_1 and Y_2 be i.i.d. with the above distribution. A procedure for 'accepting' and 'rejecting' H_0 is defined by: accept H_0 for $y_1 = y_2 = 0$, accept H_A for $y_1 = y_2 = 1$, and otherwise randomize with equal probability between acceptance and rejection. Show that the size and power are identical to those with just one observation.

It is argued that this shows that, for comparing H_0 and H_A, 'one binary observation is as good as two'. Refute this by examining the levels of significance achievable in testing H_0.

Solution

For a single observation, we have for the size and power respectively

$$\mathrm{pr}(\text{'prefer' } H_A; H_0) = \mathrm{pr}(Y = 1; H_0) = \varepsilon,$$

$$\text{pr}(\text{'prefer'}\,H_A; H_A) = \text{pr}(Y = 1; H_A) = 1 - \varepsilon.$$

When there are two observations and the suggested procedure is used,

$$\text{pr}(\text{'prefer'}\,H_A; H_0) = \text{pr}(Y_1 = Y_2 = 1; H_0) + \tfrac{1}{2}\text{pr}(Y_1 + Y_2 = 1; H_0) = \varepsilon,$$
$$\text{pr}(\text{'prefer'}\,H_A; H_A) = \text{pr}(Y_1 = Y_2 = 1; H_A) + \tfrac{1}{2}\text{pr}(Y_1 + Y_2 = 1; H_A) = 1 - \varepsilon.$$

The qualitative conclusion suggested is false. With one observation we have two possible outcomes

'moderate' evidence against H_0, 'moderate' evidence against H_A;(1)

whereas with two observations the possible outcomes are

'strong' evidence against H_0, neutral evidence, 'strong' evidence against H_A. (2)

For assessing strengths of evidence for and against H_0, (1) and (2) are by no means equivalent.

[*Theoretical Statistics*, Section 4.5; Cohen, 1958]

4.7.* The random variables $Y_1, \ldots, Y_n$ are i.i.d. in the exponential distribution with density $\rho e^{-\rho y}(y \geq 0)$. Obtain the uniformly most powerful test of $\rho = \rho_0$ against alternatives $\rho < \rho_0$, and derive the power function of the test.

To reduce dependence on possible outliers, it is proposed to replace the largest k observations by the $(k + 1)$st largest. Show that the loss of power corresponds exactly to the replacement of n by $n - k$.

Solution

Let $\rho_A < \rho_0$ represent a particular alternative. The likelihood ratio for observations $y_1, \ldots, y_n$ is

$$\text{lr}_{A0}(y) = \{\rho_A^n \exp(-\rho_A \Sigma y_j)\} / \{\rho_0^n \exp(-\rho_0 \Sigma y_j)\}$$

so that the likelihood ratio critical region $\text{lr}_{A0}(y) \geq c_\alpha$ has the form $\Sigma y_j \geq d_\alpha$ for all $\rho_A < \rho_0$. By computing the moment generating function we find that $2\rho \, \Sigma Y_j$ has the chi-squared distribution with $2n$ degrees of freedom. Thus the α level significance point for Σy_j is $(2\rho_0)^{-1} c^*_{2n,\alpha}$ and the power is $\text{pr}(X_{2n} \geq \rho_A c^*_{2n,\alpha} / \rho_0)$, where X_{2n} has the chi-squared distribution with $2n$ degrees of freedom, and $c^*_{2n,\alpha}$ denotes the upper α point of the chi-squared distribution with $2n$ degrees of freedom.

When the k largest observations are each replaced by $Y_{(n,n-k)}$, the test

*Amended version.

statistic becomes

$$\sum_{j=1}^{n-k} Y_{(n,j)} + k Y_{(n,n-k)}.$$

Now the order statistics $Z_{(n,j)}$ from a unit exponential distribution have the representation (*Theoretical Statistics*, Appendix 2)

$$Z_{(n,j)} = \frac{W_1}{n} + \dots + \frac{W_j}{n-j+1} \quad (j=1,\dots,n), \tag{1}$$

where $W_1, \dots, W_n$ are i.i.d. with the unit exponential distribution. Writing $\rho Y_{(n,j)} = Z_{(n,j)}$ and using (1), we have

$$2\rho\left(\sum_{j=1}^{n-k} Y_{(n,j)} + k Y_{(n,n-k)}\right) = 2\sum_{j=1}^{n-k} W_j = X_{2n-2k}.$$

Therefore the size and power are calculated as before, the effective sample size being $n-k$.

[*Theoretical Statistics*, Section 4.6]

4.8. Let $Y_1, \dots, Y_n$ be i.i.d. with density proportional to $\exp\left(-\frac{1}{2}y^2 - \theta y^4\right)$. Obtain the uniformly most powerful test of $H_0: \theta = 0$ versus alternatives $\theta > 0$. Examine the distribution of the test statistic under H_0. For what practical situation might the test be useful?

Solution

Let $\theta_A > 0$ be a particular alternative. The likelihood ratio is

$$\mathrm{lr}_{A0}(y) = \exp(-\theta_A \Sigma y_j^4),$$

and the corresponding critical region is equivalent to $\Sigma y_j^4 \leq d_\alpha$ for all $\theta_A > 0$.

To obtain the distribution under H_0 the central limit theorem, or modifications thereof, can be used (*Theoretical Statistics*, Appendix 1). If Y has the $N(0,1)$ distribution

$$E(Y^{4m}) = (4m)!/\{2^{2m}(2m)!\},$$

so that $E(Y^4) = 3$, $\mathrm{var}(Y^4) = 96$. Thus $T = (\Sigma Y_j^4 - 3n)/\sqrt{(96n)}$, is approximately $N(0,1)$ under H_0. However the skewness coefficient is $\gamma_{1T} = 99/\sqrt{(96n)}$, large enough to indicate very slow convergence of T to normality.

The main application is likely to be when the Y_j are test statistics, but there seems to be no obvious reason for considering this kind of symmetric alternative in preference to one in which the Y_j are normal with changing variances; thus the problem seems rather an academic one.

[*Theoretical Statistics*, Section 4.6]

4.9. Let $Y_1, \ldots, Y_n$ be i.i.d. in $N(0, \sigma^2)$ and consider $H_0: \sigma^2 = 1$ versus $H_A: \sigma^2 \neq 1$. Obtain the most powerful unbiased test and compare its form numerically with the equitailed test for the special case $\alpha = 0.05, n = 5$.

Solution

For an arbitrary alternative hypothesis the density of Y is

$$(2\pi\sigma^2)^{-\frac{1}{2}n} \exp\left(-\frac{1}{2}\Sigma y_j^2/\sigma^2\right) = q(y, \sigma),$$

say. We therefore apply the general result of Problem 4.2 with $m = 2$, $k_1(y) = q(y, 1), k_2(y) = [\partial q(y, \sigma)/\partial\sigma]_{\sigma=1}, k_3(y) = q(y, \sigma), a_1 = \alpha, a_2 = 0$. The critical region is defined by a quadratic equation in $t = \Sigma y_j^2$ and has the form $\{t \leqslant t_1^*, t \geqslant t_2^*\}$. Because T/σ^2 has the chi-squared distribution with n degrees of freedom, with density $p_n(t)$, say, the constraints defining t_1^* and t_2^* may be written

$$\int_{t_1^*}^{t_2^*} p_n(t)dt = 1 - \alpha, \quad \int_{t_1^*}^{t_2^*} (t - n)p_n(t)dt = 0.$$

Integration by parts in the second constraint leads to the alternative form

$$(t_1^*)^{\frac{1}{2}n}e^{-\frac{1}{2}t_1^*} = (t_2^*)^{\frac{1}{2}n}e^{-\frac{1}{2}t_2^*}.$$

Further progress has to be numerical. Lindley *et al.* (1960) have tabulated t_1^* and t_2^*; for $n = 5$, $\alpha = 0.05$, $t_1^* = 0.989$, $t_2^* = 14.37$. This compares with equitailed limits 0.831 and 12.83. The tail areas corresponding to t_1^* and t_2^* are approximately 0.037 and 0.013.

[*Theoretical Statistics*, Section 4.7; Lehmann, Section 5.2]

4.10. Apply higher terms of a series expansion to find an improvement on the locally most powerful test for testing $H_0: \theta = 0$ versus $H_A: \theta > 0$ when $Y_1, \ldots, Y_n$ are i.i.d. in $N(0, 1 + a\theta^2)$, where a is a known positive constant.

Solution

For a single random variable Y_j the log density is

$$l_j(\theta) = -\frac{1}{2}\log(2\pi) - \frac{1}{2}\log(1 + a\theta^2) - \frac{(Y_j - \theta)^2}{2(1 + a\theta^2)},$$

whose first derivative is

$$U_j(\theta) = -\frac{a\theta}{1 + a\theta^2} + \frac{Y_j - \theta}{1 + a\theta^2} + \frac{a\theta(Y_j - \theta)^2}{(1 + a\theta^2)^2}.$$

Thus $U_j(0) = Y_j$. The second derivative of $l_j(\theta)$ at $\theta = 0$ is

$$U_j'(0) = -a - 1 + aY_j^2,$$

and $i_j(0) = 1$.

An approximation to the log likelihood ratio for $\theta = \delta$ versus $\theta = 0$ is, by Taylor expansion to two terms,

$$\delta\Sigma U_j(0) + \tfrac{1}{2}\delta^2 \Sigma U_j'(0),$$

which leads to the test statistic

$$\Sigma Y_j + \tfrac{1}{2}\delta a\Sigma(Y_j^2 - 1). \tag{1}$$

The choice of δ is somewhat arbitrary, but a reasonable procedure is to maximize α level power near the point where power is β. Because the test statistic (1) is approximately $N(\delta n, n)$, this leads to

$$\delta \simeq (k_\alpha^* + k_\beta^*)/\sqrt{n}.$$

Probably as good a general choice as any is $\delta = 2/\sqrt{n}$, which leads from (1) to the statistic

$$T = \Sigma\left(Y_j + \frac{1}{2a}\sqrt{n}\right)^2.$$

The exact distribution of T is that of $(1 + a\theta^2)X_n(\phi_n)$, where $X_n(\phi_n)$ is non-central chi-squared with n degrees of freedom and non-centrality parameter

$$\phi_n = n(2a\theta + \sqrt{n})^2/\{4a^2(1 + a\theta^2)\}.$$

The score statistic ΣY_j has exact distribution $N(n\theta, n + na\theta^2)$. As an example of the comparison, the 0.05 level powers for $n = 10$, $a = 1$, are

θ		$\frac{1}{8}$	$\frac{1}{4}$	$\frac{1}{2}$	$\frac{3}{4}$	1	$1\frac{1}{4}$	$1\frac{1}{2}$
power of	T	0.11	0.22	0.59	0.87	0.97	0.99	1.00
power of	ΣY_j	0.11	0.20	0.48	0.72	0.86	0.93	0.96

The calculations show clearly the greater power of T in the regions of moderate to high power but are not quite accurate enough to reveal the higher power of ΣY_j near the origin.

[*Theoretical Statistics*, Section 4.8; Efron, 1975; Rao, Section 7a.4]

4.11. A multinomial distribution has four cells with probabilities respectively $\{\frac{1}{6}(1-\theta), \frac{1}{6}(1+\theta), \frac{1}{6}(2-\theta), \frac{1}{6}(2+\theta)\}$. Show that for n independent trials the information is

$$i_.(\theta) = \frac{(2-\theta^2)n}{(1-\theta^2)(4-\theta^2)}.$$

Show that there are two possible ancillary statistics and use the variance of the conditional information to choose between them.

Solution

Let N_j $(j=1,\ldots,4)$ represent the sample frequencies, which have a multinomial distribution with given cell probabilities $p_j(\theta)$. Thus, except for a constant,

$$\log f_Y(y;\theta) = n_1 \log(1-\theta) + n_2 \log(1+\theta) + n_3 \log(2-\theta) + n_4 \log(2+\theta),$$

$$U_.(\theta) = -\frac{N_1}{1-\theta} + \frac{N_2}{1+\theta} - \frac{N_3}{2-\theta} + \frac{N_4}{2+\theta}$$

and

$$-U_.'(\theta) = \frac{N_1}{(1-\theta)^2} + \frac{N_2}{(1+\theta)^2} + \frac{N_3}{(2-\theta)^2} + \frac{N_4}{(2+\theta)^2}.$$

The expectation of the latter is the total information, which using $E(N_j) = np_j(\theta)$ is calculated to be

$$i_.(\theta) = n(2-\theta^2)/\{(1-\theta^2)(4-\theta^2)\}.$$

There are in this case two possible ancillary statistics

$$A = (A_1, A_2) \text{ with } A_1 = N_1 + N_2, A_2 = n - A_1 = N_3 + N_4;$$
$$B = (B_1, B_2) \text{ with } B_1 = N_1 + N_4, B_2 = n - B_1 = N_2 + N_3;$$

for example, A_1 has a binomial distribution of index n and parameter $\frac{1}{3}$, not depending on θ. Now conditionally on A the information is obtained from the conditional expectation of $-U_.'(\theta)$, which is

$$i_.(\theta|A=a) = \{3a_1 + n(1-\theta^2)\}/\{(1-\theta^2)(4-\theta^2)\};$$

for example, N_1 is conditionally binomial with index a_1 and parameter $\frac{1}{2}(1 - \theta)$. The expectation of $i\,(\theta|A)$ with respect to A is, of course, $i\,(\theta)$ and its variance is

$$2n/\{(1 - \theta^2)(4 - \theta^2)\}^2.$$

For the ancillary statistic B the expected conditional information is again $i\,(\theta)$ and the variance is

$$\theta^2 n/\{(1 - \theta^2)(4 - \theta^2)\}^2.$$

Thus, because $\theta^2 < 2$, A is more selective than B in sorting the data into sets of different information contents and on this basis A is preferable.

[*Theoretical Statistics*, Sections 4.8, 2.2 (viii); Basu, 1964; Cox, 1971]

4.12. A finite Markov chain has transition probabilities $((p_{jk}(\theta)))$ depending on a scalar parameter θ. The chain is ergodic and at time zero the state has the stationary distribution of the chain. By examining the log likelihood, find the total information function $i\,(\theta)$ for observation at times $0, 1, \ldots, n$.

Solution

Denote the equilibrium distribution over states of the chain by $\{\pi_j(\theta)\}$. Let the initial state be j_0, and let m_{jk} be the number of transitions from state j to state k out of the n sample transitions. Then the full log likelihood is

$$\log \pi_0(\theta) + \Sigma\Sigma m_{jk} \log p_{jk}(\theta). \tag{1}$$

Now if M_{jk} is the random variable corresponding to m_{jk}, then because the initial state and subsequent states all have equilibrium marginal distributions,

$$E(M_{jk}) = n\pi_j(\theta)p_{jk}(\theta).$$

Thus if n is large, the average information per observation is obtained by taking $-n^{-1}$ times the second derivative of (1), ignoring the first term, and replacing m_{jk} by $n\pi_j(\theta)p_{jk}(\theta)$. The result is

$$\Sigma\Sigma \pi_j(\theta)p_{jk}(\theta)\left\{ -\frac{\partial^2 \log p_{jk}(\theta)}{\partial \theta^2} \right\} = \Sigma\pi_j(\theta)i(\theta|j),$$

where $i(\theta|j)$ is the information calculated from the probability distribution in the jth row of the transition matrix.

[*Theoretical Statistics*, Section 4.8]

4.13. Let $Y_1, \ldots, Y_n$ have independent Poisson distributions of means μ, $\mu\rho, \ldots, \mu\rho^{n-1}$. Show how to obtain locally optimum tests (a) for $\mu = \mu_0$ when ρ is known and (b) for $\rho = \rho_0$ when μ is known.

Solution

The log density for Y_j is

$$-\mu\rho^{j-1} + y_j \log(\mu\rho^{j-1}) - \log y_j!.$$

Thus in case (a) the contribution to the efficient score is, by partial differentiation with respect to μ, $U_j(\mu_0) = -\rho^{j-1} + Y_j/\mu_0$, whose variance is the information contribution $i_j(\mu_0) = \rho^{j-1}/\mu_0$.

Therefore the test statistic is

$$U_.(\mu_0) = \frac{1}{\mu_0} \sum_{j=1}^{n} (Y_j - \mu_0\rho^{j-1}),$$

which under the null hypothesis has mean zero and variance $\Sigma\rho^{j-1}/\mu_0$, as can be verified directly. Asymptotic normality holds if $\rho \geqslant 1$. A normal approximation may be reasonable if ρ is not much smaller than 1 and μ_0 is not small; note that by the additive properties of cumulants $U_.(\mu_0)$ has sth cumulant

$$\Sigma\rho^{j-1}/\mu_0^{s-1}.$$

In case (b), when the roles of μ and ρ are interchanged, it is convenient to use the distinguishing notation $U_j^*(\rho_0)$ for the efficient score with respect to ρ. The details are different but the argument identical to that for case (a), and we obtain

$$U_j^*(\rho_0) = -\mu(j-1)\rho_0^{j-2} + (j-1)Y_j/\rho_0$$
$$i_j^*(\rho_0) = \mu\rho_0^{j-3}(j-1)^2.$$

The case with known ρ corresponds to observation of a dilution series and the above solution provides, in principle, confidence intervals for the unknown μ; see Chapter 7.

[*Theoretical Statistics*, Section 4.8; Rao, Section 7a. 4]

4.14. The independent random variables $Y_1, \ldots, Y_n$ are independently normally distributed with constant variance σ^2 and with $E(Y_j) = e^{\beta x_j}$, where $x_1, \ldots, x_n$ are known constants. Obtain the information matrix for $\theta = (\beta, \sigma^2)$. Find the locally most powerful test for $\beta = \beta_0$ versus $\beta \neq \beta_0$ with σ^2 known to be equal to σ_0^2.

The constants $x_1, \ldots, x_n$ can be chosen in $[0, 1]$, and it is proposed in fact to select them to maximize $i_{\cdot}(\beta_0)$. Justify this and, assuming that all x_j's are taken equal, find the common value.

Solution

The log density for Y_j is

$$-\tfrac{1}{2}\log(2\pi) - \log\sigma - \tfrac{1}{2}(Y_j - e^{\beta x_j})^2/\sigma^2,$$

so that the components of the contribution to the efficient score are, in an obvious notation,

$$U_{j\beta} = x_j e^{\beta x_j}(Y_j - e^{\beta x_j})/\sigma^2, \quad U_{j\sigma} = \{(Y_j - e^{\beta x_j})^2 - \sigma^2\}/\sigma^3.$$

The contribution to the information matrix is the covariance matrix of these components, namely

$$i_j = \mathrm{diag}(x_j^2\, e^{2\beta x_j}/\sigma^2, 2/\sigma^2).$$

To test the null hypothesis $\beta = \beta_0$ for known σ^2, the efficient score statistic is therefore equivalent to

$$T = \Sigma x_j e^{\beta_0 x_j}(Y_j - e^{\beta_0 x_j}),$$

which under the null hypothesis is $N(0, \sigma^2 \Sigma x_j^2 e^{2\beta_0 x_j})$. Note that the optimal property of the test statistic is relatively weak.

One justification for maximizing $i_{\cdot}(\beta_0)$ is that the local power is maximized; when $\beta = \beta_0 + \delta$ the standardized test statistic is normally distributed with approximate mean $\delta\sqrt{\{i_{\cdot}(\beta_0)\}}/\sigma$ and variance 1. Equivalently, the asymptotic properties of the maximum likelihood estimate of β are optimized near $\beta = \beta_0$; see Chapter 9. To maximize $i_{\cdot}(\beta_0)$ by a design with all observations at $\tilde{x}$ we have to maximize $\tilde{x}^2 \exp(2\beta_0\tilde{x})$ with $0 \leqslant \tilde{x} \leqslant 1$. It is easily shown that

$$\tilde{x} = \begin{cases} 1 & (\beta_0 \geqslant -1), \\ -1/\beta_0 & (\beta_0 < -1), \end{cases}$$

the qualitative form being plausible on general grounds. To prove that the optimum design is indeed concentrated at one point is difficult from first principles; an elegant general approach is via a generalization to non-linear models of the Kiefer–Wolfowitz general equivalence theorem for linear designs (White, 1973).

[*Theoretical Statistics*, Section 4.8]

4.15. Generalize the result (c) of the Summary to vector parameters by showing that $E\{U_{.}(\theta_0);\theta_0 + \delta\} = i_{.}(\theta)\delta + o(\delta)$, where δ is a column vector. Check this for the normal-theory linear model with known variance. A vector parameter θ is transformed into a new parameter ϕ by a one–one differentiable transformation. Show that the new information matrix is

$$\left(\frac{\partial\theta}{\partial\phi}\right)^{\mathrm{T}} i_{.}(\theta) \left(\frac{\partial\theta}{\partial\phi}\right).$$

Solution

The first part is an immediate consequence of the expansion of $U_{.}(\theta) - U_{.}(\theta + \delta)$ and the continuity assumption $i_{.}(\theta + \delta) = i_{.}(\theta) + o(1)$.

For the normal-theory linear model with known variance σ_0^2 the log likelihood is, except for a constant,

$$-\frac{(\hat\beta - \beta)^{\mathrm{T}}(\mathbf{x}^{\mathrm{T}}\mathbf{x})(\hat\beta - \beta)}{2\sigma_0^2},$$

where $\hat\beta = (\mathbf{x}^{\mathrm{T}}\mathbf{x})^{-1}\mathbf{x}^{\mathrm{T}}Y$. At the reference value β_0, partial differentiation gives

$$U_{.}(\beta_0) = (\mathbf{x}^{\mathrm{T}}\mathbf{x})(\hat\beta - \beta_0)/\sigma_0^2.$$

Since $E(\hat\beta) = \beta$ for all β,

$$E\{U_{.}(\beta_0);\beta_0 + \delta\} = (\mathbf{x}^{\mathrm{T}}\mathbf{x})\delta/\sigma_0^2 = i_{.}\delta,$$

which is exact for all δ. Note that the efficient score is a scaled deviation of the least squares estimate from a parameter value; the discussion of asymptotic likelihood theory in Chapter 9 hinges on the fact that the same relation holds approximately for all regular maximum likelihood estimates.

The effect of transforming parameters is found directly from

$$i_{.rs}(\theta) = E\left\{\frac{\partial \log f_Y(Y;\theta)}{\partial\theta_r}\frac{\partial \log f_Y(Y;\theta)}{\partial\theta_s};\theta\right\}$$

and the corresponding expression in terms of $\phi = \phi(\theta)$, together with the chain rule

$$\frac{\partial}{\partial\phi_k} = \sum_j \left(\frac{\partial\theta_j}{\partial\phi_k}\frac{\partial}{\partial\theta_j}\right).$$

[*Theoretical Statistics*, Section 4.8(ii); Rao, Sections 5a.3, 4a.4]

4.16. Show that the expected log likelihood ratio

$$\int \log\left\{\frac{f_1(y)}{f_0(y)}\right\} f_0(y) dy$$

is negative, unless the distributions concerned are identical, when it is zero. Hence show that a symmetrical positive distance between the two distributions is

$$\int \log\left\{\frac{f_1(y)}{f_0(y)}\right\} \{f_1(y) - f_0(y)\} dy.$$

Prove that if the distributions belong to the same regular parametric family, i.e. $f_0(y) = f(y;\theta)$ and $f_1(y) = f(y;\theta + \delta)$, then, as $\delta \to 0$, the distance measure is $i(\theta)\delta^2 + o(\delta^2)$.

Solution

The first part is a case of Jensen's inequality.

The function specified is unaffected by interchanging f_0 and f_1, and hence is a symmetric measure. It is strictly positive, unless f_0 and f_1 are identical, since the signs of the two factors are always the same.

Now with $f_1(y) = f(y;\theta + \delta)$ and $f_0(y) = f(y;\theta)$, we expand

$$f_1(y) - f_0(y) = \delta(\partial f/\partial \theta) + o(\delta), \quad \log\{f_1(y)/f_0(y)\} = \delta\frac{1}{f}\left(\frac{\partial f}{\partial \theta}\right) + o(\delta),$$

so that the distance measure is

$$\delta^2 \int \frac{1}{f}\left(\frac{\partial f}{\partial \theta}\right)^2 dy + o(\delta^2)$$

as required.

The word 'distance' is not totally appropriate in that the triangle inequality may not be satisfied.

[*Theoretical Statistics*, Section 4.8(ii); Kendall, 1973; Kullback, 1968; Rao, Section 5a.4]

5 SIGNIFICANCE TESTS: COMPOSITE NULL HYPOTHESES

Summary

In Chapter 4 we supposed that the null hypothesis H_0 is simple, i.e. completely specifies the distribution of Y. In practice, however, null hypotheses are usually composite, and do not completely specify the distribution of Y, but rather only limit the distribution to a set with one or more unknown parameters. We now discuss the main methods for deriving tests for such composite null hypotheses, again supposing alternatives are available representing directions of departures from H_0 that are of particular interest.

Suppose that possible distributions for Y are indexed by the parameter $\theta = (\psi, \lambda)$, $\theta \in \Omega = \Omega_\psi \times \Omega_\lambda$, where the null hypothesis takes the form H_0: $\psi = \psi_0$ with λ an unknown nuisance parameter. A size α critical region w_α is called similar if

$$\mathrm{pr}(Y \in w_\alpha; \psi_0, \lambda) = \alpha$$

for all λ, and the test defined by the system of such critical regions, assumed nested, is called a similar test.

If under H_0 a boundedly complete minimal sufficient statistic $S_\lambda(\psi_0)$ exists, then any similar critical region of size α must have size α conditional on $S_\lambda(\psi_0) = s(\psi_0)$ for almost all $s(\psi_0)$, so that similar tests are obtainable from the distribution of Y conditional on the value of $S_\lambda(\psi_0)$. Such critical regions are said to have Neyman structure. The optimal test against a specific alternative is the likelihood ratio test, which in general will depend on the particular alternative parameter value (ψ_1, λ_1) selected. If the likelihood ratio critical regions are independent of both ψ_1 and λ_1 the resulting test is called uniformly most powerful similar. If the likelihood ratio critical regions are independent of λ_1, but not of ψ_1, the other approaches discussed in Chapter 4 are available; for example if ψ is one-dimensional, we may consider maximizing power for alternatives close to $\psi = \psi_0$. If the l.r. critical region depends on λ_1 there is no general theory for obtaining good similar tests, but one method is to compute the likelihood ratio $f_{Y|S_\lambda(\psi_1)}(y|s(\psi_1); \psi_1)/f_{Y|S_\lambda(\psi_0)}(y|s(\psi_0); \psi_0)$.

One general class of problems where the use of similar regions succeeds consists of those where the null hypothesis specifies a linear restriction on natural parameters of an exponential family. Two types of problem where the similar region approach fails are (i) those where S_λ is not boundedly complete and (ii) those where S_λ is minimal sufficient for all θ; this latter difficulty will occur when H_0 does not restrict θ to lie in a subspace of Ω. In case (i) similar tests may exist, and must be found by other methods.

A second general approach to the construction of tests for a composite hypothesis is via invariance considerations, typified by the requirement that in suitable cases conclusions should not depend on the units used for measurement. Suppose again that distributions of Y are indexed by θ and that H_0 specifies $\theta \in \Omega_0$, the alternative hypothesis H_A specifying $\theta \in \Omega_A$. Then the testing problem is invariant under a group $\mathcal{G}$ of transformations acting on the sample space if for any transformation $g \in \mathcal{G}$ and any set B in the sample space

$$\mathrm{pr}\,(g\,Y \in B; \theta) = \mathrm{pr}\,(Y \in B; g^* \theta),$$

where g^* is in a group of transformations acting on Ω, such that $g^* \Omega_0 = \Omega_0$ and $g^* \Omega_A = \Omega_A$. Thus, in particular, H_0 is true for gY, for all g, if it is true for Y. A test with size α critical region w_α is invariant if $Y \in w_\alpha$ implies $g\,Y \in w_\alpha$ for any $g \in \mathcal{G}$. The statistic $t(Y)$ which defines an invariant critical region is maximal invariant if $t(y) = t(y')$ implies $y' = gy$ for some $g \in \mathcal{G}$. Thus to construct a suitable invariant test, we choose as test statistic a function of the observations y which is constant for the orbit of points gy as g varies in $\mathcal{G}$ and which changes from one orbit to the other. For simplicity, in general we first reduce y by sufficiency arguments before applying invariance arguments. The reduction to a maximal invariant statistic produces a similar reduction of θ. Earlier arguments concerning optimal tests now apply to the reduced testing problem based on $t\,(\cdot)$.

Where conditioning or invariance arguments do not uniquely define optimal tests, one general method for constructing a test is to form the maximum likelihood ratio

$$\sup_{\Omega_A} \mathrm{lik}\,(\theta; y) / \sup_{\Omega_0} \mathrm{lik}\,(\theta; y)$$

which has large-sample optimality properties (Chapter 9). Another approach useful in some multivariate problems is to work with the largest (most significant) test statistic based on linear transformations of the multivariate variable.

Problems

5.1. The random variables $Y_1, \ldots, Y_{n_1}$ are i.i.d. in a geometric distribution of parameter θ_1 and independently $Y_{n_1+1}, \ldots, Y_{n_1+n_2}$ are i.i.d. in a geometric distribution of parameter θ_2. Obtain a uniformly most powerful similar test of $\theta_1 = \theta_2$ versus the alternative $\theta_1 > \theta_2$. What more general null hypothesis can be tested similarly?

Solution

We have $f(y;\theta) = \theta^y(1-\theta)(y=0,1,\ldots)$ with $\theta = \theta_1$ for $Y_1, \ldots, Y_{n_1}$ and $\theta = \theta_2$ for $Y_{n_1+1}, \ldots, Y_{n_1+n_2}$. The sufficient statistic for (θ_1,θ_2) is $(S_1 = Y_1 + \ldots + Y_{n_1}, S_2 = Y_{n_1+1} + \ldots + Y_{n_1+n_2})$ and the sufficient statistic under $\theta_1 = \theta_2$ is $S = S_1 + S_2$.

If H_A is $\theta_1 > \theta_2$, then $\log \theta_1 > \log \theta_2$, an inequality in the natural parameters, and it can be shown that a uniformly most powerful similar test is obtained from any particular alternative. Similar tests have Neyman structure, since S is complete, an exponential family property. The likelihood ratio for particular (θ_1,θ_2) versus (θ_1,θ_1) is

$$\frac{f_{S_1|S}(s_1|s;\theta_1,\theta_2)}{f_{S_1|S}(s_1|s;\theta_1,\theta_1)} = \frac{\left(\dfrac{\theta_1}{\theta_2}\right)^{s_1} \sum \dbinom{r-1}{n_1-1}\dbinom{s-r-1}{n_2-1}}{\sum \dbinom{r-1}{n_1-1}\dbinom{s-r-1}{n_2-1}\left(\dfrac{\theta_1}{\theta_2}\right)^r},$$

an increasing function of s_1 for $\theta_1 > \theta_2$. Thus the size α critical region is $w_\alpha = \{(s_1,s_2) : s_1 \geqslant c_\alpha(s)\}$. The one-sided significance level for $s_{1,\,\text{obs}}$ is

$$\sum_{r=s_{1,\text{obs}}}^{s} \dbinom{s-1}{n_1-1}\dbinom{s-r-1}{n_2-1} \bigg/ \dbinom{s-1}{n_1+n_2-1}.$$

The natural parameters are $\log \theta_1$ and $\log \theta_2$ so that the same form of similar test is appropriate for $H_0 : \theta_1 = \gamma_0\theta_2$ versus $H_A : \theta_1 > \gamma_0\theta_2$. We can also test the ratio of natural parameters, e.g. null hypotheses of the form $H_0 : \theta_1 = \theta_2^{\gamma_0}$, although this is not often likely to be physically interesting and the resulting critical regions have some peculiar properties.

For tests of the adequacy of the geometric distribution, see Problem 3.11.

[*Theoretical Statistics*, Section 5.2; Lehmann, Sections 4.3, 4.4]

5.2. Events occur in a time-dependent Poisson process of rate $\rho e^{\beta t}$, where ρ and β are unknown. The instants of occurrence of events are observed for the interval $(0, t_0)$. Obtain a uniformly most powerful similar test of $\beta = \beta_0$ versus alternatives $\beta > \beta_0$. Examine in more detail the form of the test in the special case $\beta_0 = 0$.

Solution

The likelihood for the general time-dependent Poisson process with rate $\rho(t)$ and producing events at $y_1, \ldots, y_n$ is obtained by taking a factor $1 - \rho(t)\Delta t + o(\Delta t)$ for every small time interval $(t, t + \Delta t)$ without an event and $\rho(t)\Delta t + o(\Delta t)$ for every small time interval with an event. Thus, we have, on combining factors and letting $\Delta t \to 0$, that the likelihood is

$$\left\{ \prod_{i=1}^{n} \rho(y_i) \right\} \exp\left\{ - \int_{0}^{t_0} \rho(t)dt \right\}.$$

In the special case this leads to

$$\operatorname{lik}(\rho, \beta; y_1, \ldots, y_n) = \exp\left\{ n \log \rho + \beta \Sigma y_j - \rho\beta^{-1}(e^{\beta t_0} - 1) \right\},$$

so that the minimal sufficient statistic is $(N, \Sigma Y_j)$. Under $H_0 : \beta = \beta_0$, N is sufficient, and similar tests are obtained from the distribution of ΣY_j conditional on $N = n$. The marginal distribution of N is a Poisson distribution of mean $\rho(e^{\beta t_0} - 1)/\beta$, so that $f_{Y_1, \ldots, Y_N | N}(y_1, \ldots, y_n | n; \rho, \beta) \propto e^{\beta \Sigma y_j}$. This conditional distribution has natural parameter β and monotone increasing likelihood ratio in H_A, so that large values of $U = \Sigma Y_j$ are significant. The distribution is that of the sum of n i.i.d. random variables with the truncated exponential density over $(0, t_0)$.

In the special case $\beta_0 = 0$, $Y_1, \ldots, Y_n$ are order statistics from the uniform distribution on $(0, t_0)$. A normal approximation for the null distribution of U has mean $\tfrac{1}{2} n t_0$ and variance $\tfrac{1}{12} n t_0^2$.

[*Theoretical Statistics*, Section 5.2; Cox and Lewis, 1966, Chapter 3; Lehmann, Sections 4.3, 4.4]

5.3. There are available m independent normal-theory estimates of variance, each with d degrees of freedom. The corresponding parameters are $\sigma_1^2, \ldots, \sigma_m^2$. If $\sigma_j^2 = 1/(\lambda + \psi j)(j = 1, \ldots, m)$, obtain a uniformly most powerful similar test of $\psi = 0$ versus alternatives $\psi > 0$. Suggest a simpler, although less efficient, procedure based on the log transformation of the variances.

Solution

Let the variance estimates be $v_1, \ldots, v_m$ and define $Y_j = V_j d$, so that $Y_j = \sigma_j^2 X_{d,j}^2 (j = 1, \ldots, m)$. Then

$$\operatorname{lik}(\psi, \lambda; y_1, \ldots, y_m) \propto \Pi(\lambda + \psi j)^{-d} \exp\left\{ -\tfrac{1}{2}\Sigma(\lambda + \psi j)y_j \right\},$$

so that $(\Sigma Y_j, \Sigma j Y_j)$ is minimal sufficient. Under $H_0: \psi = 0, \Sigma Y_j$ is minimal sufficient, and so similar tests are based on the conditional distribution of $\Sigma j Y_j$ given $\Sigma Y_j = \Sigma y_j$ which has monotone likelihood ratio. Significance for the alternative $\psi > 0$ is obtained from large values of $\Sigma j Y_j$ in the conditional distribution.

If m is reasonably large, a normal approximation to the null distribution might be used. Following use of completeness we easily obtain

$$E(\Sigma j Y_j | \Sigma Y_j = t) = \tfrac{1}{2}(m+1)t,$$
$$\mathrm{var}(\Sigma j Y_j | \Sigma Y_j = t) = \tfrac{1}{6}m(m^2-1)t^2 d/(2md + m^2 d^2)$$
$$\sim \tfrac{1}{6}mt^2/d.$$

A simpler test is based on $X_j = \log Y_j$, for which $\mathrm{var}(X_j)$ is independent of σ_j^2 and is approximately $2/d$ and $E(X_j) \simeq \log \sigma_j^2 - 1/d$. Then approximately, for large d and small ψ,

$$X_j = \lambda' + \psi' j + \varepsilon_j, \psi' \propto \psi,$$

and ε_j i.i.d. $N(0, 2/d)$. An approximate test of $\psi = 0$ is then the normal theory linear model test of $\psi' = 0$. For discussion of the efficiency of this, see *Theoretical Statistics*, Example 8.5.

[*Theoretical Statistics*, Section 5.2; Lehmann, Sections 4.3, 4.4]

5.4. Observations are obtained on a two-state Markov chain for times $0, \ldots, n$, the initial state i_0 being fixed. The one-step transition probability from state u to state v is $\theta_{uv}(u, v = 0, 1)$ and m_{uv} denotes the number of transitions observed from state u to state v. Prove that if $\log(\theta_{01}/\theta_{00}) = \lambda$ and $\log(\theta_{11}/\theta_{10}) = \lambda + \psi$, then the likelihood is

$$\frac{\exp(\lambda m_{.1} + \psi m_{11})}{(1+e^\lambda)^{m_0.}\cdot(1+e^{\lambda+\psi})^{m_1.}},$$

not quite of the exponential family form, leading to a uniformly most powerful similar test of the null hypothesis $\psi = \psi_0$. Show further, however, that the conditional distribution of M_{11} given the number r of occupancies of state one, and both the initial and final states, i_0 and i_n, is

$$\frac{c_{i_0 i_n}(r, m_{11})e^{\psi m_{11}}}{\Sigma c_{i_0 i_n}(r, t)e^{\psi t}},$$

where the combinatorial coefficient in the numerator is the number of distinct binary sequences with the given initial and final states, with r ones and $n+1-r$ zeroes and with the required m_{11}.

Solution

By the argument of Problem 2.2

$$\text{lik}\,(\theta;y_1,\ldots,y_n|i_0) = \prod_{u,v}\theta_{uv}^{m_{uv}}.$$

Further

$$m_{0.} = n - r - \delta_{0i_n}, m_{1.} = r - \delta_{1i_n},$$

$$m_{.0} = n - r - \delta_{0i_0}, m_{.1} = r - \delta_{1i_0},$$

where $\delta_{ab} = 1(a = b)$ and $\delta_{ab} = 0(a \neq b)$ and r is the number of 1's.
From the definition of λ and ψ

$$\theta_{01} = e^\lambda/(1 + e^\lambda), \theta_{11} = e^{\lambda+\psi}/(1 + e^{\lambda+\psi}),$$

so that the likelihood becomes

$$\frac{e^{\lambda m_{01}}e^{(\lambda+\psi)m_{11}}}{(1 + e^\lambda)^{m_0.}\cdot(1 + e^{\lambda+\psi})^{m_1.}} = \frac{e^{\lambda m_{.1} + \psi m_{11}}}{(1 + e^\lambda)^{m_0.}\cdot(1 + e^{\lambda+\psi})^{m_1.}}.$$

and $m_{.1} = m_{1.} + \delta_{1i_n} - \delta_{1i_0}.$
    The joint probability of $(R, M_{11}) = (r, m_{11})$ given (i_0, i_n) is, by definition,

$$\frac{c_{i_0 i_n}(r, m_{11})e^{\lambda m_{.1} + \psi m_{11}}}{(1 + e^\lambda)^{m_0.}\cdot(1 + e^{\lambda+\psi})^{m_1.}}.$$

and the probability of $R = r$ is therefore

$$\Sigma_i c_{i_0 i_n}(r, t)e^{\lambda m_{.1} + \psi t}/\{(1 + e^\lambda)^{m_0.}\cdot(1 + e^{\lambda+\psi})^{m_1.}\},$$

so that

$$\text{pr}\,(M_{11} = m_{11}|R = r, i_0, i_n) = \frac{c_{i_0 i_n}(r, m_{11})e^{\psi m_{11}}}{\Sigma_t c_{i_0 i_n}(r, t)e^{\psi t}};$$

note that λ is eliminated because (R, I_0, I_n) is sufficient for λ for all fixed ψ. The analysis then proceeds as for the comparison of two binomial probabilities.

[*Theoretical Statistics*, Section 5.2; Cox, 1970, Section 5.7; Billingsley, 1961a]

5.5.* Let $Y_1, \ldots, Y_n$ be i.i.d. in an exponential distribution with lower terminal θ_1 and mean $\theta_1 + \theta_2$. Construct appropriate similar or invariant tests of the hypotheses (a) $H_0 : \theta_1 = 0$ against $H_A : \theta_1 > 0$, (b) $H_0 : \theta_2 = 1$ against $H_A : \theta_2 \neq 1$.

*Amended version.

Solution

The density of a single observation is

$$\theta_2^{-1} \exp\{-(y-\theta_1)/\theta_2\}\, \mathrm{hv}(y-\theta_1),$$

so that

$$\mathrm{lik}(\theta;y_1,\ldots,y_n) = \begin{cases} \theta_2^{-n}\exp\{-(\Sigma y_j - n\theta_1)/\theta_2\} & (y_{(1)} \geq \theta_1), \\ 0 & \text{otherwise,} \end{cases}$$

and the minimal sufficient statistic is $(\Sigma Y_j, Y_{(1)})$.

(a) $H_0:\theta_1 = 0$ versus $H_A:\theta_1 > 0$. This problem is invariant under $y \to ay$ for which a maximal invariant is $Y_{(1)}/\Sigma Y_j$ or more conveniently

$$T = nY_{(1)}/(\Sigma Y_j - nY_{(1)}).$$

It follows from properties of the exponential order statistics (Problem 3.9) that $X = n(Y_{(1)} - \theta_1)$ and $X_2 = \Sigma Y_j - nY_{(1)}$ are independently distributed as $\tfrac{1}{2}\theta_2\chi_2^2$ and $\tfrac{1}{2}\theta_2\chi_{2(n-1)}^2$. The most powerful invariant test based on T rejects H_0 for large T, and under $H_0, (n-1)T$ has the standard F distribution with degrees of freedom $(2, 2n-2)$.

The same test is provided by conditioning on ΣY_j which is sufficient under H_0.

(b) $H_0:\theta_2 = 1$ versus $H_A:\theta_2 \neq 1$. This problem is invariant under $y \to y + b$, and a maximal invariant is $\Sigma Y_j - nY_{(1)} = \tfrac{1}{2}\theta_2\chi_{2(n-1)}^2$. Therefore the invariant test corresponds to the normal-theory variance test of Problem 4.9.

The same test is obtained by conditioning on $Y_{(1)}$, which is sufficient under H_0.

[*Theoretical Statistics*, Sections 5.2, 5.3; Lehmann, Sections 4.3, 4.4, Chapter 6]

5.6. Let $Y_1,\ldots,Y_n$ be independent random variables such that some unknown permutation of them have gamma distributions whose densities

$$\rho_j(\rho_j y)^{\beta-1} e^{-\rho_j y}/\Gamma(\beta)$$

depend on two unknown parameters ψ and λ through the regression relationship $\rho_j = \exp(\lambda + \psi z_j)$, where the z_j's are known. Verify that the problem of testing $H_0:\psi = 0$ against the alternative $\psi \neq 0$ is invariant under permutation and scale change of the observations, and that a maximal invariant is $(Y_{(1)}/Y_{(n)},\ldots, Y_{(n-1)}/Y_{(n)})$. Show that the locally most powerful invariant test has rejection regions determined by large values of $(\Sigma Y_j^2)/(\Sigma Y_j)^2$.

Solution

The joint p.d.f. of $Y = (Y_1, \ldots, Y_n)$ is

$$\frac{1}{n!} \Sigma^* \prod_{j=1}^{n} \rho_{i_j}(\rho_{i_j} y_j)^{\beta - 1} \exp(-\rho_{i_j} y_j)/\Gamma(\beta)$$

with $\rho_j = \exp(\lambda + \psi z_j)$, where Σ^* is summation over all permutations $(i_1, \ldots, i_n)$ of $(1, \ldots, n)$. Inference is automatically invariant under permutation, thus depending only on $Y_{(i)}$. The transformations $y \to ay, z \to z + b$ induce the transformation $(\psi, \lambda, \beta) \to (\psi, \lambda + \log a + \psi b, \beta)$ leaving H_0 and H_A unchanged. Therefore

$$T = (Y_{(1)}/Y_{(n)}, \ldots, Y_{(n-1)}/Y_{(n)})$$

is maximal invariant, and without loss of generality we can take $\bar{z} = 0$.

Let $V = Y_{(n)}$. Then the Jacobian of $Y_{(.)} \to (T, V)$ is $V^{-(n-1)}$ and the joint p.d.f. of T is

$$f_T(t; \psi, \beta) = \{\Gamma(\beta)\}^{-n} \Sigma^* \int_0^{\infty} v^{n-1} \prod_{j=1}^{n} \rho_{i_j}(\rho_{i_j} v t_j)^{\beta - 1} \exp(-\rho_{i_j} v t_j) dv,$$

where $t_n = 1$. Thus

$$f_T(t; \psi, \beta) = \frac{\Gamma(n\beta)}{\{\Gamma(\beta)\}^n} \prod_{j=1}^{n} t_j^{\beta - 1} \Sigma^* \left\{ \sum_{j=1}^{n} t_j \exp(\psi z_{i_j}) \right\}^{-n\beta},$$

$$\left[\frac{\partial f_T}{\partial \psi} \right]_{\psi = 0} \propto n! \beta(\Sigma t_j)(\Sigma z_j) - n\beta \Sigma^*(\Sigma z_{i_j} t_j) = 0,$$

so that $U(0, \beta) = 0$. Therefore the leading term in the expansion of $\log f_T(t; \psi, \beta) - \log f_T(t; 0, \beta)$ is $\psi^2 u'(0, \beta)$, so that the locally most powerful test statistic is

$$\left[\frac{\partial^2 \log f_T}{\partial \psi^2} \right]_{\psi = 0} \propto \frac{\Sigma^*\{(n\beta + 1)(\Sigma z_{i_j} t_j)^2 - (\Sigma t_k)(\Sigma z_{i_j}^2 t_l)\}}{(\Sigma t_k)^2}$$

$$= \text{const} + \frac{(n-1)\Sigma z_j^2 \Sigma t_k^2}{(\Sigma t_j)^2} \propto \text{const} + \frac{\Sigma y_j^2}{(\Sigma y_j)^2}.$$

Therefore the locally most powerful test treats large values of $\Sigma y_j^2/(\Sigma y_j)^2$ as significant.

[*Theoretical Statistics*, Section 5.3; Ferguson, 1961]

5.7. Let $Y_{jk}(j = 1, \ldots, m; k = 1, \ldots, r)$ follow a normal-theory components of variance model, i.e. $Y_{jk} = \mu + \eta_j + \varepsilon_{jk}$, where the η_j's and ε_{jk}'s are independently distributed with zero mean and with variances respectively σ_b^2 and σ_w^2. Show that the minimal sufficient statistic is $(\bar{Y}_{..}, ss_b, ss_w)$ where $ss_b = r\Sigma(\bar{Y}_{j.} - \bar{Y}_{..})^2$ and $ss_w = \Sigma(Y_{jk} - \bar{Y}_{j.})^2$. Two independent sets of data of this structure are available with the same values of m and r. It is required to test the null hypothesis that the ratio σ_b^2/σ_w^2 is the same for both sets, all other parameters being arbitrary. Formulate a relevant group of transformations for the application of invariance theory and by a reduction to the minimal sufficient statistic, followed by the calculation of the maximal invariant, show that the appropriate test statistic is the ratio of the two values of ss_b/ss_w. Suggest a simple approximation to the null distribution of the test statistic, based on a log transformation. For what kind of practical situation may this problem be relevant?

Solution

For one set of data $(\bar{Y}_{..}, ss_b, ss_w)$ is minimal sufficient by the arguments of Problem 2.4.

Now for $H_0: \sigma_{b1}^2/\sigma_{w1}^2 = \sigma_{b2}^2/\sigma_{w2}^2$, the group $\mathscr{G}: gY = aY + c$ leaves the problem invariant, with different (a, c) for each set. Thus

$$(\bar{Y}_{..1}, ss_{b1}, ss_{w1}) \to (a_1\bar{Y}_{..1} + c_1, a_1^2 ss_{b1}, a_1^2 ss_{w1}),$$

$$(\bar{Y}_{..2}, ss_{b2}, ss_{w2}) \to (a_2\bar{Y}_{..2} + c_2, a_2^2 ss_{b2}, a_2^2 ss_{w2}).$$

This gives maximal invariant $(ss_{b1}/ss_{w1}, ss_{b2}/ss_{w2}) = (T_1, T_2)$, say. However this group $\mathscr{G}$ does not reduce H_0 to a simple hypothesis; the invariant parameter function is

$$(\sigma_{b1}^2/\sigma_{w1}^2, \sigma_{b2}^2/\sigma_{w2}^2).$$

Now $T_i = (1 + r\sigma_{bi}^2/\sigma_{wi}^2)F_i(i = 1, 2)$, where F_1, F_2 are independent standard variance ratio variables. Thus, with $\lambda_i = 1 + r\sigma_{bi}^2/\sigma_{wi}^2$

$$f_{T_1, T_2}(t_1, t_2) = \lambda_1^{-1}g(t_1/\lambda_1)\lambda_2^{-1}g(t_2/\lambda_2), \qquad (1)$$

where $g(\cdot)$ is the p.d.f. of $F_{m-1, mr-m}$. But $H_0: \sigma_{b1}^2/\sigma_{w1}^2 = \sigma_{b2}^2/\sigma_{w2}^2$ is equivalent to $H_0': \lambda_1 = \lambda_2$ for (1) and this hypothesis testing problem is invariant under $T_i \to aT_i(i = 1, 2), a > 0$, giving maximal invariant T_1/T_2. This only works for common values of r, m.

The same end result can be obtained by first applying orthogonal transformations to $\{Y_{jk}; k = 1, \ldots, r\}$ to obtain independent normal variables, which gives new parameters $\sigma_{wi}^2, \lambda_i(i = 1, 2)$ and considering general location-scale transformations.

For reasonably large m normal approximations to $\log ss_{bi}$, $\log ss_{wi}$ may be used. Then, as in Problem 5.3,

$$\log(T_1/T_2) = \log ss_{b1} - \log ss_{b2} + \log ss_{w2} - \log ss_{w1}$$
$$\simeq \log(\lambda_1/\lambda_2) + \varepsilon,$$

where ε is $N\{0, 4(m-1)^{-1} + 4m^{-1}(r-1)^{-1}\}$.

The analysis is relevant to the comparison of the sensitivities of two measuring techniques.

[*Theoretical Statistics*, Section 5.3; Dar, 1962]

5.8. Suppose that $Y_1, \ldots, Y_n$ are i.i.d. random variables either in $N(\mu, \sigma^2)$ or in the uniform distribution on $(v - \frac{1}{2}\tau, v + \frac{1}{2}\tau)$, the parameters being unknown. Show that the most powerful test between these two hypothetical distributions which is invariant under location and scale changes has test statistic $(Y_{(n)} - Y_{(1)})/\{\Sigma(Y_j - \bar{Y})^2\}^{1/2}$.

Solution

For any location-scale distribution $g(\cdot)$ the maximal invariant is

$$T = \{(Y_3 - Y_2)/(Y_2 - Y_1), \ldots, (Y_n - Y_2)/(Y_2 - Y_1)\}.$$

To find its distribution write $y_2 = u$, $y_2 - y_1 = v$, so that

$$f_T(t; H_0) = \int\int v^{n-2} g(u)g(u-v) \prod_{j=3}^{n} g(vt_j + u)\, du\, dv.$$

The likelihood ratio test based on T is the ratio of the corresponding forms of this or equivalently the ratio of

$$h(y; g) = \int_0^\infty \int_{-\infty}^\infty a^{n-2} \prod_{j=1}^{n} g(ay_j - b)\, da\, db.$$

Straightforward calculation gives

$$h(y; \text{normal}) \propto \{\Sigma(y_j - \bar{y})^2\}^{-\frac{1}{2}(n-1)}$$

and

$$h(y; \text{uniform}) = \int_0^{r_n^{-1}} \int_{ay_{(n)}-1}^{ay_{(1)}} a^{n-2}\, da\, db \propto r_n^{-(n-1)},$$

where $r_n = y_{(n)} - y_{(1)}$. Thus the likelihood ratio is the $(n-1)$th power of $(y_{(n)} - y_{(1)})/\{\Sigma(y_j - \bar{y})^2\}^{1/2}$, which is often called the studentized range statistic (Pearson and Hartley, 1970, Table 29).

[*Theoretical Statistics*, Section 5.3; Uthoff, 1970]

5.9. Observations are taken independently from a multivariate normal distribution with unknown mean and covariance matrix. The null hypothesis H_0 asserts that the first q co-ordinates are independent of the remaining $p - q$ co-ordinates, the alternative hypothesis being completely general. Find a suitably wide group of transformations such that the maximal invariant statistic is the set of canonical correlations. That is, if the sample cross-product matrix SS is partitioned into $SS_{11}, SS_{12}, SS_{21}$ and SS_{22} corresponding to the first q and last $p - q$ co-ordinates, then the maximal invariant is the set of solutions of $|SS_{11} - lSS_{12}SS_{22}^{-1}SS_{21}| = 0$. What function of the maximal invariant is used in the maximum likelihood ratio test?

Solution

A minimal sufficient statistic is $(\bar{Y}, SS)$. Let

$$Y = \begin{pmatrix} Y_1 \\ Y_2 \end{pmatrix}, \mu = \begin{pmatrix} \mu_1 \\ \mu_2 \end{pmatrix}, \Sigma = \begin{bmatrix} \Sigma_{11} & \Sigma_{12} \\ \Sigma_{12}^T & \Sigma_{22} \end{bmatrix},$$

where $\Sigma_{ij} = \mathrm{cov}(Y_i, Y_j)$, and Y_1 gives the first q co-ordinates of Y. Then $H_0 : \Sigma_{12} = 0$, the parameters $\mu, \Sigma_{11}, \Sigma_{22}$ being arbitrary and unknown.

Consider general non-singular linear transformations

$$g\begin{pmatrix} Y_1 \\ Y_2 \end{pmatrix} = \begin{bmatrix} a_{11} & a_{12} \\ a_{21} & a_{22} \end{bmatrix}\begin{pmatrix} Y_1 \\ Y_2 \end{pmatrix} + \begin{pmatrix} b_1 \\ b_2 \end{pmatrix}$$

inducing

$$g^*\begin{pmatrix} \mu_1 \\ \mu_2 \end{pmatrix} = \begin{bmatrix} a_{11} & a_{12} \\ a_{21} & a_{22} \end{bmatrix}\begin{pmatrix} \mu_1 \\ \mu_2 \end{pmatrix} + \begin{pmatrix} b_1 \\ b_2 \end{pmatrix}.$$

On calculating the new covariance matrix, it follows that $g^*\Sigma_{12} = 0$ only if $a_{21} = 0, a_{12} = 0$ given $\Sigma_{12} = 0$; otherwise the transformation is arbitrary. The problem is therefore invariant under

$$g\begin{pmatrix} Y_1 \\ Y_2 \end{pmatrix} = \begin{bmatrix} a_{11} & 0 \\ 0 & a_{22} \end{bmatrix}\begin{pmatrix} Y_1 \\ Y_2 \end{pmatrix} + \begin{pmatrix} b_1 \\ b_2 \end{pmatrix},$$

and these transformations map $(\bar{Y}, SS)$ into

$$\begin{pmatrix} \mathbf{a}_{11}\bar{Y}_1 + b_1 \\ \mathbf{a}_{22}\bar{Y}_2 + b_2 \end{pmatrix}, \begin{bmatrix} \mathbf{a}_{11}SS_{11}\mathbf{a}_{11}^T & \mathbf{a}_{11}SS_{12}\mathbf{a}_{22}^T \\ \mathbf{a}_{22}SS_{12}^T\mathbf{a}_{11}^T & \mathbf{a}_{22}SS_{22}\mathbf{a}_{22}^T \end{bmatrix}.$$

Only the second matrix can yield an invariant statistic.

A particular transformation is that defined by $\mathbf{a}_{11} = SS_{11}^{-1/2}, \mathbf{a}_{22} = SS_{22}^{-1/2}$, which transforms SS into

$$\begin{bmatrix} \mathbf{I} & SS_{11}^{-1/2}SS_{12}SS_{22}^{-1/2} \\ SS_{22}^{-1/2}SS_{12}^TSS_{11}^{-1/2} & \mathbf{I} \end{bmatrix}.$$

Suppose that the matrix $\mathbf{G} = SS_{11}^{-1}SS_{12}SS_{22}^{-1}SS_{12}^T$ has the same $\min(q, p-q)$ non-zero eigenvalues for two data sets. Then there must exist a non-singular matrix $\mathbf{c}$ such that $\mathbf{G} = \mathbf{c}^{-1}\tilde{\mathbf{G}}\mathbf{c}$. A similar argument applies to $SS_{22}^{-1}SS_{12}^TSS_{11}^{-1}SS_{12}$, involving a non-singular matrix $\mathbf{d}$. These two results imply

$$\widetilde{SS} = \begin{bmatrix} \mathbf{c}^T & \mathbf{0} \\ \mathbf{0} & \mathbf{d}^T \end{bmatrix} SS \begin{bmatrix} \mathbf{c} & \mathbf{0} \\ \mathbf{0} & \mathbf{d} \end{bmatrix}.$$

The data sets are therefore related by a transformation of the above form, so that the maximal invariance of the eigenvalues is verified.

The likelihood function of (μ, Σ) given $y_1, \ldots, y_n$ is $\mathrm{lik}(\mu, \Sigma; y) \propto |\Sigma|^{-\frac{1}{2}n}$ $\times \exp\{-\frac{1}{2}\Sigma(y_j - \mu)^T\Sigma^{-1}(y_j - \mu)\}$ and is maximized with respect to μ by $\hat{\mu} = \bar{y}$, for any Σ. Further in $\Omega = \Omega_A \cup \Omega_0, \hat{\Sigma} = n^{-1}SS$ and in Ω_0

$$\hat{\Sigma} = n^{-1}\begin{bmatrix} SS_{11} & \mathbf{0} \\ \mathbf{0} & SS_{22} \end{bmatrix}.$$

It follows quite directly that the maximized likelihood ratio statistic is a function of

$$V = |SS|/\{|SS_{11}||SS_{22}|\}.$$

Now $|SS| = |SS_{11} - SS_{12}SS_{22}^{-1}SS_{12}^T||SS_{22}| = |SS_{22} - SS_{12}^TSS_{11}^{-1}SS_{12}||SS_{11}|$ so that

$$V = |\mathbf{I} - SS_{11}^{-1}SS_{12}SS_{22}^{-1}SS_{12}^T| = |\mathbf{I} - SS_{22}^{-1}SS_{12}^TSS_{11}^{-1}SS_{12}| = \Pi(1 - l_i),$$

where the l_i are the eigenvalues of the matrix $\mathbf{G}$ above. Other functions of the eigenvalues can, of course, be used.

[*Theoretical Statistics*, Sections 5.3, 5.4; Anderson, 1958, Chapter 12; Rao, Sections 8c, 8f]

5.10. The sample space of the bivariate random variable Y consists of two concentric circles and their centre point. Under the null hypothesis, H_0, the centre point has known probability p_0 and the inner and outer circles have total probabilities respectively $1 - 2p_0$ and p_0, distributions being uniform over each circle. Under the composite alternative hypothesis, the centre point has known probability $p_A > p_0$, the inner circle has zero probability and there is an arbitrary bounded distribution over the outer circle. The problem is thus invariant under rotation of the plane about the centre point. Find the maximal invariant statistic and hence describe the uniformly most powerful invariant test of H_0. Compare this test with that based on the maximum likelihood ratio.

Solution

If $Y = (Y_1, Y_2)^T$, then Ω_0 and Ω_A remain invariant under the group corresponding to

$$gY = \begin{bmatrix} \sin a & \cos a \\ \cos a & -\sin a \end{bmatrix} Y,$$

where the origin is taken to be the centre of the circles. The maximal invariant is $T = Y_1^2 + Y_2^2$ which has three possible values: $0, t_1$ and $t_2 > t_1$. We have

$$\text{pr}(T = 0; H_0) = p_0, \text{pr}(T = 0; H_A) = p_A > p_0,$$
$$\text{pr}(T = t_1; H_0) = 1 - 2p_0, \text{pr}(T = t_1; H_A) = 0,$$
$$\text{pr}(T = t_2; H_0) = p_0, \text{pr}(T = t_2; H_A) = 1 - p_A.$$

The likelihood ratio test depends on whether $1 - p_A \geq p_A$; if $p_A \leq \frac{1}{2}$, then

$$\text{lr}_{A0}(t_2) \geq \text{lr}_{A0}(0) > \text{lr}_{A0}(t_1) = 0.$$

The maximum likelihood ratio is unbounded if $T = t_2$ since the arbitrary continuous density on the outer circle can give arbitrarily high probability density to the observed y. Thus the two tests differ if $p_A > \frac{1}{2}$ although the significance attached to $T = t_1$ is the same in each case.

[*Theoretical Statistics*, Sections 5.3, 5.4; Lehmann, Section 6.12]

5.11. Let $Y_1, \ldots, Y_{n_1}$ be i.i.d. in $MN_p(\mu, \Sigma)$ and $Y'_1, \ldots, Y'_{n_2}$ be i.i.d. in $MN_p(\mu', \Sigma')$. Derive an invariant test of the hypothesis $H_0 : \Sigma = \Sigma'$ against the general alternative by finding the most significant of the test statistics $F(a)$ used in testing the corresponding hypotheses about variances of the scalar combinations $a^T Y$ and $a^T Y'$.

Solution

Now $a^{\mathrm{T}}Y_j$ is $N(a^{\mathrm{T}}\mu, a^{\mathrm{T}}\Sigma a)$ and $a^{\mathrm{T}}Y_j'$ is $N(a^{\mathrm{T}}\mu', a^{\mathrm{T}}\Sigma' a)$.

Let $a^{\mathrm{T}}\Sigma a = \sigma_a^2, a^{\mathrm{T}}\Sigma' a = \tau_a^2$. Tests of $H_0 : \sigma_a^2 = \tau_a^2$ are invariant under location and scale transformations of $a^{\mathrm{T}}Y_j$ and $a^{\mathrm{T}}Y_j'$; this leads to tests based on

$$\mathrm{MS}_a/\mathrm{MS}_a' = (a^{\mathrm{T}}\mathrm{MS}a)/(a^{\mathrm{T}}\mathrm{MS}'a) = U_a.$$

Both large and small values of U_a are evidence against H_0, so that the most significant values of U_a are the largest and smallest over choice of a.

Because of invariance with respect to scale, we suppose without loss of generality that $a^{\mathrm{T}}\mathrm{MS}'a = 1$. Then maximization of U_a is equivalent to maximization of

$$a^{\mathrm{T}}\mathrm{MS}a - \lambda a^{\mathrm{T}}\mathrm{MS}'a$$

achieved when $(\mathrm{MS} - \lambda\mathrm{MS}')a = 0$, i.e. when λ is an eigenvalue of $\mathrm{MS}\,\mathrm{MS}'^{-1}$ and a an eigenvector. The largest value of U_a is the largest eigenvalue l_p. Similarly the smallest eigenvalue l_1 of $\mathrm{MS}\,\mathrm{MS}'^{-1}$ is the smallest value of U_a. The test of $H_0 : \Sigma = \Sigma'$ therefore comprises evaluation of two significance probabilities

$$p^+ = \mathrm{pr}(L_p \geqslant l_p; \Sigma = \Sigma'), p^- = \mathrm{pr}(L_1 \leqslant l_1; \Sigma = \Sigma').$$

[*Theoretical Statistics*, Section 5.4]

6 DISTRIBUTION-FREE AND RANDOMIZATION TESTS

Summary

The terms non-parametric and distribution-free are used interchangeably for tests in which the null hypothesis involves, explicitly or implicitly, arbitrary unknown distributions. The simplest such null hypothesis is that $Y_1, \ldots, Y_n$ are i.i.d. with some unknown density. Possible departures are: (a) trend with serial order; (b) dependence on explanatory variables; (c) systematic differences between observations $1, \ldots, n_1$ and observations $n_1 + 1, \ldots, n$, i.e. the two-sample problem. A test is called distribution-free if the distribution of the test statistic is the same for some rich class of densities, e.g. in the general case all densities or all continuous densities. Such tests are obtained in the general case via the conditional distribution given the values of the order statistics; all permutations of them are, under the null hypothesis, equally likely. Tests used in this way are called permutation tests.

The simplest approach, following the discussion of Chapter 3, is to choose a test statistic in an informal way, for example, by analogy with some parametric problem. The permutation distribution under the null hypothesis can be found by enumeration or approximation via the first few moments. Often test statistics can be appreciably simplified because the order statistics are regarded as fixed. For example, for the two-sample problem the Student t statistic is equivalent to one of the sample means.

The Wilcoxon two-sample test is obtained by using rank numbers rather than the original observations and taking as the test statistic the sum (or mean) of the ranks in one of the samples. This is an important special case of tests in which observations are used only through their rank order.

One formal approach to the choice of rank test statistics is to find that rank statistic which has maximum local power for some parametric version of the problem. That is, the parametric formulation is used to determine a test statistic; the distribution under the null hypothesis is obtained by permutation, thereby retaining the distribution-free property. An important class of rank statistics are the linear rank statistics in which linear statistics $\Sigma c_j Y_j$

are replaced by $\Sigma c_j w(R_j)$, where R_j is the rank order of Y_j. For example, in the two-sample problem the particular 'scores' $w(k) = k$ give the Wilcoxon test. General results are available on the asymptotic normality of linear rank statistics.

A quite different approach to the justification of permutation tests is restricted to experiments in which treatments are allocated to experimental units at random, and probability calculations are based on the physical randomization, rather than on an assumption of i.i.d. random variables. Tests viewed from this approach are called randomization tests.

Another way of deriving tests is to define a general measure of distance for the problem in question, for example, a general measure of distance between two population distribution functions in the two-sample problem. This distance may then be estimated using sample distribution functions to give a test statistic; the distribution-free property may or may not be achieved. An alternative method is to derive the uniform minimum variance unbiased estimate of the distance by Rao-Blackwellization (see Chapter 8).

Problems

6.1. Suppose that $Y_1, \ldots, Y_n$ are i.i.d. with a density $f(y - \theta)$, where $f(\cdot)$ is an unknown continuous density symmetric about zero, and consider testing the null hypothesis $H_0 : \theta - 0$ against the alternative that $\theta > 0$. Show that H_0 is equivalent to a hypothesis comparing the sets of positive and of negative values and hence construct a rank test of H_0.

Solution

It is convenient to write $Y_j = (I_j, Z_j)$, where $Z_j = |Y_j|$ and $I_j = 1$ or 0 according as $Y_j = + Z_j$ or $- Z_j$. Under the hypothesis $\theta = 0$, the random variables I_j and Z_j are independent and $\mathrm{pr}(I_j = 1) = \frac{1}{2}$. If $\theta > 0$, Z_j is stochastically larger when $I_j = 1$, and $\mathrm{pr}(I_j = 1) > \frac{1}{2}$. Therefore if we group observations according to their signs and define $R_j = \mathrm{rank}(Z_j)$, we expect that when $\theta > 0$ (a) the ranks corresponding to positive observations will tend to be higher than those corresponding to negative observations, and (b) there will be more positive than negative observations.

One direct analogue of the two-sample Wilcoxon statistic is $T = \Sigma I_j R_j$; of course ΣI_j itself is a natural statistic, and defines the sign test. Under the null hypothesis, conditional on $\Sigma I_i = m$, T has the same distribution as the two-sample Wilcoxon statistic; see Problem 6.2. Thus, by averaging over the binomial distribution of ΣI_j, we can obtain the null distribution of T. In particular we can derive a normal approximation to the distribution of

T with, under H_0,

$$E(T) = \tfrac{1}{4}n(n+1), \text{ var}(T) = \tfrac{1}{24}n(n+1)(2n+1).$$

A general theory of optimum rank tests can be developed for a specific density $f(\cdot)$. The joint density of the (I_j, R_j) for $j = 1, \ldots, n$ is found to be

$$2^{-n}E\left[\prod_{j=1}^{n}\{f(Z^{(r_j)} + \theta)\}^{i_j}\{f(Z^{(r_j)} - \theta)\}^{1-i_j}/f(Z^{(j)}; H_0)\right],$$

where $Z^{(1)} \leqslant \ldots \leqslant Z^{(n)}$ denote ordered values of the Z_j. This leads to the locally most powerful rank statistic

$$-E\left\{\Sigma i_j \frac{f'(Z^{(r_j)})}{f(Z^{(r_j)})}; H_0\right\},$$

whose null distribution is determined by the permutation distribution of ranks R_j and the Bernoulli probabilities of the signs I_j.

[*Theoretical Statistics*, Section 6.2; Rao, Section 7e; Silvey, Section 9.3, 9.4; Lehmann, Section 6.9]

6.2. By arguments of symmetry or otherwise, obtain the first four moments of the sample mean in random samples of size n_1 drawn without replacement from the finite population $\{y_1, \ldots, y_n\}$. By examining the third and fourth cumulant ratios, show that the rate of approach to normality as $n \to \infty$, $n_1/n \to a, 0 < a < 1$, is faster than that for sampling with replacement. Give some explicit results for the finite population $\{1, \ldots, n\}$ and show the application to the two-sample Wilcoxon test.

Solution

There are various ways of computing the moments of statistics in random sampling without replacement from a finite population, of which mathematically the neatest exploit considerations of symmetry. Thus if $m_r = \Sigma(y_i - m_1)^r/n$ denote the moments about the mean of the finite population and if $\bar{Y}$ denotes the sample mean, it can be shown from such symmetry considerations first that $E(\bar{Y}) = a_1 m_1$, where a_1 is a constant independent of the population values but depending on n and n_1; consideration of the special population $y_1 = \ldots = y_n = 1$ then gives $a_1 = 1$. It follows by similar arguments that

$$\text{var}(\bar{Y}) = a_2 m_2, \mu_3(\bar{Y}) = a_3 m_3, \mu_4(\bar{Y}) = a_4 m_4 + b_4 m_2^2,$$

for suitable constants a_2, a_3, a_4, b_4. Consideration of special populations then shows that

$$a_2 = \frac{n_1(n - n_1)}{(n - 1)}, a_3 = \frac{n_1(n - n_1)(n - 2n_1)}{(n - 1)(n - 2)},$$

$$a_4 = \frac{(n^2 - 6nn_1 + n + 6n_1^2)n_1(n - n_1)}{(n - 1)(n - 2)(n - 3)},$$

$$b_4 = \frac{3(n_1 - 1)n(n - n_1 - 1)n_1(n - n_1)}{(n - 1)(n - 2)(n - 3)}.$$

We can now calculate the standardized measures of skewness and kurtosis for $\bar{Y}$. If we put $n_1/n = f$ and let $n \to \infty$ we have asymptotically

$$\frac{\mu_3(\bar{Y})}{\{\mathrm{var}(\bar{Y})\}^{3/2}} \sim \frac{(1 - 2f)m_3/m_2^{3/2}}{(1 - f)\sqrt{n_1}};$$

$$\frac{\mu_4(\bar{Y})}{\{\mathrm{var}(\bar{Y})\}^2} - 3 \sim \frac{-6}{n} + \left\{\frac{1 - 6f(1 - f)}{(1 - f)}\right\}\frac{(m_4/m_2^2 - 3)}{n_1}.$$

In sampling with replacement, thus generating i.i.d. random variables, we would have, for example,

$$\frac{\mu_3(\bar{Y})}{\{\mathrm{var}(\bar{Y})\}^{3/2}} \sim \frac{m_3/m_2^{3/2}}{\sqrt{n_1}},$$

thus indicating a more nearly normal distribution for $\bar{Y}$ in the former case. Note in particular that if $f = \frac{1}{2}$, the distribution is symmetrical, as is obvious from the relation $\frac{1}{2}\bar{Y} + \frac{1}{2}\bar{Y}' = m_1 = \mathrm{const}$, where $\bar{Y}'$ is the mean of the portion not sampled.

The application to the two-sample Wilcoxon test is as follows. Let the observations in two independent samples of sizes n_1 and n_2 be regarded as one set of $n = n_1 + n_2$ values and ranked. Let the test statistic be the mean of the ranks in the first sample. Then if a null hypothesis of identity of the underlying distribution holds, the test statistic is the mean of a sample size n_1 drawn randomly without replacement from the 'finite population' of ranks. In particular, if there are no tied values the finite population is $\{1, \dots, n\}$ and the resulting values of $m_1, \dots, m_4$ are easily obtained. The distribution under the null hypothesis approaches normality rapidly.

[*Theoretical Statistics*, Section 6.2; Rao, Section 7e; Silvey, Section 9.3]

6.3. In a randomized matched pair experiment, suppose that the observed differences between treatment A and treatment B are 8, 5, 4, -2, -2, 0 and 1. Show, by enumeration, that the exact two-sided significance level for testing the null hypothesis of treatment equivalence is 1/4. Compare this with the result of (a) applying the 'ordinary' one-sample Student t test; (b) a normal approximation to the permutation distribution, with a continuity correction; (c) an approximation to the permutation distribution using the first four moments.

Solution

The differences $(x_1, \dots, x_7) = (8, 5, 4, -2, -2, 0, 1)$ arise from randomized treatment allocation within each pair of individuals, so that the reference set for differences $(Y_1, \dots, Y_7)$ is the set of $2^7 = 128$ vectors $(\pm x_1, \dots, \pm x_7)$, all such vectors being equally likely under the null hypothesis. The table below indicates which samples $(y_1, \dots, y_7)$ have values of Σy_j at least as large as the observed value 14.

x:	-2	-2	0	1	4	5	8	Σy_j	frequency
	$-$	$-$	$\pm$	$+$	$+$	$+$	$+$	22	2
	$-$	$-$	$\pm$	$-$	$+$	$+$	$+$	20	2
	$+$	$-$	$\pm$	$+$	$+$	$+$	$+$	18	2
	$-$	$+$	$\pm$	$+$	$+$	$+$	$+$	18	2
	$-$	$+$	$\pm$	$-$	$+$	$+$	$+$	16	2
	$+$	$-$	$\pm$	$-$	$+$	$+$	$+$	16	2
	$-$	$-$	$\pm$	$+$	$-$	$+$	$+$	14	2
	$+$	$+$	$\pm$	$+$	$+$	$+$	$+$	14	2

Therefore, under the null hypothesis,

$$\mathrm{pr}(\Sigma Y_j \geqslant 14) = \tfrac{16}{128} = 0.125,$$

which is the one-sided significance probability.

For the Student t test we obtain $t = 1.40$, which with 6 degrees of freedom corresponds to one-sided significance probability 0.1.

In a normal approximation with correction for discreteness, we note that the correction for the upper tail probability is -1 because values of Σy_j differ by 2. Thus, with continuity correction, the standardized value is

$$z = (\Sigma y_j - 1)/(\Sigma x_j^2)^{1/2} = 1.22,$$

giving a one-sided significance probability of 0.111.

To obtain an improved normal approximation via the Edgeworth expansion we use the first four randomization moments of ΣY_j, which are

$$0, \Sigma x_j^2 = 114, 0, 3(\Sigma x_j^2)^2 - 2(\Sigma x_j^4) = 28968.$$

The standardized third and fourth cumulants are $\gamma_1 = 0$ and $\gamma_2 = -0.77$.

The Edgeworth expansion for upper tail probability corresponding to the (corrected) standardized variate z is, with $\gamma_1 = 0$,

$$1 - \Phi(z) + \frac{\gamma_2}{24}(z^3 - 3z)\phi(z),$$

whose value for $z = 1.22$ is 0.123, an excellent approximation.

[*Theoretical Statistics*, Section 6.2]

6.4. Let $(Y_1,Z_1),\ldots,(Y_n,Z_n)$ be n i.i.d. bivariate random variables with an arbitrary continuous distribution. Show that the rank statistic

$$T = \frac{1}{n(n-1)}\sum_{j>k}\operatorname{sgn}\{(Y_j - Y_k)(Z_j - Z_k)\} + \tfrac{1}{2},$$

equivalent to Kendall's τ, has expectation equal to the probability that $Y - Y'$ and $Z - Z'$ have the same sign, where (Y,Z) and (Y',Z') are independent pairs with the distribution in question. Show that under the null hypothesis that Y and Z are independent, the permutation distribution of T has mean $\tfrac{1}{2}$ and variance $(2n+5)/\{18n(n-1)\}$.

   Prove that if the bivariate pairs have a bivariate normal distribution of correlation coefficient ρ, then the expectation of T is $\tfrac{1}{2} + \pi^{-1}\sin^{-1}\rho$.

Solution

Denote by ξ the probability that $Y - Y'$ and $Z - Z'$ have the same sign. Let $I_{jk} = \operatorname{sgn}\{(Y_j - Y_k)(Z_j - Z_k)\}$. Then

$$E(I_{jk}) = \xi - (1 - \xi) = 2\xi - 1.$$

Now there are $\tfrac{1}{2}n(n-1)$ terms in the sum defining T, each with the same expectation, so that $E(T) = \tfrac{1}{2}(2\xi - 1) + \tfrac{1}{2} = \xi$. Kendall's rank correlation coefficient is defined to take values in $[-1, 1]$ and is $2T - 1$.
   If Y and Z are independent, $\xi = \tfrac{1}{2}$, so that $E(T) = \tfrac{1}{2}$. Further

$$\operatorname{var}(I_{jk}) = E(I_{jk}^2) - E(I_{jk}) = 1,$$

$$\operatorname{cov}(I_{jk}, I_{lm}) = 0 \quad (j \neq k \neq l \neq m);$$

and for $j \neq k \neq l$,

$$\operatorname{cov}(I_{jk}, I_{jl}) = E[\operatorname{sgn}\{(Y_j - Y_k)(Z_j - Z_k)\}\operatorname{sgn}\{(Y_j - Y_l)(Z_j - Z_l)\}]$$
$$= E[\operatorname{sgn}\{(Y_j - Y_k)(Y_j - Y_l)\}]E[\operatorname{sgn}\{(Z_j - Z_k)(Z_j - Z_l)\}].$$

Now $E[\text{sgn}\{(Y_j - Y_k)(Y_j - Y_l)\}] = \text{pr}(Y_j > Y_k, Y_l) + \text{pr}(Y_j < Y_k, Y_l)$
$$- \text{pr}(Y_k > Y_j > Y_l) - \text{pr}(Y_l > Y_j > Y_k)$$
$$= \tfrac{2}{3} - \tfrac{2}{6} = \tfrac{1}{3},$$

so that $\text{cov}(I_{jk}, I_{jl}) = \tfrac{1}{9}$.

Finally

$$\text{var}(T) = \frac{1}{n^2(n-1)^2}\text{var}\left(\sum_{j>k} I_{jk}\right) = \frac{1}{n^2(n-1)^2}\{\tfrac{1}{2}n(n-1) + \tfrac{1}{9}n(n-1)(n-2)\}$$
$$= (2n+5)/\{18n(n-1)\}.$$

In the general bivariate normal case, $\text{corr}(Y - Y', Z - Z') = \text{corr}(Y, Z)$, so that we can without loss of generality take $Y - Y' = U$ and $Z - Z' = V$ as bivariate normal of zero means, unit variances and correlation coefficient ρ. The required probability is thus $2\text{pr}(U > 0, V > 0)$. Now calculations connected with the bivariate normal distribution are often most painlessly done conditionally and for this we write $V = \rho U + \kappa W$, where $\kappa = (1 - \rho^2)^{1/2}$, and U and W are independent $N(0,1)$. The required probability is thus

$$\xi = 2\int_0^\infty \Phi(-\rho u/\kappa)\phi(u)\,du,$$

where the first factor in the integral is $\text{pr}(V > 0 | U = u)$. The integral is easily evaluated, most simply by writing $\rho/\kappa = \gamma$ and noting that

$$\frac{d\xi}{d\gamma} = -2\int_0^\infty \phi(-\gamma u)\phi(u)\,du = -\{2\pi(1 + \gamma^2)\}^{-1/2}.$$

Integration with respect to γ and use of the initial condition that $\xi = \tfrac{1}{2}$ when $\gamma = 0$ gives the required result, $\xi = \tfrac{1}{2} + \pi^{-1}\sin^{-1}\rho$, called Sheppard's formula.

[*Theoretical Statistics*, Section 6.3; Kendall, 1962]

6.5. Let $Y_1, \ldots, Y_{n_1}$ be i.i.d. with density $h(y)$, and $Y_{n_1+1}, \ldots, Y_n$ be independent i.i.d. with density $\tau^{-1}h\{(y - \mu)/\tau\}$. Develop the theory for constructing rank tests of the null hypothesis $H_0 : \tau = 1, \mu = 0$ against the alternatives (a) $H_A : \tau > 1, \mu > 0$ and (b) $H_A' : \tau > 1, \mu < 0$.

Solution

The first step is to calculate the density of the rank vector R. This is

$$f_R(r;\mu,\tau) = \int\limits_{\{y_j = y_{(r_j)}\}} \prod_{k=1}^{n_1} h(y_k) \prod_{l=n_1+1}^{n} \tau^{-1}h\{(y_l - \mu)/\tau\}\,dy.$$

By noting that the joint density of the $Y_{(r_j)}$ when $\mu = 0, \tau = 1$ is $n! \prod_{j=1}^{n} h(y_{(r_j)})$, we have that

$$f_R(r;\mu,\tau) = \frac{1}{\tau^{n_2}n!} E\left[\prod_{j=n_1+1}^{n} \frac{h\{(Y_{(r_j)} - \mu)/\tau\}}{h(Y_{(r_j)})} ;0,1\right],$$

where $n_2 = n - n_1$ and the expectation is with respect to the above joint distribution, $\mu = 0, \tau = 1$.

To obtain a local test of H_0 we calculate

$$[\partial \log f_R(r;\mu,\tau)/\partial\mu]_{\mu=0,\,\tau=1} \text{ and } [\partial \log f_R(r;\mu,\tau)/\partial\tau]_{\mu=0,\,\tau=1},$$

thus deriving test statistics

$$S = s(R) = \sum_{j=n_1+1}^{n} v_n(R_j), \quad T = t(R) = \sum_{j=n_1+1}^{n} w_n(R_j),$$

where the weights $v_n(\cdot)$ and $w_n(\cdot)$ are determined by $h(\cdot)$.

The test statistics S and T have to be combined into a single test statistic. Against a quite general alternative, a natural possibility is to take a quadratic form associated with S and T and with coefficients determined by the inverse covariance matrix. For the special alternatives, however, it is sensible to apply the appropriate one-sided tests, i.e. to take the more significant of the two components. To calculate the resulting significance level, the joint distribution of S and T under the null hypothesis is required. The exact means are $n_2\bar{v}$ and $n_2\bar{w}$, and, for example,

$$\text{var}(S;H_0) = \frac{n_1 n_2}{(n-1)} \Sigma\{v_n(j) - \bar{v}\}^2,$$

with analogous formulae for $\text{cov}(S,T)$ and $\text{var}(T)$. A bivariate normal approximation will often be adequate. For example, if the alternative is H_A the test statistic is $\max\{S/\sqrt{\text{var}(S)}, T/\sqrt{\text{var}(T)}\}$ and the chance under H_0 of this exceeding its observed value can be approximated directly from tables of the bivariate normal distribution.

[*Theoretical Statistics*, Section 6.3; Lehmann, Section 6.8]

6.6. Examine the null hypothesis distribution of the optimal two-sample rank test for exponential distributions.

Suppose that under the null hypothesis $Y_1, \ldots, Y_n$ are i.i.d. and exponentially distributed, whereas under the alternative hypothesis Y_j has mean $1/(\gamma + \beta z_j)$, where $z_1, \ldots, z_n$ are known. Obtain optimum parametric and rank tests, and suggest an approximation to the null hypothesis distribution of the latter.

Solution

The two-sample rank test which is optimal when the underlying distributions are exponential is similar in form to the Wilcoxon test outlined in Problem 6.2. The distinction is that in the present test the ith largest observation is assigned a score $e_{ni} = 1/n + 1/(n-1) + \ldots + 1/(n-i+1)$, which is the expected value of the ith largest observation in a sample of size n from the unit exponential distribution. The test statistic, instead of being the mean rank, is the mean score for the individuals in the first sample.

The exact distribution under the null hypothesis can again be obtained, this time by considering the finite population $\{e_{n1}, \ldots, e_{nn}\}$, easily shown to have unit mean. Approximations can be obtained by:

(i) using a normal approximation for the 'sample mean' $\bar{e}_1$;

(ii) 'improving' the normal approximation by finding the skewness and kurtosis from the results of Problem 6.2;

(iii) using an analogy with the exponential theory test to approximate the distribution of $\bar{e}_1/(1 - \bar{e}_1)$ as F with $(2n_1, 2n_2)$ degrees of freedom, i.e. to approximate the distribution of $\bar{e}_1$ by a particular beta distribution;

(iv) to 'improve' the approximation in (iii) by using degrees of freedom $(2n_1 l, 2n_2 l)$ and choosing l to match the exact mean and variance of $\bar{e}_1$. Detailed calculation (Cox, 1964b) gives

$$l \sim 1 + (\gamma - 2 + \log n)/n,$$

where γ is Euler's constant. All methods give reasonably good approximations even in quite small samples, although (iv) is the most accurate.

[*Theoretical Statistics*, Sections 6.3, 5.2, Lehmann, Section 6.8]

6.7.* In a simple randomized block design to compare m treatments, experimental units are arranged in b blocks each of m units. Treatments are allocated to units at random subject to each treatment occurring once in each block. Let $x_{jk,p}$ denote the observation that would be obtained were treatment p applied to the kth unit in the jth block; this is assumed to be independent of the allocation of treatments to other units. According to an assumption of treatment-unit additivity, $x_{jk,p} - x_{jk,q}$ is the same for all units,

*Amended version.

i.e. $x_{jk,p} = \tau_p + x_{jk}$, say, where x_{jk} can be regarded as, except for a constant, the observation that would be obtained in a uniformity trial and τ_p is a treatment parameter. Let Y_{jp} denote the observation obtained on the pth treatment in the jth block. Develop a linear model for Y_{jp} based solely on the randomization and examine some of the properties of the standard analysis of variance.

Solution

The usual normal-theory linear model approach to this situation is to write

$$Y_{jp} = \mu + \tau_p + \beta_j + \varepsilon'_{jp}, \tag{1}$$

where the ε'_{jp} are i.i.d. in $N(0,\sigma^2)$. Such a model refers to what would happen in some hypothetical set of repetitions, usually rather ill-defined, and is an assumption about the physical form of the random variation encountered. By contrast, the randomization model deals only with the finite set $x_{jk,p}$ and probabilistic considerations enter merely via the randomization used in treatment allocation.

In fact Y_{jp} is τ_p plus one of $x_{j1},\ldots,x_{jm}$, selected at random. We can write this

$$Y_{jp} = \tau_p + \sum_{k=1}^{m} \Delta_{jk,p} x_{jk},$$

where $\Delta_{jk,p} = 1$ if treatment p is applied to the kth unit of jth block and is zero otherwise. To obtain an 'error' of zero mean, rewrite this as

$$Y_{jp} = \tau_p + \bar{x}_{j.} + \varepsilon_{jp}, \tag{2}$$

where $\varepsilon_{jp} = \Sigma \Delta_{jk,p}(x_{jk} - \bar{x}_j)$. The formal analogy with (1) is clear. The indicator random variables $\Delta_{jk,p}$ have simple properties, for example

$$\mathrm{pr}(\Delta_{jk,p} = 1) = 1/m,\ \mathrm{pr}(\Delta_{jk,p} = 1, \Delta_{jl,q} = 1) = 1/\{m(m-1)\}\,(k \neq l, p \neq q). \tag{3}$$

This means that, superficially at least, the ε's in (2) have a quite different structure from the ε'''s in (1).

Three important results based on the normal-theory model (1) are as follows:

(a) a contrast $\Sigma l_p \tau_p$ (with $\Sigma l_p = 0$) is estimated by $\Sigma l_p \bar{Y}_{.p}$ with variance estimated by $\Sigma l_p^2 \mathrm{MS}_e / b$, where

$$\mathrm{MS}_e = \Sigma(Y_{jp} - \bar{Y}_{j.} - \bar{Y}_{.p} + \bar{Y}_{..})^2 / \{(m-1)(b-1)\};$$

(b) if $\mathrm{MS}_t = b\Sigma(\bar{Y}_{.p} - \bar{Y}_{..})^2/(m-1)$, then $E(\mathrm{MS}_t) \geqslant E(\mathrm{MS}_e)$ with equality if and only if $\tau_1 = \ldots = \tau_m$;

(c) to test null hypotheses in the situations of (a) and (b), t and F tests are available.

To examine randomization theory analogies of (a)–(c), the most direct technique is to express the relevant quantities in terms of the Δ's and to use results such as (3). Much detailed calculation can, however, be avoided by applying an argument similar to that used for Problem 6.2. Let $E_R(\cdot)$ denote expectation with respect to the randomization distribution, i.e. with respect to the distribution of the Δ's.

For example, $\Sigma l_p \bar{Y}_{.p}$ has the form $\Sigma l_p \tau_p$ + linear function of x's. Considerations of symmetry show that

$$E_R(\Sigma l_p \bar{Y}_{.p}) = \Sigma l_p \tau_p + a \sum_{j,k} x_{jk}.$$

Choice of the special population $x_{jk} = 1$ proves that $a \equiv 0$. Similarly, on taking for simplicity the simple contrast $\bar{Y}_{.1} - \bar{Y}_{.2}$, we find a randomization variance that is quadratic in the x's and considerations of the symmetry of the randomization show that

$$\begin{aligned}
\mathrm{var}_R(\bar{Y}_{.1} - \bar{Y}_{.2}) &= c'\Sigma x_{jk}^2 + d' \sum_{k \neq l} x_{jk} x_{jl} + e' \sum_{j \neq l} x_{jk} x_{lm} \\
&= c''\bar{x}^2 + d''\Sigma(\bar{x}_{j.} - \bar{x}_{..})^2 + e''\Sigma(x_{jk} - \bar{x}_{j.})^2,
\end{aligned} \tag{4}$$

where c'', d'' and e'' are constants not depending on the x's. If the x_{jk} are constant within each block, the variance is zero and this implies that $c'' = d'' = 0$.

A similar argument shows that

$$E_R(\mathrm{MS}_e) = e'''\Sigma(x_{jk} - \bar{x}_{j.})^2. \tag{5}$$

The constants e'', e''' can be calculated by considering special populations. Alternatively imagine, purely as a basis for a mathematical argument, that the x_{jk} are uncorrelated random variables of zero mean and variance τ^2. Then, with $\mathscr{E}$ denoting expectation over their distribution,

$$\mathscr{E}\{\mathrm{var}_R(\bar{Y}_{.1} - \bar{Y}_{.2})\} = 2\tau^2/b, \mathscr{E}\{E_R(\mathrm{MS}_e)\} = \tau^2,$$

$$\mathscr{E}\{\Sigma(x_{jk} - \bar{x}_{j.})^2\} = b(m-1)\tau^2,$$

from which it follows that

$$\mathrm{var}_R(\bar{Y}_{.1} - \bar{Y}_{.2}) = \frac{2\,\Sigma(x_{jk} - \bar{x}_{j.})^2}{b^2(m-1)} = \frac{2}{b}E_R(\mathrm{MS}_e).$$

Similarly

$$E_R(\mathrm{MS}_t) = \frac{b\Sigma(\tau_p - \bar{\tau})^2}{(m-1)} + E_R(\mathrm{MS}_e).$$

These are the randomization theory versions of (a) and (b). The most important general aspect of this argument is that analogous results for other designs follow from the assumption of unit-treatment additivity combined with the appropriate randomization. Thus no different physical assumption is involved in dealing with a Latin square or balanced incomplete block design from that for a randomized block or indeed a completely randomized design.

Exact significance tests based on the randomization can be obtained by enumeration or, approximately, by the evaluation of moments. Under the null hypothesis that all treatments are equivalent, the observations that would have been obtained under different treatment allocations can be calculated exactly. Further $SS_t + SS_e = \text{const}$, so that instead of considering MS_t/MS_e, we may consider SS_t or MS_t. The variances and higher moments of this can be calculated by a generalization of the previous argument. Provided that the $Y_{jp} - \bar{Y}_{j\cdot}$ have an overall distribution not too far from that expected under (1), the randomization distribution of the test statistic is close to the normal-theory distribution. This is indeed clear on general grounds in that under an 'infinite' model such as (1), the distribution of any test statistic is an average of separate randomization distributions, so that 'infinite' model theory and randomization theory agree in some average sense.

[*Theoretical Statistics*, Section 6.4; Rao, Section 7e.4; Silvey, Section 9.6; Kempthorne, 1952, 1966; Grundy and Healy, 1950]

6.8. To examine the null hypothesis that n i.i.d. observations have a given continuous cumulative distribution function $F(y)$, consider the sample distribution function $\tilde{F}_n(y)$, defined as the proportion of the n observations less than or equal to y. The Kolmogorov distance statistics are defined as

$$D_n^+ = \sup_y \{\tilde{F}_n(y) - F(y)\}, D_n^- = \sup_y \{F(y) - \tilde{F}_n(y)\}, D_n = \max(D_n^+, D_n^-).$$

Prove that the null hypothesis distribution of the Kolmogorov distance statistic is unaffected by an arbitrary monotonic transformation and hence that, without loss of generality, the null hypothesis to be tested can be taken as the uniform distribution over $(0, 1)$.

In this case, prove that the first and second moment properties of $\tilde{F}_n(y) - y$ are, as $n \to \infty$, the same as those of a tied Brownian motion (sometimes called Brownian bridge), i.e. Brownian motion starting at $(0,0)$ and conditioned to go through $(1,0)$. Hence interpret the limiting null hypothesis distribution in terms of a tied Brownian motion with absorbing barriers and show that, as $n \to \infty$,

$$\lim(D_n^+ \sqrt{n} < x) = 1 - e^{-2x^2},$$

and

$$\lim(D_n \sqrt{n} < x) = 1 + 2 \sum_{k=1}^{\infty} (-1)^k e^{-2k^2 x^2}.$$

Solution

The required invariance is seen from the form of the graphs $\tilde{F}_n(y)$, and the theoretical cumulative distribution function $F(y)$, versus y. Under arbitrary monotonic transformations, the abcissa is stretched in an arbitrary way, but the ordinates are unchanged. Thus the set of values of $\tilde{F}_n(y) - F(y)$ is unchanged by transformation. We can thus transform to a uniform distribution, $F(y) = y$.

Now $\tilde{F}_n(y)$ is the proportion of n independent trials that are 'successes', the probability of success being y. The binomial distribution thus applies, so that

$$E\{\tilde{F}_n(y)\} = y, \text{ var}\{\tilde{F}_n(y)\} = y(1-y)/n.$$

Let $y_1 < y_2$. We can classify observations as in $[0, y_1), [y_1, y_2), [y_2, 1]$ and the multinomial distribution with three 'cells' is applicable. It follows that $\text{cov}\{\tilde{F}_n(y_1), \tilde{F}_n(y_2)\} = y_1(1-y_2)/n$.

Brownian motion is a stochastic process effectively of cumulative sums of independent normally distributed random variables. The second moment properties of tied Brownian motion can be calculated from first principles by introducing independent normal random variables Z_1, Z_2, Z_3 of variances $y_1, y_2 - y_1$ and $1 - y_2$, so that before conditioning $\tilde{F}_n(y_1)$ and $\tilde{F}_n(y_2)$ are represented by Z_1 and $Z_1 + Z_2$, whereas the value at $y = 1$ is $Z_1 + Z_2 + Z_3$. The required covariance matrix is that of Z_1 and $Z_1 + Z_2$ conditionally on $Z_1 + Z_2 + Z_3 = 1$ and this is easily calculated from standard properties of the trivariate normal distribution.

That the properties of the binomially distributed process $\{\tilde{F}_n(y)\}$ are approximated by the normally distributed process with the same covariance structure should be taken as 'obvious' for the purpose of heuristic arguments of the kind so valuable in applied mathematics. Rigorous proof, which is of considerable mathematical interest, is best via the ideas of weak convergence (Billingsley, 1968). The distribution problem for the statistics D_n and D_n^+ thus corresponds approximately to a problem with absorbing barriers; books on stochastic processes describe the relevant techniques.

[*Theoretical Statistics*, Sections 6.5, 3.2; Rao, Section 6f; Silvey, Section 9.1; Bartlett, 1966, Section 4.1]

6.9. To test whether random variables Y and Z are independent is to test whether their joint cumulative distribution function is of the form $F_{Y,Z}(y, z) = G_Y(y)K_Z(z)$, where $G_Y(\cdot)$ and $K_Z(\cdot)$ are the marginal cumulative distribution functions. Construct a distribution-free permutation test of monotonic dependence based on the measure of dependence

$$\Delta = \int\int \{F_{Y,Z}(y, z) - G_Y(y)K_Z(z)\} dG_Y(y)dK_Z(z),$$

giving the sampling distribution of the test under the null hypothesis of independence.

Solution

One direct method is to estimate Δ using the relevant sample distribution functions. We examine the alternative U-statistic method of constructing a minimum variance unbiased estimate of Δ. To do this, we note that

$$\Delta = \text{pr}(Y < Y', Z < Z'') - \tfrac{1}{4},$$

where (Y, Z), Y' and Z'' are independent. Therefore an unbiased estimate of Δ based on three independent pairs $(Y_1, Z_1), (Y_2, Z_2), (Y_3, Z_3)$ is

$$t\{(Y_1, Z_1), (Y_2, Z_2), (Y_3, Z_3)\} = \tfrac{1}{2}\{\text{hv}(Y_2 - Y_1)\text{hv}(Z_3 - Z_1) + \text{hv}(Y_3 - Y_1) \\ \times \text{hv}(Z_2 - Z_1)\} - \tfrac{1}{4}.$$

The corresponding symmetric estimate is

$$k\{(Y_1, Z_1), (Y_2, Z_2), (Y_3, Z_3)\} = \tfrac{1}{3}[t\{(Y_1, Z_1), (Y_2, Z_2), (Y_3, Z_3)\} \\ + t\{(Y_2, Z_2), (Y_3, Z_3), (Y_1, Z_1)\} \\ + t\{(Y_3, Z_3), (Y_1, Z_1), (Y_2, Z_2)\}].$$

Given n pairs $(Y_1, Z_1), \ldots, (Y_n, Z_n)$ with $n \geqslant 3$, the complete minimal sufficient statistic for F is the set of ordered Y_j's and matched Z_j's. Therefore the uniformly minimum variance unbiased estimate of Δ is obtained by the process of Rao-Blackwellization described in Chapter 8 as

$$T = \frac{1}{\binom{n}{3}} \sum k\{(Y_{j1}, Z_{j1}), (Y_{j2}, Z_{j2}), (Y_{j3}, Z_{j3})\},$$

where summation is over $1 \leqslant j_1 \leqslant j_2 \leqslant j_3 \leqslant n$.

In principle the exact sampling distribution of T may be found under the null hypothesis of independence. We use the fact that, conditionally on the order statistics $y_{(1)} \leqslant \ldots \leqslant y_{(n)}$ and $z_{(1)} \leqslant \ldots \leqslant z_{(n)}$, all permutations of $(y_{(1)}, \ldots, y_{(n)})$ are equally likely values of $(Y_1, \ldots, Y_n)$ and that all permutations of $(z_{(1)}, \ldots, z_{(n)})$ are equally likely values of $(Z_1, \ldots, Z_n)$ given $(Y_1, \ldots, Y_n) = (y_{(1)}, \ldots, y_{(n)})$.

In practice a normal approximation to the null distribution of T will probably be adequate for n greater than 10, say. For this we have zero mean and the large-sample variance approximation (Hoeffding, 1948)

$$9n^{-1} \operatorname{var}(E[k\{(Y_1, Z_1), (Y_2, Z_2), (Y_3, Z_3)\} | (Y_1, Z_1)]).$$

A straightforward calculation shows that this is equal to $(16n)^{-1}$.

[*Theoretical Statistics*, Section 6.5]

7 INTERVAL ESTIMATION

Summary

In many ways a central problem of statistical inference is to summarize what can be learned from data about the value of an unknown parameter, treating all points in the parameter space on an equal footing *a priori*. This is done by specifying, at various probability levels, those parameter values consistent with the data. In a sampling theory approach, such parameter values are specified by confidence limits, intervals and regions.

Suppose first that there is a one-dimensional unknown parameter θ indexing the distribution of Y, and for $\alpha > 0$ let $T^{\alpha} = t^{\alpha}(Y)$ be a statistic such that for all $\theta \in \Omega$

$$\mathrm{pr}(T^{\alpha} \geqslant \theta; \theta) = 1 - \alpha, \tag{1}$$

and that if $\alpha_1 > \alpha_2$ then $T^{\alpha_1} \leqslant T^{\alpha_2}$. We then call T^{α} a $1 - \alpha$ upper confidence limit for θ. If $g(\cdot)$ is strictly increasing, then $g(T^{\alpha})$ is a $1 - \alpha$ upper confidence limit for $g(\theta)$. Lower confidence limits T_{α} are defined similarly. If in (1) the equality sign is replaced by a greater than or equals sign then the limits are called conservative. (1) gives a hypothetical interpretation to the limits, which is verifiable experimentally in principle.

In applications we explicitly or implicitly give confidence limits for a range of values of α, rather than choosing a specific single value α_0.

Optimal limits are defined by requiring $\mathrm{pr}(T^{\alpha} \geqslant \theta'; \theta)$ to be small for $\theta' > \theta$, if possible to be minimal for all pairs (θ, θ'), so that T^{α} is 'close' to θ. This leads to a general procedure for constructing good or best confidence limits: to obtain 'good' $1 - \alpha$ upper confidence limits, take all those parameter values not 'rejected' at level α in a 'good' significance test against lower alternatives.

For discrete distributions, where only a discrete set of levels α are achievable, conservative limits are normally used.

The above definitions generalize to confidence intervals and regions. Thus $[T_{.}, T^{.}]$ specifies a $1 - \alpha$ confidence interval if for all θ

$$\mathrm{pr}(T_{.} \leqslant \theta \leqslant T^{.}; \theta) = 1 - \alpha,$$

a nesting condition being required in addition. In the continuous case, a combination of upper and lower limits $[T_{\alpha_1}, T^{\alpha_2}]$ with $\alpha_1 + \alpha_2 = \alpha$ gives such an interval. For the majority of purposes, the convention $\alpha_1 = \alpha_2 = \frac{1}{2}\alpha$ is sensible in that lower and upper limits of separately known levels are being given.

In situations lacking a natural monotonicity property, confidence regions are not restricted to be intervals. The nested set of regions $R_\alpha(Y)$ are $1 - \alpha$ confidence regions if for all θ

$$\mathrm{pr}\{\theta \in R_\alpha(Y); \theta\} = 1 - \alpha. \tag{2}$$

A useful convention in forming such regions is to arrange, if possible, that all parameter values in R_α have higher likelihood than those outside; the region is then called likelihood-based. A general procedure for constructing good intervals and regions is via corresponding two-sided tests, the interval or region consisting of all parameter values not rejected at the level in question.

When the parameter θ is multidimensional, confidence regions for θ are defined by a direct generalization of (2). More commonly it will be required to find confidence limits, intervals or regions for a single component ψ of θ, the remainder λ of θ being a nuisance parameter. The ideas of similarity and invariance in Chapter 5 then apply directly to the tests used in construction of confidence sets.

Where ancillary statistics are available, the probability calculations (1) and (2) are made conditionally on the ancillary statistics.

There are a number of points of interpretation that need careful discussion in a full treatment of confidence regions. In particular, it is possible that a particular confidence region is the whole parameter space; an interpretation is that at the given level all possible parameter values are consistent with the data.

A final closely related idea is that of $1 - \alpha$ prediction regions for an as yet unobserved random variable $Y†$ having a distribution depending on the same parameter θ as the observed random variable Y. This too can be converted formally into a problem in the theory of tests by supposing that Y and $Y†$ have distributions corresponding to parameter values θ and $\theta†$, and then finding w_α, the best critical region of size α for testing the composite null hypothesis $\theta = \theta†$. For given y, let the prediction region $P_\alpha(y)$ be the set of $y†$ values such that $(y, y†)$ is not in w_α, i.e. such that y and $y†$ are consistent at level α with a common parameter value. Then $P_\alpha(Y)$ has the property that for all θ

$$\mathrm{pr}\{Y† \in P_\alpha(Y); \theta\} = 1 - \alpha,$$

a reasonable requirement for a prediction region.

Problems

7.1. The random variable Y has a binomial distribution of parameter $\frac{1}{2}$ and with an unknown number θ of trials. Obtain confidence limits for θ.

Solution

To derive an upper confidence limit we consider the null hypothesis $\theta = \theta_0$ with alternatives $\theta < \theta_0$. A conservative size α critical region is then of the form $y < y^\alpha(\theta_0)$, where

$$\sum_{r=0}^{y^\alpha(\theta_0)} \binom{\theta_0}{r} 2^{-\theta_0} \leqslant \alpha.$$

For a given observation y, the value of θ_0 that is just not rejected at level α, say $\tilde{\theta}^\alpha$, is the largest θ_0 such that

$$\sum_{r=0}^{y} \binom{\theta_0}{r} 2^{-\theta_0} \geqslant \alpha. \tag{1}$$

Then $\tilde{\theta}^\alpha$ is the upper confidence limit with conservative confidence coefficient $1 - \alpha$. Corresponding lower confidence limits $\tilde{\theta}_\alpha$ are determined via critical regions of the form $y > y_\alpha(\theta_0)$.

An approximate upper confidence limit is obtained by using a normal approximation to the left-hand side of (1), which with continuity correction gives

$$\Phi\left(\frac{y + \frac{1}{2} - \frac{1}{2}\tilde{\theta}^\alpha}{\frac{1}{2}\sqrt{\tilde{\theta}^\alpha}} \right) = \Phi(-k_\alpha^*),$$

leading to a quadratic equation for $\tilde{\theta}^\alpha$ with solution

$$2y + 1 + \tfrac{1}{2}k_\alpha^{*2} + k_\alpha^*(2y + 1 + \tfrac{1}{4}k_\alpha^{*2})^{1/2}.$$

[*Theoretical Statistics*, Section 7.2; Rao, Section 7b.2]

7.2. Let $Y_1, \ldots, Y_n$ be i.i.d. with p.d.f. $h(y - \theta)$, where $h(y)$ is an unknown density symmetrical about zero. Explain how the null hypothesis $\theta = 0$ can be tested by using the statistic ΣY_j. To obtain a confidence region for θ, this test is applied to $\Sigma(Y_j - \theta_0)$. Show that the inversion of this test at any fixed level of significance yields an interval of θ values.

Solution

Under the null hypothesis $\theta = 0$, values y and $-y$ of y_j have equal probability. Thus if $T = \Sigma Y_j$ is taken as test statistic, and if the observed values are

$y_1, \ldots, y_n$, then the null distribution of T is found by attaching equal probabilities 2^{-n} to the 2^n points $\{\pm y_1, \ldots, \pm y_n\}$. More formally, we note that $(|Y_1|, \ldots, |Y_n|)$ is minimal sufficient for the unknown nuisance function $h(\cdot)$, so that a conditional argument treats only the signs of the Y_j as random. Of course, there remains considerable flexibility in the choice of test statistic.

The null distribution of T can be obtained by enumeration. Alternatively a normal approximation can be used, with moments found by noting that T is, conditionally, the sum of n independent symmetric binary random variables. Thus

$$E(T; \theta = 0) = 0, \text{ var}(T; \theta = 0) = \Sigma y_j^2.$$

To obtain confidence intervals, we consider the arbitrary null hypothesis $\theta = \theta_0$ and take the test statistic $T(\theta_0) = \Sigma(Y_j - \theta_0)$, with conditional sample space $\{\theta_0 \pm (y_1 - \theta_0), \ldots, \theta_0 \pm (y_n - \theta_0)\}$. Then

$$E\{T(\theta_0); \theta = \theta_0\} = 0, \text{ var}\{T(\theta_0); \theta = \theta_0\} = \Sigma(y_j - \theta_0)^2.$$

To determine a conservative $1 - \alpha$ upper confidence limit, we test $\theta = \theta_0$ versus alternatives $\theta < \theta_0$, for which the small values of $T(\theta_0)$ are significant. Now let $T_\alpha^*(\theta_0)$ be the conservative lower α point for $T(\theta_0)$, i.e. the largest value of t such that

$$\text{pr}\{T(\theta_0) \leqslant t; \theta = \theta_0\} \leqslant \alpha.$$

Then the conservative upper confidence region for θ is the set of θ_0 values for which $T(\theta_0) > T_\alpha^*(\theta_0)$, since these values are consistent with the hypothesis $\theta = \theta_0$ at conservative level α. If we use a normal approximation based on the exact mean and variance, then the confidence region is approximated by the semi-infinite interval $\theta \leqslant \tilde{\theta}^\alpha$ where

$$\tilde{\theta}^\alpha = \bar{y}_. + \frac{k_\alpha^* \{\Sigma(y_j - \bar{y}_.)^2\}^{1/2}}{\{n(n - k_\alpha^{*2})\}^{1/2}}.$$

A more elaborate argument with the exact distribution of $T(\theta)$ shows that the confidence region is of the form $\theta \leqslant \bar{y}_. + c_\alpha(y)$. The corresponding two-sided test gives a confidence interval around $\bar{y}_.$. For further details, see Kempthorne and Doerfler (1969).

[*Theoretical Statistics*, Section 7.2; Rao, Sections 7b, 7e.4]

7.3. Let $Y_1, \ldots, Y_n$ be i.i.d. with the unknown continuous cumulative distribution function $F_Y(y)$. For $0 < p < 1$, the p-quantile ξ_p of the distribution is defined by $p = F_Y(\xi_p)$; any reasonable convention can be used to make ξ_p unique should this equation not have a single solution. Show how to test the null hypothesis $\xi_p = \xi_{p0}$ against (a) one-sided and (b) two-sided alternatives by counting the number of observations exceeding ξ_{p0}. Show that for large n and for one-sided alternatives $\xi_p > \xi_{p0}$, the data fall in the size α critical region if and only if the rth order statistic exceeds ξ_{p0}, where r is the integer part of

$$np - k_\alpha^*\{np(1-p)\}^{1/2} + \tfrac{1}{2}.$$

Hence obtain confidence limits for ξ_p.

Solution

Let R denote the number of observations less than ξ_{p0}. If the null hypothesis $\xi_p = \xi_{p0}$ is true, then R has a binomial distribution of index n and parameter p. For alternatives $\xi_p > \xi_{p0}$ a critical region is formed from small values of R. Using a normal approximation with continuity correction we obtain the size α critical region as the set of r such that

$$\frac{r - np + \tfrac{1}{2}}{\{np(1-p)\}^{1/2}} < - k_\alpha^*. \tag{1}$$

Now $R < r'$ is equivalent to the r'th order statistic $Y_{(r')}$ falling above ξ_{p0}. Hence the data fall in the size α critical region if and only if the order statistic $Y_{(s)}$ exceeds ξ_{p0}, where s is the smallest value of r violating (1); i.e.

$$s = \left[- k_\alpha^*\{np(1-p)\}^{1/2} + np - \tfrac{1}{2}\right] + 1,$$

where $[\cdot]$ denotes the integer part. All values of ξ_{p0} not rejected in this way form the approximate one-sided confidence region, which is therefore the interval $[Y_{(s)}, \infty]$. An exact conservative interval can be obtained using the exact binomial distribution. An upper confidence limit can be obtained similarly.

The confidence limits in this non-parametric approach depend only on order statistics near to $Y_{([np])}$, which constitute a small part of the data. The dependence is not usually localized in this way when the distribution is restricted to a parametric family. A particularly critical case is that of very small or very large p; then the parametric approach is much more precise if correct, but is likely to be very wrong if the parametric model has incorrect tail behaviour.

[*Theoretical Statistics*, Section 7.2; Rao, Sections 7b.2; 6f.2]

7.4. Let $Y_{(1)}, \ldots, Y_{(n)}$ be order statistics from the uniform distribution on $(\theta, \theta + 1)$. Using the unconditional uniformly most powerful one-sided test, show that the associated lower confidence limit is $T_\alpha = \max(Y_{(1)} - c, Y_{(n)} - 1)$, where $\alpha = (1 - c)^n$. Comment on the fact that

$$\mathrm{pr}(T_\alpha \leqslant \theta \mid Y_{(n)} - Y_{(1)} \geqslant 1 - c) = 1$$

and suggest a more relevant lower confidence limit for θ.

Solution

The minimal sufficient statistic is the pair of extreme order statistics $(Y_{(1)}, Y_{(n)})$, and $A = Y_{(n)} - Y_{(1)}$ is ancillary, as follows from the invariance of A under location transformation of the data.

To derive a lower confidence limit, we consider the null hypothesis $\theta = \theta_0$ with alternatives $\theta > \theta_0$. Now for any fixed $\theta_A > \theta_0$, the possible values of the likelihood ratio $\mathrm{lr}_{A0}(y)$ are 0, 1, and ∞, corresponding respectively to the events

$$\theta_0 \leqslant y_{(1)} < \theta_A, \theta_A \leqslant y_{(1)} \leqslant y_{(n)} \leqslant \theta_0 + 1 \text{ and } \theta_0 + 1 < y_{(n)} < \theta_A + 1.$$

The latter possibility cannot occur when $\theta = \theta_0$, so that likelihood ratio critical regions have achievable levels

$$1, (\theta_0 + 1 - \theta_A)^n, 0,$$

where the middle level is determined by the particular alternative chosen. To obtain a size α critical region we must randomize, and the best way to do this is to choose that size α region which contributes most to power when $\theta > \theta_0$. This leads immediately to the uniformly most powerful critical region of the form

$$w_\alpha = \{y : y_{(1)} > \theta_0 + c \text{ or } y_{(n)} > \theta_0 + 1\}, \tag{1}$$

where direct calculation of $\mathrm{pr}(Y \in w_\alpha; \theta_0)$ shows that $\alpha = (1 - c)^n$.

All values of θ_0 not in the critical region (1) make up the required confidence region, which is therefore the set of θ_0 values exceeding

$$T_\alpha = \max(y_{(1)} - c, y_{(n)} - 1).$$

The critical region (1) is a triangle in the upper right-hand corner of the triangle defining the range of $(y_{(1)}, y_{(n)})$. The latter triangle has vertices (θ_0, θ_0), $(\theta_0, \theta_0 + 1)$ and $(\theta_0 + 1, \theta_0 + 1)$; the region (1) rests on the diagonal $y_{(1)} = y_{(n)}$ with the left-hand side parallel to the $y_{(n)}$ axis and passing through the point $(\theta_0 + c, \theta_0 + 1)$. Samples for which the ancillary statistic is equal to a correspond to points on the line $y_{(n)} = y_{(1)} + a$, which do not intersect region (1) if $a > 1 - c$. Thus the conditional level of (1) is zero if $a > 1 - c$, which gives the desired result for the lower confidence limit.

In our view it would not be relevant to attach the uncertainty associated with unconditional confidence limits when in fact T_α is known with certainty to exceed θ, as happens if $a > 1 - c$. The value of a measures how accurately θ may be located: conditionally on $A = a$, $M = \frac{1}{2}(Y_{(1)} + Y_{(n)})$ is uniformly distributed over $[\theta + \frac{1}{2}a, \theta + 1 - \frac{1}{2}a]$. Consideration of the likelihood suggests that the whole interval $[M - 1 + \frac{1}{2}a, M - \frac{1}{2}a]$ be given as a confidence interval; an exact best lower confidence limit would be $M - \frac{1}{2}a - \alpha(1 - a)$.

G.A. Barnard has recently shown that the confidence interval with shortest average length is determined by a system of conditional intervals with $\alpha = 0$ or 1 depending on the value of a. For an earlier reference and general discussion, see Pierce (1973).

[*Theoretical Statistics*, Section 7.2; Rao, Section 7b.2]

7.5. Suppose that Y_1 and Y_2 are i.i.d. in the standard Cauchy distribution of unknown location. Show that the likelihood is bimodal if and only if $c = y_{(2)} - y_{(1)} > 2$. Examine the forms of conditioned confidence region for the location parameter when $c \leqslant 2$ and when $c > 2$, and comment on the value of the mean as a location statistic.

Solution

Except for a constant, the log likelihood is

$$- \log\{1 + (y_1 - \theta)^2\} - \log\{1 + (y_2 - \theta)^2\}.$$

Write $\bar{y} = \frac{1}{2}(y_1 + y_2)$, $c = y_{(2)} - y_{(1)}$ and $\theta = \bar{y} + \delta$. Then the log likelihood is

$$l(\delta) = - \log\{1 + (\delta + \tfrac{1}{2}c)^2\} - \log\{1 + (\delta - \tfrac{1}{2}c)^2\},$$

which is an even function of δ.

Simple calculation gives

$$l'(\delta) = - 2\left\{\frac{(\delta + \frac{1}{2}c)}{1 + (\delta + \frac{1}{2}c)^2} + \frac{(\delta - \frac{1}{2}c)}{1 + (\delta - \frac{1}{2}c)^2}\right\}$$

$$l''(\delta) = - 2\left[\frac{1 - (\delta + \frac{1}{2}c)^2}{\{1 + (\delta + \frac{1}{2}c_2)^2\}^2} + \frac{1 - (\delta - \frac{1}{2}c)^2}{\{1 + (\delta - \frac{1}{2}c)^2\}^2}\right],$$

and in particular $l''(0) = - 4(1 - \frac{1}{4}c^2)(1 + \frac{1}{4}c^2)^{-2}$. Thus the stationary points are at roots of the cubic equation $l'(\delta) = 0$, one root being zero. The condition for bimodality can be obtained either via the condition that the other two roots are real, or alternatively from the condition that zero is a minimum of the likelihood because $l''(0) > 0$.

Conditional confidence intervals are obtained by rescaling the likelihood to have total integral equal to one. When $c \leqslant 2$, and also for $c > 2$ with sufficiently small α, the likelihood-based confidence regions will be intervals symmetrical about $\theta = \bar{y}$, whereas, for $c > 2$ and sufficiently large α the confidence regions will consist of two intervals symmetrically placed about, but not including, $\theta = \bar{y}$. Thus if $c \leqslant 2$, $\bar{y}$ is in a sense the only reasonable single measure of location, whereas for $c > 2$ the form of the likelihood function needs explicit consideration, although $\bar{y}$ is still the centre of symmetry.

Of course, for sample size greater than 2 the situation is more complicated. However, for sample size 20 and above the likelihood is usually well approximated by a normal curve centred at $\hat{\theta}$ with variance $\{-l''(\hat{\theta})\}^{-1}$, from which approximate conditional confidence intervals may be obtained. For further details, see Efron and Hinkley (1978).

[*Theoretical Statistics*, Section 7.2; Rao, Section 7b.2; Barnard and Sprott, 1971]

7.6. Show that if the scalar random variable Y has the distribution $N(\mu, 1)$ and if we observe $Y = y$, then μ is distributed in $N(y, 1)$ in the following frequency sense. Imagine hypothetical repetitions $(y^{(1)}, \mu^{(1)}), (y^{(2)}, \mu^{(2)}), \ldots$, each $y^{(j)}$ being the observed value of a random variable $Y^{(j)}$ having the distribution $N(\mu^{(j)}, 1)$ and the $\mu^{(j)}$ being arbitrary. Suppose now that all pairs are translated so that the observed value is y. That is, the jth pair is translated to $(y, \mu^{(j)} + y - y^{(j)}) = (y, \mu^{(j)'})$, say. Then the $\mu^{(j)'}$ have the frequency distribution $N(y, 1)$; this is the hypothetical frequency distribution of true means in a set of repetitions all having the observed value y. Use a similar argument starting from $Y_1, \ldots, Y_n$ i.i.d. in $N(\mu, \sigma^2)$ to show that μ has a Student t distribution, when samples are rescaled to have the observed mean and mean square.

Solution

The mathematical derivation is straightforward. We can write $Y^{(j)} = \mu^{(j)} + \varepsilon^{(j)}$, where $\varepsilon^{(j)}$ is a $N(0, 1)$ random variable. Hence after translation such that the observed value is a fixed y, the value of the parameter is $y - \varepsilon^{(j)}$, which has the $N(y, 1)$ frequency distribution. The essential point is that there is a hypothetical frequency distribution for the parameter, regardless of the physical distribution of the $\mu^{(j)}$; in particular it might be taken that all the $\mu^{(j)}$ are equal to the unknown μ under analysis, but this is not necessary.

When scale and location are both unknown, we consider general linear transformations. Let $\bar{y}$ and $\sqrt{\text{MS}}$ be the observed mean and estimate of standard deviation obtained from n observations from $N(\mu, \sigma^2)$. Consider hypothetical repetitions, the jth being $(\bar{y}^{(j)}, \sqrt{MS^{(j)}}, \mu^{(j)}, \sigma^{(j)})$. To transform the jth set to agree with the data, we use the transformation

$$y \text{ into } \sqrt{(MS/MS^{(j)})}y + \bar{y} - \sqrt{(MS/MS^{(j)})}\bar{y}^{(j)}.$$

Thus $\mu^{(j)}$ is transformed into

$$\bar{y} + \sqrt{(MS/MS^{(j)})}(\mu^{(j)} - \bar{y}^{(j)})$$

which implies that the transformed means have a frequency distribution of the form

$$\bar{y} + T_{n-1}\sqrt{(MS/n)}$$

where T_{n-1} is a random variable with the Student t distribution with $n-1$ degrees of freedom.

This argument (Fraser, 1961) gives an explicit frequency interpretation to the fiducial distribution of μ.

[*Theoretical Statistics*, Section 7.2; Rao, Section 5b.5]

7.7. The parameter μ is an unknown integer and is observed with an error equally likely to be $+1$ or -1. On the basis of an observation y it is claimed that

$$\mathrm{pr}(\mu = y - 1) = \mathrm{pr}(\mu = y + 1) = \tfrac{1}{2}.$$

Show that this 'probability' statement does not have the full properties of an ordinary probability statement in that it can be defeated by the following betting strategy:

> if $y \geq 1$, bet even money that $\mu = y - 1$;
>
> if $y < 1$, refuse to bet.

Prove that if $\mu = 0$ or 1 this strategy 'wins', whereas if $\mu \neq 0$ or 1 it breaks 'even'. Note that the strategy wins for all μ if the cut-off is chosen to be $y = m$ with probability $\pi_m > 0$, $m = 0, \pm 1, \ldots$.

Solution

Fiducial probability, and to some extent structural probability (Fraser, 1968), aim to use data to derive a probability distribution for unknown parameters, without the explicit assumptions of the Bayesian theory. A pure sampling theory approach, however, insists that, while confidence statements may often be similar to probability statements, there is an essential difference:

unknown parameters are unique constants and as such are not random variables.

It is reasonable to think that if it is meaningful to deal with unknown parameters as random variables, then it should be possible to do this in the very simple situation indicated here, but the calculation shows that the betting strategy of accepting an even bet on $\mu = y - 1$ can be defeated, so that the claimed probability of $\frac{1}{2}$ does not have one of the usual 'practical' interpretations.

If $\mu = 0$, the expected gain with betting stake c is

$$c \times \mathrm{pr}(y = +1|\mu = 0) + 0 \times \mathrm{pr}(y = -1|\mu = 0)$$

which is positive; there is a similar argument if $\mu = 1$. For $\mu < 0$, no bet takes place because then y is always less than one. For $\mu > 1$, the expected gain is zero. Under the extended strategy, let M be the random cut-off point. Then for betting stake c the expected gain is

$$\{c\mathrm{pr}(y = \mu + 1|\mu) - c\mathrm{pr}(y = \mu - 1|\mu)\}\mathrm{pr}(M < \mu + 1)$$
$$+ c\mathrm{pr}(y = \mu + 1|\mu)\mathrm{pr}(M = \mu + 1) = c\mathrm{pr}(y = \mu + 1|\mu)\mathrm{pr}(M = \mu + 1)$$

which is positive for all μ such that $\mu + 1$ is a possible value of M.

[*Theoretical Statistics*, Section 7.2; Rao, Section 5b.5; Buehler, 1971]

7.9*. Suppose that it is required to obtain a $1 - \alpha$ confidence interval of preassigned width $2l$ for the unknown mean μ of a normal distribution, the variance also being unknown. To achieve this, n_0 observations are taken; let MS_0 be the estimate of variance from these observations. Now take further observations so that the total number of observations is

$$\max(n_0, [4t^{*2}_{n_0 - 1, \frac{1}{2}\alpha}\mathrm{MS}_0/l^2] + 1),$$

where $[x]$ is the integer part of x. Show, by first arguing conditionally on MS_0, that if $\bar{Y}$ is the mean of the combined data, then ($\bar{Y} - l, \bar{Y} + l$) defines a conservative $1 - \alpha$ confidence interval for μ. Outline how, by suitable randomization, the confidence interval can be made exact. Comment on more efficient uses of the data obtained by such a procedure.

Solution

There are several ways of converting what will typically be conservative intervals into exact intervals. One is randomization. Another is as follows.

For each n define constants $a_1, \ldots, a_n$ depending on MS_0 and such that

* Problem 7.8 omitted.

$$a_1 + \dots + a_n = 1, \; a_1 = \dots = a_{n_0}, \; \mathrm{MS}_0(a_1^2 + \dots + a_n^2) = \tfrac{1}{4}l^2/t^{*2}_{n_0-1,\frac{1}{2}\alpha}.$$

This is clearly possible. Now $(\Sigma a_i Y_i - \mu)/(a_1^2 + \dots + a_n^2)^{1/2}$ has, conditionally on MS_0, the distribution $N(0, \sigma^2)$, and hence has this distribution unconditionally and independently of MS_0. Thus

$$T = (\Sigma a_i Y_i - \mu)/\{\mathrm{MS}_0(a_1^2 + \dots + a_n^2)\}^{1/2}$$

has the Student t distribution with $n_0 - 1$ degrees of freedom. Hence the exact confidence interval of length $2l$ is obtained.

Use of the mean of all observations, rather than the 'inefficient' statistic $\Sigma a_i Y_i$, leads to a conservative interval. A more important point is that the information about σ^2 in the second sample, if taken, is ignored. In practice one would be tempted, subject to internal consistency, to take the ordinary confidence intervals obtained from the full data as summarizing the information about μ.

A general point raised by the example is that frequency properties unattainable for fixed sample size are sometimes attainable in the extended sample space where sample size may vary in an appropriate manner.

[*Theoretical Statistics*, Section 7.3; Rao, Section 7c.6; Stein, 1945]

7.10. The random variables $Y_1, \dots, Y_n$ are independently normally distributed with unknown variance σ^2 and with $E(Y_j) = \gamma + \beta e^{-\rho x_j}$, where $x_1, \dots, x_n$ are known constants and γ, β and ρ are unknown parameters. Show that there is no minimal sufficient statistic of low dimension. Consider the null hypothesis $\rho = \rho_0$ and show that for local departures $\rho = \rho_0 + \delta$, the model becomes $E(Y_j) = \gamma + \beta e^{-\rho_0 x_j} - \beta \delta x_j e^{-\rho_0 x_j}$. Hence, show that an exact locally most powerful test of $\rho = \rho_0$ is obtained by considering the model $E(Y_j) = \gamma + \beta e^{-\rho_0 x_j} + \psi x_j e^{-\rho_0 x_j}$ and by applying the normal-theory linear model test of $\psi = 0$ using Student's t. Thence obtain a $1 - \alpha$ confidence region for ρ. Give a general formulation of the argument of which this problem is a special case.

Solution

The log likelihood is

$$-\tfrac{1}{2}n \log(2\pi\sigma^2) - \frac{\Sigma(Y_j - \gamma - \beta e^{-\rho x_j})^2}{2\sigma^2}$$

and, so long as ρ is unknown, there is no reduction of the data by sufficiency.
    For $\rho = \rho_0 + \delta$ we can write

$$e^{-\rho x_j} = (1 - \delta x_j)e^{-\rho_0 x_j} + O(\delta^2),$$

thereby obtaining the model in the linearized form

$$E(Y_j) = \gamma + \beta e^{-\rho_0 x_j} + \psi x_j e^{-\rho_0 x_j} + O(\delta^2),$$

where $\psi = -\rho_0 \delta$. Thus the Student t statistic for testing $\psi = 0$ will, for $\rho_0 \neq 0$, be locally most powerful for testing $\rho = \rho_0$. Note especially that the test is 'exact' in the sense that under the null hypothesis the test statistic has the indicated Student t distribution. The optimum power property is only local; in principle this is shown by applying the Neyman–Pearson lemma to the conditional distribution of the data given the minimal sufficient statistic under $\rho = \rho_0$, although it is implicit in the absence of a reduction by sufficiency.

An exact confidence region for ρ is obtained as the set of ρ_0 not 'rejected' in the above test. Numerical solution is straightforward in principle. It is not clear that the region will always be an interval, although this will normally be so.

One more general formulation is to consider normal-theory models with

$$E(Y_j) = g_j(\beta_1, \ldots, \beta_p, \rho),$$

where the dependence on $\beta_1, \ldots, \beta_p$, but not that on ρ, is linear. More generally ρ might be a vector, and an exact test of $\rho = \rho_0$ is still possible based on the F distribution. Exact tests cease to be possible if the dependence on nuisance parameters $\beta_1, \ldots, \beta_p$ is non-linear.

There is also the possibility of generalization to members of the exponential family other than the normal.

[*Theoretical Statistics*, Sections 7.3; Rao, Section 7b.2; Williams, 1962]

7.11. Independent binary trials are made with constant but unknown probability of success. In a fixed number n of trials, r successes are observed. What can be said about the number of successes to be observed in a further fixed number m trials?

Solution

We consider independent random variables R and $R\dagger$ having binomial distributions with fixed indices n and m and parameters θ and $\theta\dagger$. Then to obtain a lower $1 - \alpha$ confidence limit on $R\dagger$ we construct a size α critical region for testing $\theta = \theta\dagger$ against alternatives $\theta > \theta\dagger$. The set of values $(r, r\dagger)$ not in the critical region specifies future $r\dagger$ consistent with the observed r.

An 'exact' solution is provided by Fisher's test. That is, if as judged by

Fisher's test, the 2×2 contingency table

	Successes	Failures	Total
	r	$n - r$	n
	$r\dagger$	$m - r\dagger$	m

shows no significant difference between rows, then $r\dagger$ is a possible value for $R\dagger$.

An approximate solution is given by a normal approximation to the distribution of $R\dagger/m - R/n$ with continuity correction. Thus, in a two-sided procedure, the values of $r\dagger$ consistent with r at level α satisfy

$$\frac{\left\{ \left| r\dagger - \frac{m(r + r\dagger)}{m + n} \right| - \frac{1}{2} \right\}^2}{\left\{ \frac{mn(r + r\dagger)(m + n - r - r\dagger)}{(m + n)^3} \right\}} \leqslant k^*_{\frac{1}{2}\alpha}.$$

Note the symmetry implicit in this problem in that if

$$r = a, n = b; r\dagger = a', m = b'$$

are consistent at level α, then so are

$$r = a', n = b'; r\dagger = a, m = b.$$

In this sense the process is time-reversible.

[*Theoretical Statistics*, Section 7.5]

8 POINT ESTIMATION

Summary

Chapter 7 outlined methods for estimating parameters by specifying a range of values consistent with the data. Point estimation involves the specification of a single value. Special care is required in formulating point estimation problems and at least three types of application may be distinguished:

(a) Often, possibly after transformation of the parameter, upper and lower $1 - \alpha$ confidence limits for θ are approximately of the form $t \pm k^*_{\frac{1}{2}\alpha}\sigma_t$. Then the value of t, supplemented by the precision measure σ_t, is a convenient way of summarizing information about θ. It seems best, however, to regard this as a device for concise presentation of confidence limits rather than as a technique of point estimation *per se*.

(b) In a decision problem it may be required, in effect, to give a single value, e.g. as a basis for some control criterion. Here the full formulation of decisions is required if somewhat arbitrary choices are to be avoided (Chapter 11).

(c) In the analysis of large sets of data, it may be sensible to calculate a point estimate T of some parameter θ from each portion of the data, and then in a second stage to examine how θ varies across the sets. If the second-stage analysis is linear it will be required that in each first-stage analysis the bias $b(\theta) = E(T;\theta) - \theta$ is small.

In general the mean squared error of an estimator is

$$E\{(T - \theta)^2;\theta\} = \{b(\theta)\}^2 + \mathrm{var}(T;\theta).$$

One common procedure for obtaining point estimates is to restrict the class of estimates, e.g. by requiring invariance under a particular type of transformation, and to search for estimates of minimum mean squared error within the class.

Some elegant theory, which should be treated critically in application, requires unbiased estimators, i.e. $b(\theta) = 0$, and then aims to choose T to minimize $\mathrm{var}(T;\theta)$, leading to a minimum variance unbiased estimate.

According to the Cramér–Rao inequality, in a regular problem with

θ one-dimensional

$$\mathrm{var}(T;\theta) \geqslant \{1 + b'(\theta)\}^2/i_.(\theta),$$

where $i_.(\theta)$ is the total Fisher information (Chapter 4). For unbiased estimates

$$\mathrm{var}(T;\theta) \geqslant 1/i_.(\theta).$$

The lower bound is achieved if and only if T is a linear function of the efficient score $U_.(\theta)$. For a vector parameter an unbiased estimate T_1 of a particular component θ_1, say, is such that

$$\mathrm{var}(T_1;\theta) \geqslant i^{11}(\theta),$$

where $i^{rs}(\theta)$ is the (r,s)th element of $\{\mathbf{i}_.(\theta)\}^{-1}$. The lower bound is achieved if and only if T_1 is a linear function of the components of $U_.(\theta)$. More generally an unbiased estimate of the linear parametric function $l^T\theta$ has variance at least $l^T\{\mathbf{i}_.(\theta)\}^{-1}l_.$

If there is a complete sufficient statistic S for the parameter θ, minimum variance unbiased estimation is possible by the following construction, often called Rao–Blackwellization. Let V be any unbiased estimate of θ and $T = E(V|S)$. It is easily shown that $E(T;\theta) = \theta$ and $\mathrm{var}(T;\theta) \leqslant \mathrm{var}(V;\theta)$; uniqueness of T is a consequence of the completeness of S. Thus any function of a complete sufficient statistic is a minimum variance unbiased estimate of its expectation.

Two important techniques for the approximate elimination of estimation bias are series expansion and the jackknife. In the first, suppose that sample size n is large and that we can find an estimate T such that

$$E(T;\theta) = \theta + a(\theta)/n + O(n^{-2}). \tag{1}$$

Then $T - a(T)/n$ has a bias of smaller order in n^{-1}. This often applies with $T = g(S), \theta = g(\varphi)$ and S unbiased for φ with variance of order n^{-1}, in which case $a(\theta)/n = \frac{1}{2}\{g'(\varphi)\}^2 \mathrm{var}(S;\varphi)$. For the jackknife, let T_n be an estimate obtained from $Y_1,\ldots,Y_n$ and $T_{n-1,j}$ the corresponding estimate obtained when Y_j is omitted. Then if (1) holds for sample sizes n and $n-1$, it is easy to show that with $\bar{T}_{n-1,.} = \Sigma T_{n-1,j}/n$

$$T_n^J = n T_n - (n-1)\bar{T}_{n-1,.} \tag{2}$$

has bias of smaller order in n^{-1} than T_n. It is possible to estimate $\mathrm{var}(T_n^J;\theta)$ and $\mathrm{var}(T_n;\theta)$ by

$$\frac{n-1}{n} \Sigma (T_{n-1,j} - \bar{T}_{n-1,.})^2. \tag{3}$$

Although the jackknife is useful when distributional properties are not

known precisely, it does not work well for radically non-linear statistics
or radically non-homogeneous data.

The topic of robust estimation arises when we require that estimates
are not sensitive to barely-detectable deviations from distributional assumptions, e.g. when a few aberrant observations occur. For estimating location
parameters, robust replacements for the sample mean de-emphasize or
remove extreme order statistics in an appropriate (e.g. symmetric) way.

Problems

8.1 Suppose for simplicity that there is a scalar parameter. Let the likelihood
attain its largest value at a point where the second derivative exists; call the
value at which the maximum is attained the maximum likelihood estimate.
For sufficiently large α, the $1 - \alpha$ likelihood-based confidence interval is
approximately symmetrical about the maximum likelihood estimate and
according to the view that point estimates are sometimes useful as indicating
the centres of confidence intervals this provides a special status to the maximum likelihood estimate. What further property of the likelihood function
would make this more compelling?

Solution

The argument outlined provides a weak justification of maximum likelihood
estimates in cases where the overall maximum of the likelihood is at a stationary point. If the likelihood function is unimodal and approximately
symmetrical about the maximum then the justification is strengthened,
because the $1 - \alpha$ likelihood-based confidence regions will, for all α, be
approximately symmetrical about the maximum likelihood estimate.

Note that in such cases the likelihood function can be made exactly
symmetrical for any particular sample point y by transformation of the
parameter. Such a transformation typically depends on y. One data-
independent transformation that will tend to symmetrize the likelihood is
that which makes the third derivative of the log likelihood have zero expected
value at the true parameter point.

[*Theoretical Statistics*, Section 8.1; Rao, Section 5d.3; Silvey, Chapter 4]

8.2. For continuous distributions, an estimate T is called median unbiased
for θ if, for all θ,

$$\mathrm{pr}(T < \theta; \theta) = \mathrm{pr}(T > \theta; \theta) = \tfrac{1}{2}.$$

Prove that if $g(.)$ is strictly monotonic, $g(T)$ is median unbiased for $g(\theta)$. Show that if ss_d is a normal-theory sum of squares based on d degrees of freedom, then the median unbiased estimate of variance is ss_d/c_d, where $c_d \simeq d - \frac{2}{3}$. Show also that the same value of c_d applies approximately if the estimate is that $\tilde{\theta}$ such that $\mathrm{pr}\,(T \leqslant t_{\mathrm{obs}}; \tilde{\theta}) = \frac{1}{2}$, leading to another median-based estimate. Discuss critically the circumstances under which these requirements might be relevant.

Solution

The fact that median unbiasedness is invariant under strictly monotonic transformations follows from the equivalence of the events $T < \theta$ and $g(T) < g(\theta)$, taking increasing $g(\cdot)$ without loss of generality. This makes median unbiasedness superficially attractive as one concept for forcing uniqueness in a point estimation problem. Nevertheless, we consider that the concept is not particularly important, particularly when the point estimate is used in summarization of confidence intervals or in preliminary data reduction. Note, however, that if it were required to test $H_0 : \theta = \theta_0$ from a large number of independent sets of data, then reduction of each set to the median unbiased estimate would allow simple application of the sign test.

Similar remarks apply to the second criterion. One is asking: what value of θ would make t_{obs} come at the centre of its sampling distribution? While this has some intuitive appeal, it seems little more than a mathematical device for forcing uniqueness.

To form a median unbiased estimate from ss_d we use the fact that ss_d/σ^2 has the chi-squared distribution with d degrees of freedom. If the median of this distribution is denoted $c^*_{d,\frac{1}{2}}$, then our estimate of σ^2 is $T = \mathrm{ss}_d/c^*_{d,\frac{1}{2}}$. Tables may be used to obtain $c^*_{d,\frac{1}{2}}$. Alternatively we can use an Edgeworth expansion of the chi-squared distribution with mean d, variance $2d$ and standardized skewness $\gamma_1 = 2\sqrt{2}/\sqrt{d}$; by the Fisher–Cornish inversion the median is approximately

$$d - \tfrac{1}{6}\gamma_1 \sqrt{(2d)} = d - 2/3.$$

In fact this approximation is remarkably close: for $d = 2$ and $d = 10$ the true medians are 1.39 and 9.34 respectively.

[*Theoretical Statistics*, Section 8.2]

8.3. Show that if $Y_1, \dots, Y_n$ are i.i.d. with density

$$\exp\{a(\theta)b(y) + c(\theta) + d(y)\},$$

then $n^{-1}\Sigma b(Y_j)$ attains the Cramér–Rao lower bound for an unbiased estimate of its expectation.

Solution

The total efficient score is

$$U_.(\theta) = a'(\theta)\Sigma b(Y_j) + nc'(\theta).$$

Because $n^{-1}\Sigma b(Y_j)$ is a linear function of $U_.(\theta)$, equality holds in the Cramér–Rao inequality.

[*Theoretical Statistics*, Section 8.3; Rao, Section 5a.2; Silvey, Section 2.10]

8.4. Explain qualitatively the presence of the term $\{1 + b'(\theta)\}^2$ in the general form of the Cramér–Rao inequality, as follows:
  (a) explain why $b'(\cdot)$ rather than $b(\cdot)$ occurs;
  (b) explain why the bound must vanish when $b'(\theta) = -1$;
  (c) explain why the term is squared rather than of degree one.
Discuss why the vanishing of $b(\cdot)$ at an isolated θ_0 is not enough to justify the simplified version of the bound at θ_0.

Solution

(a) Adding an arbitrary constant to an estimate (i) leaves the variance unchanged, (ii) leaves $b'(\cdot)$ unchanged, (iii) changes $b(\cdot)$ arbitrarily. This suggests that the bound depends on $b'(\cdot)$ rather than on $b(\cdot)$.
  (b) The estimate taking a constant value has zero variance and $b'(\theta) = -1$.
  (c) The bound must be non-negative.
  For estimating the mean μ of $N(\mu, 1)$ the degenerate estimate that is identically zero has zero bias at $\mu = 0$. Thus at $\mu = 0$ the zero variance contradicts the simple lower bound n^{-1} for the variance of an unbiased estimate. Examination of the proof shows that the simple bound requires zero bias in an open neighbourhood of the parameter value in question.

[*Theoretical Statistics*, Section 8.3; Rao, Section 5a.2; Silvey, Section 2.10]

8.5. Subject to some regularity conditions, the equation $k(y, \tilde\theta) = 0$, considered as an equation for $\tilde\theta$, is called an estimating equation for θ if $E\{k(Y, \theta); \theta\} = 0$, for all θ. Such an equation is called optimum if it has the smallest value of the index

$$E\{k^2(Y, \theta); \theta\} / [E\{\partial k(Y, \theta)/\partial \theta; \theta\}]^2.$$

Defend this definition. Show that the value of the index is at least $1/i_.(\theta)$, the lower bound being attained if and only if $k(\cdot,\cdot)$ is proportional to the efficient score. Generalize to the multiparameter case.

Solution

The availability of fast iterative procedures for solving non-linear equations means that estimates need not be defined explicitly and makes natural the study of estimating equations as such. The condition $E\{k(Y,\theta);\theta\}=0$ is a standardizing condition ensuring, roughly speaking, that if there is negligible random variation then the correct value of θ is recovered. If $k(Y,\theta)$ is exactly or approximately linear in θ for each Y then we can write

$$k(Y,\theta)+(\tilde\theta-\theta)\frac{\partial k(Y,\theta)}{\partial\theta}=0. \tag{1}$$

Assuming S.D. $\{\partial k(Y,\theta)/\partial\theta;\theta\}\ll|E\{\partial k(Y,\theta)/\partial\theta;\theta\}|$the proposed index is thus a first-order approximation to var $(\tilde\theta)$, whose minimization is sensible.

The required lower bound is found directly from Schwarz's inequality

$$\text{var}\{k(Y,\theta);\theta\}\,\text{var}\{U_.(\theta);\theta\}\geq[\text{cov}\{k(Y,\theta),U_.(\theta);\theta\}]^2$$

by noting that the right-hand side is the square of

$$\int k(y,\theta)\frac{1}{f_Y(y;\theta)}\frac{\partial f_Y(y;\theta)}{\partial\theta}f_Y(y;\theta)dy=\int\frac{\partial k(y,\theta)}{\partial\theta}f_Y(y;\theta)dy$$

after integrating by parts.

When θ is a column vector with q components we require q estimating functions $k_1(Y,\theta),\ldots,k_q(Y,\theta)$. If these form the column vector $k(Y,\theta)$ and if $g(Y,\theta)$ is the matrix with elements $g_{rs}(Y,\theta)=\partial k_r(Y,\theta)/\partial\theta_s$, then (1) becomes

$$k(Y,\theta)+g(Y,\theta)(\tilde\theta-\theta)=0$$

and

$$\tilde\theta-\theta=-\{g(Y,\theta)\}^{-1}k(Y,\theta).$$

A suitable index for the estimation of θ_s is thus

$$\sum_{r,t}E\{k_r(Y,\theta)k_t(Y,\theta);\theta\}E\{g^{rs}(Y,\theta);\theta\}E\{g^{ts}(Y,\theta);\theta\}$$

if we assume   S.D.$\{g_{rs}(Y,\theta);\theta\}\ll|E\{g_{rs}(Y,\theta);\theta\}|.$

[*Theoretical Statistics*, Section 8.3; Rao, Section 5a.1,2; Godambe, 1960]

8.6. Examine the special case of Problem 8.5 holding when the estimate is given explicitly by the equation $g_1(Y) - \tilde{\theta} g_2(Y) = 0$ with the requirement that, for all θ, $E\{g_1(Y); \theta\} = \theta E\{g_2(Y); \theta\}$. The equation is then called an unbiased estimating equation. Given several sets of data with a common value of θ how would a combined estimate be formed?

Solution

The condition for an unbiased estimating equation is a special case of the requirement $E\{k(Y, \theta); \theta\} = 0$ in Problem 8.5.

If $g_{1j}(Y_j) - \tilde{\theta} g_{2j}(Y_j) = 0$ denotes the estimating equation for the jth set of data $Y_j(j = 1, \dots, m)$, then an unbiased estimating equation is

$$\Sigma w_j g_{1j}(Y_j) - \tilde{\theta} \Sigma w_j g_{2j}(Y_j) = 0,$$

where the w_j are arbitrary constants. This corresponds to the previous exercise with

$$k(Y, \theta) = \Sigma w_j g_{1j}(Y_j) - \theta \Sigma w_j g_{2j}(Y_j),$$

so that if the Y_j are independent the index of Problem 8.5 becomes

$$\frac{\Sigma w_j^2 \, \text{var} \, \{g_{1j}(Y_j) - \theta g_{2j}(Y); \theta\}}{[\Sigma w_j E\{g_{2j}(Y_j); \theta\}]^2}. \tag{1}$$

In particular cases it may be possible to choose the w_j to minimize this exactly. In general, if the data sets are of similar structure, the jth set containing n_j observations, and if $g_{1j}(\cdot)$ and $g_{2j}(\cdot)$ are equivalent to totals of homogeneous observations, then (1) is approximately proportional to

$$\Sigma n_j w_j^2 / (\Sigma n_j w_j)^2.$$

This is minimized by taking w_j to be constant, equivalent to simple addition of the individual estimating equations.

[*Theoretical Statistics*, Section 8.3; Rao, Sections 5a, 6a.2; Durbin, 1960]

8.7. In the first order autoregressive process

$$Y_{j+1} - \theta Y_j = \varepsilon_{j+1},$$

where $Y_0 = y_0$ is a constant and $\varepsilon_1, \dots, \varepsilon_n$ are i.i.d. with normal distributions of zero mean, show that

$$\Sigma Y_j Y_{j+1} - T \Sigma Y_j^2 = 0$$

is an unbiased estimating equation attaining the lower bound of Problem 8.5.

Solution

We have $Y_j = \theta^j y_0 + \theta^{j-1}\varepsilon_1 + \ldots + \varepsilon_j$ for $j = 1, \ldots, n$, so that if $\text{var}(\varepsilon_j) = \sigma^2$

$$E(Y_j Y_{j+r}) = \theta^{2j+r} y_0^2 + \sigma^2(1 + \theta^2 + \ldots + \theta^{2j-2})\theta^r \quad (r = 0, 1).$$

It follows immediately that

$$E\left(\sum_{j=0}^{n-1} Y_j Y_{j+1}\right) = \theta E\left(\sum_{j=0}^{n-1} Y_j^2\right)$$

and hence that the estimating equation is unbiased.

Because of the special Markov property of the process, the log likelihood is

$$\log f_Y(y;\theta) = \sum_{j=0}^{n-1} \log f_{Y_{j+1}|Y_j}(y_{j+1}|y_j;\theta)$$

$$= -\tfrac{1}{2}n\log\sigma^2 - \tfrac{1}{2}\sum_{j=0}^{n-1}(y_{j+1} - \theta y_j)^2/\sigma^2$$

and the efficient score is, on differentiating with respect to θ,

$$\tfrac{1}{2}\sum_{j=0}^{n-1} y_j(y_{j+1} - \theta y_j)/\sigma^2.$$

This is proportional to the estimating function, so that by Problem 8.5 the lower bound on variance is attained.

The effect of random y_0 would be negligible for large n.

[*Theoretical Statistics*, Section 8.3; Rao, Section 5a; Silvey, Chapter 2; Durbin, 1960]

8.8.* Obtain the efficient score and information for a set of n i.i.d. random variables having an exponential density written first in terms of the mean μ as $\mu^{-1}\exp(-\mu^{-1}y)$ and then in terms of $\rho = \mu^{-1}$ as $\rho e^{-\rho y}$.

Solution

If $Y_1, \ldots, Y_n$ are i.i.d. in an exponential distribution of mean μ, the p.d.f. of a single observation is $\mu^{-1}\exp(-\mu^{-1}y)$. Hence the contribution of Y_j to the total efficient score is

$$U_j(\mu) = \frac{\partial}{\partial\mu}(-\log\mu - Y_j/\mu) = -\mu^{-1} + \mu^{-2}Y_j$$

*Amended version.

and

$$U_.(\mu) = -n\mu^{-1} + \mu^{-2}\Sigma Y_j.$$

Further the information from Y_j is

$$E\{-\partial U_j(\mu)/\partial\mu;\mu\} = -\mu^{-2} + 2\mu^{-3}E(Y_j;\mu) = \mu^{-2}$$

and the total information is thus $i_.(\mu) = n\mu^{-2}$.

If, however, the p.d.f. is written in the form $\rho e^{-\rho y}$, we can calculate efficient score and information for ρ. Using the distinguishing superscript *, we have that

$$U_j^*(\rho) = \frac{\partial}{\partial\rho}(\log\rho - Y_j) = \frac{1}{\rho} - Y_j, \partial U_j^*(\rho)/\partial\rho = -\rho^{-2},$$

so that

$$U_.^*(\rho) = n\rho^{-1} - \Sigma Y_j, i_.^*(\rho) = n\rho^{-2}.$$

These illustrate the general relations for reparametrization given in Chapter 4, which in our special case become

$$U^* = U(d\mu/d\rho), i^* = i(d\mu/d\rho)^2$$

with $d\mu/d\rho = -\rho^{-2}$.

[*Theoretical Statistics*, Sections 8.3, 4.8; Rao, Section 5a; Silvey, Sections 2.8, 2.9]

8.10*. Let $Y_1, \ldots, Y_n$ be i.i.d. in the exponential density $\rho e^{-\rho y}$. Show that the minimum variance unbiased estimate of the cumulative distribution function evaluated at y is

$$1 - \{1 - \min(y, S)/S\}^n,$$

where $S = \Sigma Y_j$.

Solution

We use the general technique of Rao–Blackwellization, starting with the complete sufficient statistic $S = \Sigma Y_j$ and the simple unbiased estimate V defined by

$$V = \begin{cases} 1 & (Y_1 \leqslant y), \\ 0 & (Y_1 > y). \end{cases}$$

---

* Problem 8.9 omitted.

To compute the minimum variance unbiased estimate $T = E(V|S)$, we need the conditional density of Y_1 given $S = s$, which is computed as

$$\frac{f_{Y_1}(y;\rho)f_{S-Y_1}(s-y;\rho)}{f_S(s;\rho)} = \frac{e^{-\rho y}\rho\{\rho(s-y)\}^{n-1}\rho\exp\{-\rho(s-y)\}/(n-1)!}{\rho(\rho s)^n e^{-\rho s}/n!}$$

$$= n(1-y/s)^{n-1} \qquad (0 \leqslant y \leqslant s).$$

It follows that

$$T = E(V|S) = \mathrm{pr}(V = 1|S) = \begin{cases} 1 & (y \geqslant S), \\ 1 - (1 - y/S)^n & (y < S). \end{cases}$$

For large n, T will be approximately $1 - \exp(-ny/S)$, which is the maximum likelihood estimate.

[*Theoretical Statistics*, Section 8.4; Rao, Section 5a.2; Silvey, Sections 2.4–2.6]

8.11. In connexion with the estimation of the variance σ^2 of a normal distribution, obtain an unbiased estimator of $\log \sigma$ using (a) exact, and (b) approximate arguments. When would the results be relevant? Suggest also an application to the analysis of data from Poisson processes.

Solution

Let MS be a normal-theory estimate of variance σ^2 based on d degrees of freedom. Then $\mathrm{MS}d/\sigma^2$ has the chi-squared distribution with d degrees of freedom, so that

$$E(\tfrac{1}{2}\log \mathrm{MS}) = \log \sigma - \tfrac{1}{2}\log d + \int\limits_0^\infty (\tfrac{1}{2}\log x)\frac{\frac{1}{2}(\frac{1}{2}x)^{\frac{1}{2}d-1}e^{-\frac{1}{2}x}}{\Gamma(\frac{1}{2}d)}dx$$

$$= \log \sigma - \tfrac{1}{2}\log d + \Gamma'(\tfrac{1}{2}d)/\Gamma(\tfrac{1}{2}d).$$

Thus the required unbiased estimate is $\tfrac{1}{2}\log \mathrm{MS} + \tfrac{1}{2}\log d - \psi(\tfrac{1}{2}d)$; tables and approximations for the digamma function $\psi = \Gamma'/\Gamma$ are available (Abramowitz and Stegun, 1965).

For the approximate argument, note that by properties of the chi-squared distribution $E(\mathrm{MS}) = \sigma^2$, $\mathrm{var}(\mathrm{MS}) = 2\sigma^4/d$. Therefore, using result (1) of Problem 8.12 with $\theta = \sigma^2$ and $g(\theta) = \tfrac{1}{2}\log \theta$, we find

$$E(\tfrac{1}{2}\log \mathrm{MS}) = \log \sigma - 1/(2d) + \dots,$$

so that the required estimate is approximately $\tfrac{1}{2}\log \mathrm{MS} + 1/(2d)$.

An advantage of the second approach, quite apart from its simplicity, is that it extends to estimates based on non-normal data.

The results are relevant when several such estimates are available and it is required to represent $\log \sigma$ by a linear model in explanatory variables, i.e. a multiplicative model for σ. The bias correction could then be important if the estimates are not all based on the same degrees of freedom.

In a Poisson process of rate ρ, the time T_m to the mth event from 'now' is such that $2\rho T_m$ has the chi-squared distribution with $2m$ degrees of freedom, so that the above discussion applies with $d = 2m$, MS $= T_m/m$ and $\sigma^2 = 1/\rho$.

[*Theoretical Statistics*, Section 8.4; Rao, Sections 6a, 6g]

8.12. By considering the Taylor expansion of $g(t)$ about $t = \theta$ show that if $E(T;\theta) = \theta$, and if var $(T;\theta)$ is small, then

$$\text{var}\{g(T);\theta\} \simeq \{g'(\theta)\}^2 \text{var}(T;\theta),$$

and hence suggest how independent estimates of several parameters $\theta_1,\ldots,$ θ_m with variances $v(\theta_1),\ldots,v(\theta_m)$ can be transformed to have approximately constant variability.

Solution

We use the Taylor series expansion

$$g(T) = g(\theta) + (T-\theta)g'(\theta) + \tfrac{1}{2}(T-\theta)^2 g''(\theta) + \ldots,$$

so that first

$$E\{g(T);\theta\} = g(\theta) + \tfrac{1}{2}\text{var}(T;\theta)g''(\theta) + \ldots. \qquad (1)$$

Then

$$[g(T) - E\{g(T);\theta\}]^2 = (T-\theta)^2\{g'(\theta)\}^2$$
$$+ \{(T-\theta)^3 - (T-\theta)\text{var}(T;\theta)\}g'(\theta)g''(\theta) + \ldots$$

and on taking expectations

$$\text{var}\{g(T);\theta\} = \{g'(\theta)\}^2 \text{var}(T;\theta) + \ldots. \qquad (2)$$

The second term of (1) represents a bias correction, while (2) is the required first-order variance; further terms can be calculated. A rigorous argument requires explicit consideration of a limiting operation.

The extension to vector T is immediate, and may be used in particular to obtain corresponding useful results for ratios.

The simplest way to achieve approximately constant variance is to find a fairly simple form for the relation between $v(\theta)$ and θ. This can often be done by plotting estimates $\log v(\tilde{\theta}_i)$ versus corresponding estimates $\log \tilde{\theta}_i$ searching for a relation of the form $v(\theta) = a\theta^b$ by choice of b. If $g(T)$ has approximately constant variance, say 1, we have from (2) that

$$1 = \{g'(\theta)\}^2 v(\theta),$$

from which

$$g(\theta) = \int^{\theta} dx/\sqrt{v(x)}.$$

For the special form $v(\theta) = a\theta^b$ this gives

$$g(T) \propto \begin{cases} \log T & (b = 2), \\ T^{1 - \frac{1}{2}b} & (b \neq 2). \end{cases}$$

Standard transformations derived from this argument include the square root transformation for Poisson variables, log transformation for normal-theory estimate of variance, and the inverse hyperbolic tangent of the sample product-moment correlation.

[*Theoretical Statistics*, Section 8.4; Rao, Sections 6a.2, 6g]

8.13. The random variable Y is said to be log normally distributed if $Z = \log Y$ is normal with, say, mean λ and variance τ^2. Prove that $E(Y) = \exp(\lambda + \frac{1}{2}\tau^2)$. For a set of i.i.d. variables $Y_1, \ldots, Y_n$ with the above distribution, the sufficient statistic is the estimates of mean and variance $\bar{Z}_.$ and MS_z from the logs. Thus an approximately unbiased estimate of $E(Y)$ is $\exp(\bar{Z}_. + \frac{1}{2}\text{MS}_z)$. Examine bias-removing techniques as applied to this problem.

Solution

Two useful elementary results are that if Z and Q_d are respectively distributed as $N(\mu, \sigma^2)$ and as chi-squared with d degrees of freedom, then

$$E(e^{sZ}) = \exp(\mu s + \tfrac{1}{2}\sigma^2 s^2), E(e^{sQ}) = (1 - 2s)^{-\frac{1}{2}d}.$$

Thus if $Z = \log Y$ is $N(\lambda, \tau^2)$, then using the first moment generating function

$$E(Y) = E(e^Z) = \exp(\lambda + \tfrac{1}{2}\tau^2). \tag{1}$$

The minimal sufficient statistic based on $Y_1, \ldots, Y_n$ is $(\bar{Z}_., \text{MS}_z)$, with $E(\bar{Z}_.)$ $= \lambda$ and $E(\text{MS}_z) = \tau^2$. The first-order estimate of $E(Y)$ is thus $T = \exp(\bar{Z}_. + \frac{1}{2}\text{MS}_z)$.

Because $\bar{Z}$ and MS_z are independent the exact expectation of T is easily calculated: since $\bar{Z}$ is $N(\lambda, \tau^2/n)$ and $\mathrm{MS}_z = \tau^2 Q_{n-1}/(n-1)$,

$$E(e^{\bar{Z}\cdot}) = \exp(\lambda + \tfrac{1}{2}\tau^2/n), E(e^{\frac{1}{2}\mathrm{MS}_z}) = \{1 - \tau^2/(n-1)\}^{-\frac{1}{2}(n-1)}.$$

Thus

$$E(T) = \exp[\lambda + \tfrac{1}{2}\tau^2/n - \tfrac{1}{2}(n-1)\log\{1 - \tau^2/(n-1)\}]$$
$$= \exp\{\lambda + \tfrac{1}{2}\tau^2 + \tfrac{1}{2}\tau^2/n + \tfrac{1}{4}\tau^4/n + O(1/n^2)\}. \tag{2}$$

An alternative approach is via the vector form of expansion (1) in Problem 8.12, equivalent to Taylor expansion of T as a function of $(\bar{Z}, \mathrm{MS}_z)$ and (λ, τ^2).

Consideration of (2) shows that bias of order n^{-1} is removed by the modification

$$T \exp\{-(\tfrac{1}{2}\mathrm{MS}_z + \tfrac{1}{4}\mathrm{MS}_z^2)/n\}.$$

While the jackknife is an alternative, general arguments of sufficiency suggest it to be inferior.

An exactly unbiased estimate of minimum variance is defined in principle by $E(Y_1 | \bar{Z}, \mathrm{MS}_z)$. An alternative approach (Neyman and Scott, 1960) is to write

$$\exp(\lambda + \tfrac{1}{2}\tau^2) = \sum_{r,s=0}^{\infty} \frac{\lambda^r}{r!} \frac{\tau^{2s}}{2^s s!}$$

and to then substitute unbiased estimates of $\lambda^r \tau^{2s}$ formed from $\bar{Z}$ and MS_z.

[*Theoretical Statistics*, Section 8.4; Rao, Section 6a]

8.14. Examine the jackknifed estimate (2) for the range of the uniform distribution $(0, \theta)$. Take T_n to be the maximum observation in the data. Compare the estimate with that based on the sufficient statistic. Show that the point estimate is very inadequate as a summary of the confidence regions in such a case.

Solution

Let the ordered values corresponding to $Y_1, \ldots, Y_n$ be $Y_{(1)} \leqslant \ldots \leqslant Y_{(n)}$. Then $T_n = Y_{(n)}$, whose mean is $n\theta/(n+1)$. Thus the jackknife technique is applicable for bias reduction, although exact removal of bias is simply achieved by taking $(n+1)T_n/n$.

When single observations are omitted, in $n-1$ cases we obtain the estimate T_n and in the remaining case we obtain $Y_{(n-1)}$. Therefore the jack-knifed estimate is

$$n Y_{(n)} - \frac{(n-1)}{n}\{(n-1)Y_{(n)} + Y_{(n-1)}\} = \frac{2n-1}{n}Y_{(n)} - \frac{n-1}{n}Y_{(n-1)},$$

whose expected value is $\theta[1 - \{n(n+1)\}^{-1}]$.

The jackknife estimate of variance for T_n is not applicable because T_n is radically non-linear. In any case, confidence limits for θ of the form $T_n \pm k \{\text{var}(T_n)\}^{1/2}$ are not appropriate in this problem, since T_n is a certain lower limit for θ, and the likelihood for θ decreases as $\theta - T_n$ increases. Thus appropriate confidence intervals are of the form $[T_n, (1 + c)T_n]$.

[*Theoretical Statistics*, Section 8.4]

8.15. Prove that in estimating a variance starting from the biased estimate $\Sigma(Y_j - \bar{Y})^2/n$, the jackknifed estimate (2) exactly eliminates bias. Examine the usefulness of the jackknife estimate (3) of variance.

Solution

We start from $T_n = \Sigma(Y_j - \bar{Y})^2/n$. Direct calculations are straightforward but messy, and can be avoided by considerations of symmetry. Necessarily the jackknifed estimate T_n^J is symmetric, quadratic and invariant under addition of a constant to all observations. Thus

$$T_n^J = a_n \Sigma(Y_j - \bar{Y})^2.$$

To determine the constant a_n we consider any special case, for instance $Y_1 = 1$, $Y_j = 0 (j \geq 2)$. Then in the latter case $\Sigma(Y_j - \bar{Y}_0)^2 = (n-1)/n$, $T_n = (n-1)/n^2$ and $T_{n-1,j} = (n-2)/(n-1)^2$ except for $j = 1$, when $T_{n-1,1} = 0$. It follows that $a_n = 1/(n-1)$.

If $Y_1, \ldots, Y_n$ are i.i.d. with variance σ^2 and standardized fourth cumulant (kurtosis) γ_2, then

$$\text{var}\left\{\frac{\Sigma(Y_j - \bar{Y})^2}{n-1}\right\} \sim \frac{2\sigma^4}{n}(1 + \tfrac{1}{2}\gamma_2). \tag{1}$$

To obtain an estimate of variance for T_n^J via the jackknife, we consider the 'pseudo-values'

$$T_j^P = nT_n - (n-1)T_{n-1,j}$$

and estimate the variance of the estimate of σ^2 by

$$V^J = \Sigma(T_j^P - T_n^J)^2/\{n(n-1)\}.$$

Considerations of degree, symmetry and invariance under addition of a constant to the observations shows that

$$V^{\text{J}} = b_n \Sigma (Y_j - \bar{Y}_{.})^4 + c_n \{ \Sigma (Y_j - \bar{Y})^2 \}^2.$$

The constants b_n and c_n are obtained by evaluation of V^{J} in two simple special cases. The resulting V^{J} agrees asymptotically with (1).

In this case, therefore, the jackknife method of estimating variance has no obvious advantages over the direct use of the standard estimates of σ^2 and γ_2 to estimate $\text{var}(T_n)$ directly.

Note that however we estimate $\text{var}(T_n)$, approximate normal confidence limits are best obtained by working with an approximately normal version of T_n. Thus in the present case the logarithm or cube root of sample variance would be preferable to the sample variance itself.

[*Theoretical Statistics*, Section 8.4]

8.16. Observations $y_{jk}(j = 1, \ldots, m; k = 1, \ldots, r)$ are represented by random variables Y_{jk} with unknown location parameters μ_j and unknown constant dispersion. The values of the μ_j's being possibly close together, the linear combination

$$\tilde{\mu}_j(a) = a \bar{y}_{j.} + (1 - a) \bar{y}_{..}$$

is considered as a suitable estimate for μ_j. Show that the squared prediction error criterion $\Sigma\Sigma \{ y_{jk} - \mu_j(a) \}^2$ is minimized when $a = 1$.

Denote the estimate $\tilde{\mu}_j(a)$ based on the data with y_{jk} omitted by $\tilde{\mu}_{j,k}(a)$. Then the prediction error for y_{jk} may be measured by the pseudo-value $y_{jk} - \tilde{\mu}_{j,k}(a)$, leading to the overall squared error criterion $\Sigma\Sigma \{ y_{jk} - \tilde{\mu}_{j,k}(a) \}^2$. Show that the value of a which minimizes this criterion is a monotone increasing function of $\text{MS}_b / \text{MS}_w$. Comment on the explicit form of the resulting estimate for μ_j and the method of derivation.

Solution

For the first part we have

$$\Sigma\Sigma \{ y_{jk} - \tilde{\mu}_j(a) \}^2 = \Sigma\Sigma \{ (y_{jk} - \bar{y}_{j.}) + (1 - a)(\bar{y}_{j.} - \bar{y}_{..}) \}^2$$
$$= \Sigma\Sigma (y_{jk} - \bar{y}_{j.})^2 + r(1 - a)^2 \Sigma (\bar{y}_{j.} - \bar{y}_{..})^2.$$

The second positive term is removed when $a = 1$, which gives the usual linear estimate $\bar{y}_{j.}$.

If we take μ_j as the best predictor for Y_{jk}, then it seems reasonable to measure how well the estimators for μ_j predict independent additional observations. This naturally leads to comparison of $\tilde{\mu}_{j,k}(a)$ with y_{jk}, and to the symmetric balanced criterion

$$S(a) = \Sigma\Sigma\{y_{jk} - \tilde{\mu}_{j,k}(a)\}^2.$$

We may express $\tilde{\mu}_{j,k}(a)$ as

$$\frac{a}{r-1}(r\bar{y}_{j.} - y_{jk}) + \frac{1-a}{rm-1}(rm\bar{y}_{..} - y_{jk}),$$

from which it follows that

$$S(a) = \left\{\frac{ar}{r-1} + \frac{(1-a)rm}{rm-1}\right\}^2 ss_w + \frac{(1-a)^2(rm)^2}{(rm-1)^2} ss_b,$$

with $ss_w = \Sigma\Sigma(y_{jk} - \bar{y}_{j.})^2$, $ss_b = \Sigma(\bar{y}_{j.} - \bar{y}_{..})^2$. The quadratic $S(a)$ is minimized at

$$a^* = \frac{F-1}{F + \dfrac{m-1}{m(r-1)}}$$

with

$$F = \left\{\frac{r ss_b}{(m-1)}\right\} \Big/ \left\{\frac{ss_w}{m(r-1)}\right\}.$$

When $F = 1$, usually taken as evidence that the means are nearly equal, $a^* = 0$ and all estimates are equal to $\bar{y}_{..}$. When F is very large, evidence that the μ_j are unequal, $a^* \simeq 1$ and the μ_j are essentially estimated by individual averages $\bar{y}_{j.}$. These results are similar to those obtained in an empirical Bayes analysis when the μ_j have a common normal distribution with unknown parameters.

Although the present method seems to involve few formal assumptions, it does implicitly assume (i) an additive model for the μ_j and (ii) homogeneous variability of the y_{jk}. Nevertheless, when used with caution, the general methods of internal comparison can be very informative as an aid in model fitting and model assessment. A detailed discussion of these methods is given by Stone (1974, 1977).

[*Theoretical Statistics*, Sections 8.4, 8.5]

8.17. Consider a stationary Poisson process with rate ρ, and suppose that on the basis of observation for a time t we wish to estimate $\theta = e^{-\rho x}$. If the number of events in $(0, t)$ is $N(t)$, then a 'natural' estimate of θ is

$$\hat{\theta} = \exp\{-N(t)x/t\}.$$

Now split the time interval up into r equal sub-intervals of length t/r and calculate the jackknifed estimate $\tilde{\theta}_r$ of θ obtained by successively deleting single sub-intervals. Show that as r increases, with t fixed,

$$\tilde{\theta}_r \to \hat{\theta}\{1 - N(t)(e^{x/t} - 1 - x/t)\} \, ;$$

that is, with very fine subdivision of $(0, t)$ the jackknifed estimate $\tilde{\theta}_r$ is equivalent to $\hat{\theta}$ with first-order bias correction.

Solution

If the number r of intervals is large, so that at most one event occurs in any interval, then the estimate obtained by omitting the jth interval is

$$\exp\{ - (n - \delta_j)x/(t - t/r)\},$$

where $N(t)$ of the δ_j are equal to one and the other δ_j are zero. Therefore the jackknifed estimate is

$$\exp\left\{ - \frac{N(t)xr}{(r - 1)t}\right\}\left[1 - \frac{N(t)}{r} + \frac{N(t)}{r}\exp\left\{\frac{rx}{(r - 1)t}\right\}\right],$$

which is approximately

$$\exp\left\{ - \frac{N(t)x}{t}\right\}\{1 - N(t)(e^{x/t} - 1 - x/t)\}.$$

A more direct argument uses (1) of Problem 8.12 with $T = N(t)/t$, $\theta = \rho$, $g(T) = e^{-Tx}$. Thus, since $N(t)$ has a Poisson distribution with mean and variance equal to ρt,

$$E(\hat{\theta}) \sim e^{-\rho x} + \tfrac{1}{2}\rho t^{-1}x^2 e^{-\rho x}.$$

Substitution of $N(t)/t$ for ρ leads to the bias-corrected estimate

$$\hat{\theta}\{1 - \tfrac{1}{2}N(t)x^2/t^2\},$$

which is equivalent to the jackknifed estimate when a three-term expansion is used for $e^{x/t}$.

[*Theoretical Statistics*, Section 8.4; Gaver and Hoel, 1970]

8.18. Let T_n be an estimate from a full set of n observations, and let $T'_{\frac{1}{2}n}$ and $T''_{\frac{1}{2}n}$ denote the corresponding estimates from the two halves of the data when the data are randomly split into two. If for a random sample of size m

$$E(T_m ; \theta) = \theta + a_1(\theta)/m + a_2(\theta)/m^2 + \ldots,$$

show that

$$2T_n - \tfrac{1}{2}(T''_{\frac{1}{2}n} + T''_{\frac{1}{2}n})$$

has a smaller order of bias than T_n. Comment on the method of splitting the data.

Solution

The result follows directly from the fact that, under random splitting of the data, both $T'_{\frac{1}{2}n}$ and $T''_{\frac{1}{2}n}$ are equivalent to estimates based on random samples of size $\tfrac{1}{2}n$.

Note that certain systematic methods of data-splitting would not give the same result. For example, if $T_n = \bar{Y}$ and if the ordered sample $Y_{(1)} \leqslant \ldots \leqslant Y_{(n)}$ is split into the sets

$$\{Y_{(2j-1)} ; j = 1, \ldots, \tfrac{1}{2}n\}, \{Y_{(2j)} ; j = 1, \ldots, \tfrac{1}{2}n\}$$

then the averages of these sets are biased estimates of $E(Y)$.
[*Theoretical Statistics*, Section 8.4; Quenouille, 1949, 1956]

8.19. The linear model $E(Y) = \mathbf{x}\beta$ is called quadratically balanced if the diagonal elements of the matrix $\mathbf{x}(\mathbf{x}^T\mathbf{x})^{-1}\mathbf{x}^T$ are all equal. Let the errors be independent with constant variance and with constant kurtosis γ_2. Prove that of all quadratic forms that are unbiased estimates of the error variance, the usual residual mean square has minimum variance, provided either that the model is quadratically balanced or that $\gamma_2 = 0$.

Solution

We start with the general quadratic form $Q = Y^T\mathbf{a}Y$, for which

$$E(Q) = E\{(Y - \mathbf{x}\beta)^T\mathbf{a}(Y - \mathbf{x}\beta)\} + \beta^T\mathbf{x}^T\mathbf{ax}\beta = \sigma^2 \mathrm{tr}(\mathbf{a}) + \beta^T\mathbf{x}^T\mathbf{ax}\beta.$$

The estimate Q is unbiased provided that $\mathrm{tr}(\mathbf{a}) = 1$ and $\mathbf{x}^T\mathbf{ax} = 0$, that is if $\mathbf{ax} = 0$.

When the rank of $\mathbf{x}$ is p, the residual mean square estimate $\mathrm{MS}_{\mathrm{res}}$ corresponds to

$$\mathbf{a}_{\mathrm{res}} = \frac{1}{n - p}\{\mathbf{I} - \mathbf{x}(\mathbf{x}^T\mathbf{x})^{-1}\mathbf{x}^T\},$$

which satisfies the unbiasedness conditions.

In general the variance of Q may be expressed as

$$2\sigma^4\{\mathrm{tr}(\mathbf{a}^2) + \tfrac{1}{2}\gamma_2\mathbf{d}^T\mathbf{d}\} + 4\sigma^2\beta^T\mathbf{x}^T\mathbf{a}^2\mathbf{x}\beta + 4\gamma_1\sigma^3\beta^T\mathbf{x}^T\mathbf{ad}$$

with $\mathbf{d} = \text{diag}(\mathbf{a})$ and γ_1, γ_2 the standardized third and fourth cumulants of Y. Because unbiasedness requires $\mathbf{ax} = 0$, the last two terms vanish and the required variance is $2\sigma^4 \{\text{tr}(\mathbf{a}^2) + \frac{1}{2}\gamma_2 \mathbf{d}^T \mathbf{d}\}$. We now write $\mathbf{a} = \mathbf{a}_{res} + \mathbf{b}$, and note that $\mathbf{bx} = 0$, $\text{tr}(\mathbf{b}) = 0$, $\mathbf{a}_{res}\mathbf{b} = \mathbf{b}/(n-p)$ and $\text{diag}(\mathbf{a}) = \text{diag}(\mathbf{a}_{res}) + \text{diag}(\mathbf{b})$. It follows that $\text{tr}(\mathbf{a}^2) = 1 + \text{tr}(\mathbf{b}^2)$, so that the variance of an unbiased Q becomes

$$\text{var}(\text{MS}_{res}) + 2\sigma^4 \{\Sigma\Sigma b_{ij}^2 + \gamma_2(\Sigma b_{ii} a_{res,ii} + \tfrac{1}{2}\Sigma b_{ii}^2)\}. \tag{1}$$

The optimality of MS_{res} is immediate if $\gamma_2 = 0$. Next, if the diagonal elements of $\mathbf{x}(\mathbf{x}^T\mathbf{x})^{-1}\mathbf{x}^T$ are equal, then every diagonal element of $\mathbf{a}_{res}$ is n^{-1} and (1) reduces to

$$\text{var}(\text{MS}_{res}) + 2\sigma^4 \{(1 + \tfrac{1}{2}\gamma_2)\Sigma b_{ii}^2 + \sum_{i \neq j} b_{ij}^2\}$$

since $\text{tr}(\mathbf{b}) = 0$. Optimality of MS_{res} now follows from the fact that $1 + \frac{1}{2}\gamma_2 \geqslant 0$, which is equivalent to the inequality $E(Z^4) \geqslant \{E(Z^2)\}^2$ when $E(Z) = 0$.

[*Theoretical Statistics*, Section 8.5; Rao, Section 4a.5; Atiqullah, 1962]

8.20. Prove Gauss's theorem that for a linear model with uncorrelated errors of constant variance the least squares estimators are of minimum variance among all linear unbiased estimates. Compare this to the optimum property of least squares estimators when errors are also normally distributed. Show that a linear estimate that is not unbiased has unbounded mean squared error over the whole parameter space and that therefore the requirement of unbiasedness in Gauss's theorem could be replaced by that of bounded mean squared error.

Solution

Most introductory courses on theoretical statistics contain a proof of Gauss's (or the Gauss–Markov) theorem, so that a detailed answer will not be given here. There are various methods, namely, minimization of variance subjected to the linear unbiasedness constraint introduced via a Lagrange multiplier, matrix proofs, and a geometrical proof. In the last, we take an arbitrary linear combination $l^T Y$ of the observations, and argue as follows:

    (a) $l = l_x + l_{\perp x}$, where l_x and $l_{\perp x}$ are in and orthogonal to the space spanned by columns of $\mathbf{x}$;
    (b) $E(l_{\perp x}^T Y) = 0$;

(c) $\operatorname{cov}(l_x^T Y, l_{\downarrow x}^T Y) = 0,$ so that $\operatorname{var}(l_x^T Y) = \operatorname{var}(l_x^T Y) + \operatorname{var}(l_{\downarrow x}^T Y);$

(d) from (b) and (c) the minimum variance unbiased estimate is defined by an l in the space spanned by columns of $\mathbf{x}$;

(e) since the required vectors have the form $a^T \mathbf{x}^T$, the corresponding linear function of Y is a linear combination of the right-hand sides of the least squares equations;

(f) there is at most one combination of the right-hand sides of the least squares equations estimating a given β_r.

In comparing this result with that from the Cramér–Rao inequality, note first that both involve a restriction to unbiased estimates and the measurement of error by expected squared error, the first in particular being rather artificial. Gauss's theorem involves an assumption of linear estimates but requires only weak assumptions about the error distribution; the Cramér–Rao inequality assumes normality but proves that then the optimum estimate is linear. In general the optimum unbiased estimate will not be linear.

Linear estimates that are not unbiased have a squared bias contribution to mean squared error that is a quadratic form in β, which is unbounded because the parameter space is unbounded. Hence bounded mean squared error implies unbiasedness.

[*Theoretical Statistics*, Section 8.5; Rao, Section 4a; Silvey, Section 3.5; Barnard, 1963]

8.21. Random variables X and Y are such that the marginal distribution of Y and the conditional distribution of Y given X can be observed. Show that these two distributions determine the conditional distribution of X given Y if and only if a certain Fredholm integral equation has a unique solution. If the conditional distribution of Y given $X = x$ is normal with mean $\gamma + \beta x$ and constant variance, show that the conditional distribution of X given Y is always determined and examine in more detail the special case when the marginal distribution of Y too is normal. Discuss the possible relevance of these results to the problem of estimating the value $x\dagger$ corresponding to a new observation $Y\dagger$, given observations $(x_1, Y_1), \ldots, (x_n, Y_n)$ on the normal-theory linear model $E(Y) = \gamma + \beta x$.

Solution

The joint p.d.f. of X and Y is expressible as both

$$f_X(x)f_{Y|X}(y|x) \text{ and } f_Y(y)f_{X|Y}(x|y),$$

so that

$$f_{X|Y}(x|y) = f_X(x)f_{Y|X}(y|x)/f_Y(y),$$

where on the right-hand side only $f_X(x)$ is unknown. But, because the left-hand side integrates to one, we have

$$\int f_X(x) f_{Y|X}(y|x) dx = f_Y(y),$$

which corresponds to the general Fredholm equation

$$\int a(x) k(x, y) dx = b(y)$$

to be solved for $a(x)$. If a unique solution for $a(x) = f_X(x)$ is available, then $f_{X|Y}(x|y)$ is determined.

Now suppose that $f_{Y|X}(y|x)$ is the $N(\gamma + \beta x, 1)$ density, which substituted into the integral equation gives

$$\int \{f_X(x) \exp(-\tfrac{1}{2}\beta^2 x^2 - \gamma\beta x)\} e^{\beta yx} dx = (2\pi)^{\frac{1}{2}} e^{\frac{1}{2}\gamma^2 - \gamma y} f_Y(y).$$

This is of the form

$$\int g(x) e^{sx} dx = h(s),$$

i.e. $h(s)$ is a Laplace transform of $g(\cdot)$, and $g(x)$ is determined by the unique inversion of $h(\cdot)$.

For the special case where $f_Y(y)$ is a normal density, it is easy to show that if $\beta \neq 0$, then $f_X(x)$ is also a normal density, so that X and Y have a bivariate normal density. To be more general, suppose that Y given $X = x$ is $N(\gamma + \beta x, \sigma^2)$ and that Y is $N(\mu, \tau^2)$. Then because $E(Y) = E\{E(Y|X)\}$ we have that $\mu = \gamma + \beta E(X)$; and because $\mathrm{var}(Y) = E\{\mathrm{var}(Y|X)\} + \mathrm{var}\{E(Y|X)\}$ we have that $\tau^2 = \sigma^2 + \beta^2 \mathrm{var}(X)$. These relationships show that X is normal with mean $(\mu - \gamma)/\beta$ and variance $(\tau^2 - \sigma^2)/\beta^2$ when $\beta \neq 0$.

If the covariance between X and Y is δ, then

$$E(Y|X = x) = \mathrm{const} + \frac{\delta}{\mathrm{var}(X)} x, \quad E(X|Y = y) = \mathrm{const} + \frac{\delta}{\mathrm{var}(Y)} y$$

from which we obtain $\delta = (\tau^2 - \sigma^2)/\beta$ and hence

$$E(X|Y = y) = (\mu - \gamma)/\beta + (\tau^2 - \sigma^2)(y - \mu)/(\beta\tau^2).$$

The variance of the conditional normal distribution for X given $Y = y$ is

$$\mathrm{var}(X|Y = y) = \mathrm{var}(X) - \mathrm{var}\{E(X|Y)\} = \sigma^2(\tau^2 - \sigma^2)/(\beta^2\tau^2).$$

For the calibration problem in its simplest form, data $(x_1, Y_1), \ldots, (x_n, Y_n)$ are available such that the Y_j are independent and conditionally $N(\gamma + \beta x_j, \sigma^2)$. The problem is to estimate the value $x\dagger$ of x corresponding to a further observation $Y\dagger$ which is $N(\gamma + \beta x\dagger, \sigma^2)$. If the values $x_1, \ldots, x_n$ constitute a random sample from the same population as $x\dagger$, then we can reasonably speak of a p.d.f. $f_X(x)$ for X and, regardless of the form of $f_X(\cdot)$, we can in principle obtain $f_{X|Y}(x|y)$ given $f_Y(y)$ and $f_X(x)$. It should be noted that X

conditional on $Y = y$ has linear expectation in y only if Y has a marginal normal distribution. The data provide estimates of γ, β and σ^2 in the usual way; and the values $(x_1, \dots, x_n)$ and $(y_1, \dots, y_n)$ may be used to estimate $f_X(x)$ and $f_Y(y)$, possibly by non-parametric methods.

Of course, if the data strongly suggest that Y has a marginal normal distribution, then it would be reasonable to work directly with the normal-theory linear regression of X on Y and to apply standard interval estimation for $E(X|Y=y\dagger)$. The assumption that $x_1, \dots, x_n$ and $x\dagger$ come from the same distribution will often be entirely inappropriate.

[*Theoretical Statistics*, Section 8.5; Tallis, 1969]

9 ASYMPTOTIC THEORY

Summary

In Chapters 4–8 we have discussed significance tests, interval estimates and point estimates and we have shown how to obtain procedures that satisfy various exact criteria of optimality. There are many situations, however, where the preceding discussion is inadequate, either because of complex distributional problems, or because techniques for eliminating nuisance parameters (Chapter 5) do not work. We now discuss approximate procedures based on large-sample properties of the likelihood function.

Suppose that θ is of fixed dimension, denoted $\dim(\theta)$, and that the number of observations n increases indefinitely. Then under very general conditions the maximum likelihood estimate (m.l.e) $\hat{\theta}$, which maximizes the log likelihood $l_Y(\theta';y)$, converges in probability to θ; this property we refer to as consistency. To proceed further with the general theory, several fairly strong regularity conditions are required of the likelihood. In particular, θ is an interior point of the parameter space Ω and the total information $\mathbf{i}_.(\theta) = \mathrm{var}\,\{U_.(\theta);\theta\}$ is positive definite, increases indefinitely with n, and is equal to minus the mean of the second derivative of $l_Y(\theta;Y)$ with respect to θ. Now the m.l.e. is asymptotically equivalent to the consistent solution of the likelihood equation $U_.(\theta') = 0$, and Taylor expansion of $U_.(\hat{\theta}) - U_.(\theta)$ gives as a first-order approximation

$$\mathbf{i}_.(\theta)(\hat{\theta} - \theta) \sim U_.(\theta).$$

If the central limit theorem applies to $U_.(\theta)$, as it does for i.i.d. variables, we can conclude that for large n, $\hat{\theta}$ is asymptotically $N\{\theta, \mathbf{i}^{-1}_.(\theta)\}$. Minus the observed second derivative of $l_Y(\theta';y)$ at $\theta' = \hat{\theta}$ may be used in place of $\mathbf{i}_.(\theta)$ to obtain a consistent normal approximation.

A corresponding property for the likelihood is that for θ' near θ

$$\mathrm{lik}_Y(\theta';Y) \sim \mathrm{lik}_Y(\hat{\theta};Y)\exp\{-\tfrac{1}{2}(\hat{\theta} - \theta')^{\mathrm{T}}\mathbf{i}_.(\hat{\theta})(\hat{\theta} - \theta')\}, \tag{1}$$

which indicates approximate sufficiency of $\hat{\theta}$ for large n. Consistent approximations to $\mathbf{i}_.(\theta)$ may be used.

For problems involving infinitely many nuisance parameters, the above results do not generally apply, but for models of the form

$$\text{lik}_Y(\theta\,;y) = \prod_{j=1}^{n} \text{lik}_{Y_j|S_j}(\psi\,;y_j|s_j)\,\text{lik}_{S_j}(\psi, \lambda_j\,;s_j)$$

the theory does apply to the conditional likelihood

$$\text{lik}_{Y|S}(\psi\,;y|s) = \prod_{j=1}^{n} \text{lik}_{Y_j|S_j}(\psi\,;y_j|s_j).$$

For multinomial models with cell probabilities $\pi_j(\theta)$ and sample frequencies $N_j(j = 1, \ldots, m), \Sigma N_j = n$, statistics asymptotically equivalent to the m.l.e. are obtained by minimizing, for example, either of the statistics

$$\Sigma\{N_j - n\pi_j(\theta)\}^2/\{n\pi_j(\theta)\}, \Sigma\{N_j - n\pi_j(\theta)\}^2/N_j.$$

More refined normal approximations for $\hat{\theta}$ can be obtained through higher-order expansion of $U_{\cdot}(\hat{\theta}) - U_{\cdot}(\theta)$. The finite information difference $i_{\cdot}(\theta) - i_{\hat{\theta}}(\theta)$ can be computed and related to second-order variance approximation for $\hat{\theta}$.

The large-sample approximate theory of significance tests (and hence of interval estimation) is built on the above asymptotic normal form (1) of the likelihood for regular problems. For a simple null hypothesis $H_0 : \theta = \theta_0$ with alternative $H_A : \theta \neq \theta_0$ the maximum likelihood ratio approach yields the test statistic $W = 2\{l_Y(\hat{\theta}\,;Y) - l_Y(\theta_0\,;Y)\}$. By Taylor expansion, or appeal to the normal approximation, we have both

$$W \sim W_e = (\hat{\theta} - \theta_0)^{\mathrm{T}}\mathbf{i}_{\cdot}(\theta_0)(\hat{\theta} - \theta_0)$$

and

$$W \sim W_u = U^{\mathrm{T}}(\theta_0)\mathbf{i}_{\cdot}^{-1}(\theta_0)U_{\cdot}(\theta_0), \tag{2}$$

each with asymptotic chi-squared distributions on $\dim(\theta)$ degrees of freedom under H_0. Tests using critical regions based on these statistics have optimum local power properties, essentially extending the Neyman–Pearson results of Chapter 4. The advantage of the W_u statistic is that $\hat{\theta}$ need not be computed; W and W_u, but not W_e, are exactly invariant under reparameterization.

The main type of composite hypothesis involves the restriction of θ to a subspace, which in its simplest form is linear, so that with $\theta = (\psi, \lambda)$ we have $H_0 : \psi = \psi_0$ with alternative $H_A : \psi \neq \psi_0$ and λ is a nuisance parameter. The maximum likelihood ratio approach now leads to the statistic $W = 2\{l_Y(\hat{\psi}, \hat{\lambda}; Y) - l_Y(\psi_0, \hat{\lambda}_0; Y)\}$, where $\hat{\lambda}_0$ is the m.l.e. of λ subject to $\psi = \psi_0$. The previous methods of expansion lead to the asymptotically equivalent statistics

$$W_e = (\hat{\psi} - \psi_0)^{\mathrm{T}}\{\mathbf{i}_{\cdot}^{\psi\psi}(\psi_0, \hat{\lambda}_0)\}^{-1}(\hat{\psi} - \psi_0)$$

and

$$W_u = U_{\cdot\psi}^{\mathrm{T}}(\psi_0, \hat{\lambda}_0) \mathbf{i}^{\psi\psi}(\psi_0, \hat{\lambda}_0) U_{\cdot\psi}(\psi_0, \hat{\lambda}_0), \tag{3}$$

and their asymptotic distribution under H_0 is chi-squared on $\dim(\psi)$ degrees of freedom. Thus the tests defined by these statistics are asymptotically similar. Note that W_u does not involve calculation of $\hat{\theta} = (\hat{\psi}, \hat{\lambda})$, and that again W and W_u, but not W_e, are invariant under reparameterization.

Corresponding statistics for non-linear hypothetical restrictions on θ are described in Problem 10 of this chapter.

For hypotheses concerning the goodness of fit of multinomial models, W_u and W_e lead to chi-squared statistics.

The asymptotic local power of the W, W_u and W_e statistics is determined by the chi-squared non-centrality parameter $(\psi - \psi_0)^{\mathrm{T}} \{\mathbf{i}^{\psi\psi}(\psi, \lambda)\}^{-1} (\psi - \psi_0)$. The large-sample relative efficiency of two statistics both with limiting chi-squared distributions under the null hypothesis with the same degrees of freedom is defined to be the ratio of non-centrality parameters. In particular, for scalar θ and test statistics T_1, T_2 which are approximately $N\{\mu_j(\theta), \sigma_j^2(\theta)\}$ $(j = 1, 2)$, the Pitman asymptotic relative efficiency $e(T_1 : T_2)$ is equal to $[\{\mu_1'(\theta_0)\}^2/\sigma_1^2(\theta_0)]/[\{\mu_2'(\theta_0)\}^2/\sigma_2^2(\theta_0)]$.

Two rather different types of composite hypotheses that can arise are (i) those where H_0 specifies a subset of Ω that is not a subspace, such as $\|\theta\| \leqslant c$, and (ii) those where H_0 and H_A specify disjoint families of distributions. In case (i), the large-sample normal approximation to the likelihood can be used, but in case (ii) this is not so. When H_0 and H_A specify separate regular families of distributions, the maximum log likelihood ratio can again be expanded to produce asymptotic properties via those of maximum likelihood estimates.

Most of the following problems deal with developments of asymptotic theory and somewhat non-standard applications. It is to be stressed that in applications much can be achieved by careful and critical use of a few simple results, in particular those for the asymptotic variance of maximum likelihood estimates, and for tests based on the comparison of maximized log likelihoods.

Problems

9.2*. Let $Y_1, \ldots, Y_n$ be i.i.d. with p.d.f. indexed by a scalar parameter θ, and assume that the following regularity conditions hold: (a) the parameter space Ω is a closed subset of the real line and the true parameter value is an interior point of Ω; (b) the probability distributions defined by any two different values of θ are distinct; (c) the first three derivatives of $l(\theta; Y)$ with respect to θ exist in the neighbourhood of the true parameter value almost

*Problem 9.1 omitted

surely. Further, in such a neighbourhood, n^{-1} times the absolute value of the third derivative is bounded above by a function of Y whose expectation exists; (d) $i_.(\theta) = \text{var}\{U_.(\theta);\theta\} = E\{-\partial U_.(\theta)/\partial\theta;\theta\}$, which is finite and positive in the neighbourhood of the true parameter value. Show that the likelihood equation $U_.(\theta') = 0$ has a consistent solution.

Solution

Note especially the difference between the statement in this problem and the consistency of the m.l.e. The present result says, qualitatively, that for very large n the likelihood equation will have a solution close to the true value θ and leaves open the possibility that distant from θ there may be solutions achieving larger likelihood.

A detailed proof will not be given. It is, however, enough to show that as $n \to \infty$ for any fixed $\delta > 0$

$$\text{pr}\{U_.(\theta - \delta) > 0 > U_.(\theta + \delta);\theta\} \to 1.$$

To prove this we write

$$U_.(\theta') = U_.(\theta) + (\theta' - \theta)U_.'(\theta) + \tfrac{1}{2}(\theta' - \theta)^2 U_.''(\tilde\theta),$$

with $\tilde\theta$ between θ and θ', and note that, by the weak law of large numbers, we have in probability

$$U_.(\theta)/n \to 0, \ U_.'(\theta)/n \to -i(\theta), U_.''(\tilde\theta)/n - M(\theta) \to 0$$

for some bounded function $M(\theta)$, the last requiring the regularity condition on the third derivative of the underlying density. It is easy then to show that

$$\text{pr}\{U_.(\theta - \delta) < 0;\theta\} \text{ and } \text{pr}\{U_.(\theta + \delta) > 0;\theta\}$$

both tend to zero as $n \to \infty$.

The same method works, expanding component by component, for finite dimensional vector θ and, under additional conditions, for non-independent and non-identically distributed random variables. It fails for components with density $\tfrac{1}{2}\exp(-|y - \theta|)$, when the necessary expansions with respect to θ cannot be made.

[*Theoretical Statistics*, Section 9.2; Rao, Section 5f; Silvey, Section 4.5; Cramér, 1946, p. 500]

9.3. Let $Y_{jk}(k = 1, \ldots, r_j; j = 1, \ldots, m)$ be independent with Y_{jk} distributed in $N(\mu, \sigma_j^2)$, all parameters being unknown. The minimal sufficient statistic is $(\bar Y_{1.}, \ldots, \bar Y_{m.}, \text{ss}_1, \ldots, \text{ss}_m)$, where, as usual, $\text{ss}_j = \Sigma(Y_{jk} - \bar Y_{j.})^2$. For estimating

μ, verify that the likelihood equation is a special case of the equation

$$\sum_{j=1}^{m} \frac{a_j(\bar{Y}_{j.} - \mu')}{\text{ss}_j + r_j(\bar{Y}_{j.} - \mu')^2} = 0.$$

Notice that each term on the left-hand side has zero expectation when $\mu' = \mu$, the true value. Now assume $r_1, r_2, \ldots$ to be fixed with m becoming large. Using a generalization of the result of Problem 9.2, show that the solution $\tilde{\mu}_a$ of the estimating equation is consistent under appropriate conditions on the a_j's and the r_j's. Hence, show that under these conditions $\tilde{\mu}_a$ has a limiting normal distribution whose variance can be made uniformly lower than that for the m.l.e., by a suitable choice of the a_j's.

Comment on this result and its connexion with Bartlett's similar test of the hypothesis $H_0 : \mu = \mu_0$ (explained in *Theoretical Statistics*, p. 147).

Solution

The log likelihood function for $(\mu, \sigma_1^2, \ldots, \sigma_m^2)$ may be written as

$$\text{const} - \Sigma r_j \log \sigma_j - \tfrac{1}{2}\Sigma r_j(\bar{y}_{j.} - \mu)^2/\sigma_j^2 - \tfrac{1}{2}\Sigma \text{ss}_j/\sigma_j^2,$$

for which we obtain the likelihood equations

$$\Sigma r_j(\bar{y}_{j.} - \hat{\mu})/\hat{\sigma}_j^2 = 0, \, r_j\hat{\sigma}_j^2 = \text{ss}_j + r_j(\bar{y}_{j.} - \hat{\mu})^2,$$

leading to the equation for $\hat{\mu}$

$$\Sigma \frac{r_j^2(\bar{y}_{j.} - \hat{\mu})}{\text{ss}_j + r_j(\bar{y}_{j.} - \hat{\mu})^2} = 0,$$

the special case with $a_j = r_j^2$.

For simplicity, write

$$B_j(\mu) = \frac{a_j(\bar{Y}_{j.} - \mu)}{\text{ss}_j + r_j(\bar{Y}_{j.} - \mu)^2},$$

so that the general estimating equation is $\Sigma B_j(\tilde{\mu}_a) = 0$. Proof of consistency of the solution proceeds by analogy with Problem 9.2, where now we must show that, writing $\theta = (\mu, \sigma_1^2, \ldots)$,

$$E\{B_j(\mu); \theta\} = 0, \text{var}\{m^{-1}\Sigma B_j(\mu); \theta\} \to 0$$

in order to apply the law of large numbers to $\Sigma B_j(\mu)/m$; and in addition we use the regularity properties that

$$m^{-1}\Sigma B_j'(\mu) = K + o_p(1), K \neq 0,$$

where $o_p(1)$ denotes a random variable converging in probability to zero, and that $m^{-1}|\Sigma B_j''(\mu)|$ is bounded by a function independent of θ with bounded mean. These conditions are analogous to those for $U(\theta)$ used in connexion with the m.l.e.

Expansion of the consistent estimating equation in Taylor series gives

$$m^{-1}\Sigma B_j(\tilde{\mu}_a) = m^{-1}\Sigma B_j(\mu) + (\tilde{\mu}_a - \mu)\{m^{-1}\Sigma B'_j(\mu) + o_p(1)\},$$

so that application of the central limit theorem to $m^{-1}\Sigma B_j(\mu)$ and the weak law of large numbers to $m^{-1}\Sigma B'_j(\mu)$ yields the asymptotic normal distribution for $\tilde{\mu}_a - \mu$ with variance

$$V_a = \frac{\text{var}\{\Sigma B_j(\mu);\theta\}}{[E\{\Sigma B'_j(\mu);\theta\}]^2} = \frac{\Sigma a_j^2/\{r_j^2(r_j - 2)\sigma_j^2\}}{\{\Sigma a_j/(r_j\sigma_j^2)\}^2}.$$

Finiteness of V_a requires that $a_j = 0$ if $r_j = 1,2$. It is easily verified that V_a is minimized at $a_j = r_j(r_j - 2)$, where V_a is uniformly smaller than at $a_j = r_j^2$ corresponding to the consistent m.l.e. Detailed investigation shows that the regularity condition required for $B''_j(\mu)$ follows after showing that $|B''_j(\mu)| \leq 8a_j r_j^2 ss_j^{-3}$.

Thus, in this particular case, the presence of infinitely many nuisance parameters leads to the m.l.e. being inefficient. Note that substitution of a particular value μ_0 in the estimating equation leads to a test statistic for $H_0 : \mu = \mu_0$. The estimating equation weights $a_j = r_j(r_j - 2)$ correspond exactly to those used in the Bartlett (1936) statistic for testing H_0; the reason for this is unclear. If $r_j = 1$ or 2, no information about μ is contributed to the statistic by $\bar{Y}_{j.}$; this leaves open the possibility that some estimate not within the class considered here is an improvement, especially when there is an appreciable proportion of sets of data with $r_j = 2$.

In applications in which the variance is not stable and the mean changes, it is important to consider the possibility that the variance is related to the mean. In other cases an empirical Bayes model for the σ_j^2 may be used; under suitable assumptions this leads to a generalization of the equation under study here (Problem 10.12).

[*Theoretical Statistics*, Sections 5.2, 9.2; Rao, Sections 5f, 6a.2; Silvey, Chapter 7; Neyman and Scott, 1948; Bartlett, 1936]

9.4. In a linear model under the usual assumptions, the regression parameter β is estimated with covariance matrix $(\mathbf{x}^T\mathbf{x})^{-1}\sigma^2$; show that the response to be observed at an arbitrary point $\tilde{x}$ in the factor space can be predicted with mean squared error $\sigma^2\{1 + \tilde{x}^T(\mathbf{x}^T\mathbf{x})^{-1}\tilde{x}\}$, where the second term represents the uncertainty arising from not knowing β.

Consider, now, a more general situation in which at a point x in factor space the corresponding response Y_x has p.d.f. $f_{Y_x}(y;x,\theta)$. From some data, θ

is estimated by maximum likelihood with asymptotic covariance matrix $i^{-1}(\theta)$. It is required to measure the uncertainty arising in predicting the response at an arbitrary point $\tilde{x}$ in factor space and attributable to lack of knowledge of θ. Justify the measurement of uncertainty with θ known by $E\{-\log f_{Y_x}(Y;\tilde{x},\theta);\theta\}$. Show further that when θ is estimated a reasonable measure of total uncertainty is $E\{-\log f_{Y_x}(Y;\tilde{x},\hat{\theta});\theta\}$. Define the component of uncertainty attributable to lack of knowledge of θ by the difference of these quantities, and show by the usual large-sample approximations that this is $\frac{1}{2}\mathrm{tr}\{i(\theta;\tilde{x})i^{-1}(\theta)\}$, where $i(\theta;\tilde{x})$ is the information matrix calculated from one observation at $\tilde{x}$. Verify that this gives the previous results for the linear model.

Solution

For an observation vector $Y = \mathbf{x}\beta + \varepsilon$, the least squares estimate $b = (\mathbf{x}^T\mathbf{x})^{-1}\mathbf{x}^T Y$ has covariance matrix $(\mathbf{x}^T\mathbf{x})^{-1}\sigma^2$, from which we deduce that $\hat{Y} = \tilde{x}^T b$ has variance $\tilde{x}^T \mathrm{var}(b)\tilde{x} = \tilde{x}^T(\mathbf{x}^T\mathbf{x})^{-1}\tilde{x}\sigma^2$ and is unbiased for $\tilde{Y} = \tilde{x}^T\beta + \tilde{\varepsilon}$. Since $\tilde{Y}$ and Y are independent

$$E(\tilde{Y} - \hat{Y})^2 = \mathrm{var}(\tilde{Y}) + \mathrm{var}(\hat{Y}) = \sigma^2\{1 + \tilde{x}^T(\mathbf{x}^T\mathbf{x})^{-1}\tilde{x}\}.$$

For the non-linear case, where Y_x has p.d.f. $f_{Y_x}(y;x,\theta)$, the measure

$$E\{-\log f_{Y_x}(Y;x,\theta);\theta\}$$

is the entropy, arising in information theory, which is additive for combination of independent observations, is zero if and only if Y_x is constant, and in a scale and location family is proportional to the scale parameter. Further it has the property that it minimizes cross-entropy or information distance $E\{-\log f_{Y_x}(Y;x,\theta');\theta\}$; see Problem 4.16. This last remark relates also to the use of $K(\hat{\theta},\theta;x) = E\{-\log f_{Y_x}(Y;x,\hat{\theta});\theta\}$ as a total measure of uncertainty, since this then is also additive and is small when $\hat{\theta}$ is close to θ.

The positive difference $K(\hat{\theta},\theta;\tilde{x}) - K(\theta,\theta;\tilde{x})$ may be calculated as follows:

$$E_{\hat{\theta}}E_{\tilde{Y}}\{-\log f_{\tilde{Y}_x}(\tilde{Y};\tilde{x},\hat{\theta}) + \log f_{Y_x}(\tilde{Y};\tilde{x},\theta);\theta\}$$
$$= E_{\hat{\theta}}E_{\hat{Y}}[-\log f_{Y_x}(\hat{Y};\tilde{x},\theta) + (\hat{\theta} - \theta)^T U(\theta;\tilde{x})$$
$$\quad - \tfrac{1}{2}(\hat{\theta} - \theta)^T\{\partial U(\theta;\tilde{x})/\partial\theta\}(\hat{\theta} - \theta) + o_p(n^{-1}) + \log f_{Y_x}(\tilde{Y};\tilde{x},\theta);\theta]$$
$$= -\tfrac{1}{2}E_{\hat{\theta}}E_{\tilde{Y}}[\mathrm{tr}\{(\hat{\theta} - \theta)(\hat{\theta} - \theta)^T\partial U(\theta;\tilde{x})/\partial\theta\}] + o(n^{-1}),$$

and by the independence of $\tilde{Y}$ and $\hat{\theta}$ this is asymptotically

$$\tfrac{1}{2}\mathrm{tr}\{i^{-1}(\theta)i(\theta;\tilde{x})\}.$$

For the case of the linear model, the results are the same whether or not $\sigma^2 = \mathrm{var}(Y)$ is part of θ, since the information matrices have diagonal block structure. It is easy to check that if $\hat{\theta}$ is based on $Y = \mathbf{x}\theta + \varepsilon$ and

$\tilde{Y}_{\tilde{x}} = \tilde{x}^T\theta + \tilde{\varepsilon}$, then $\mathbf{i}\,(\theta) = (\mathbf{x}^T\mathbf{x})\sigma^2$ and $\mathbf{i}(\theta;\tilde{x}) = \tilde{x}\tilde{x}^T\sigma^2$, so that

$$\mathrm{tr}\{\mathbf{i}^{-1}(\theta)\mathbf{i}(\theta;\tilde{x})\} = \mathrm{tr}\{\tilde{x}^T(\mathbf{x}^T\mathbf{x})^{-1}\tilde{x}\},$$

by invoking the property tr $(\mathbf{ABC}) = \mathrm{tr}\ (\mathbf{CAB})$. Note that the measure is independent of σ^2 and so is strictly only a relative measure in terms of mean square.

[*Theoretical Statistics*, Section 9.2; Rao, Section 5f; Silvey, Chapter 4; White, 1973]

9.5. Let $Y_1, \ldots, Y_n$ be independent with Y_j having the p.d.f. $f(y;\psi, \lambda_j)$, and suppose that S_j is minimal sufficient for λ_j with ψ fixed, with the property that S_j is functionally independent of ψ. This is the incidental parameter problem. Show that, if ψ and λ_j are scalars, then the Cramér–Rao lower bound on the variance of an unbiased estimator of ψ is, with $\theta = (\psi, \lambda_1, \ldots, \lambda_n)$,

$$\{i_{.00}(\theta) - \Sigma i_{.0j}^2(\theta)i_{.jj}^{-1}(\theta)\}^{-1},$$

where

$$i_{.00}(\theta) = E\left\{-\frac{\partial^2 l(\theta;Y)}{\partial\psi^2};\theta\right\}, i_{.0j}(\theta) = E\left\{-\frac{\partial^2 l(\theta;Y)}{\partial\psi\partial\lambda_j};\theta\right\}$$

and

$$i_{.jj}(\theta) = E\left\{-\frac{\partial^2 l(\theta;Y)}{\partial\lambda_j^2};\theta\right\}\quad (j=1,\ldots,n).$$

It can be shown that this lower bound is attained asymptotically by the conditional m.l.e. of ψ if the p.d.f. is a member of the exponential family with S_j such that its distribution depends on λ_j but not on ψ, and such that the conditional distribution of Y_j given S_j depends only on ψ.

Investigate the asymptotic efficiency of the conditional m.l.e. of ψ for the case where the Y_j are bivariate normal with means λ_j and $\lambda_j + \psi$ and identity covariance matrix.

Solution

By independence the efficient score $U_{\cdot}$ may be written

$$U_{\cdot}(\psi, \lambda_1, \ldots, \lambda_n) = \sum_{j=1}^n U_j(\psi, \lambda_j),$$

where $U_j^T = (U_{j0}, 0, \ldots, U_{jj}, 0, \ldots, 0)(j = 1, \ldots, n)$, since λ_j appears only for

Y_j and for no other Y_k. It follows readily that

$$\mathbf{i}(\theta) = \begin{bmatrix} a & b^\mathsf{T} \\ b & \mathbf{d} \end{bmatrix},$$

where

$$a = \Sigma i_{j,00}(\theta), b^\mathsf{T} = \{i_{1,01}(\theta), \dots, i_{n,0n}(\theta)\},$$

$$\mathbf{d} = \operatorname{diag}\{i_{1,11}(\theta), \dots, i_{n,nn}(\theta)\}.$$

The Cramér–Rao lower bound for ψ, explained in the Summary for Chapter 8, is $i^{00}(\theta) = (a - b^\mathsf{T}\mathbf{d}^{-1}b)^{-1}$, which gives the desired result.

Note next that if S_j is ancillary with respect to ψ in the extended sense, that is

$$f_{Y_j}(y_j;\theta) = f_{S_j}(s_j;\lambda_j)f_{Y_j|S_j}(y_j|s_j;\psi),$$

the conditional m.l.e. equals the unconditional m.l.e. A more interesting case than the one stated is where S_j is not ancillary but is still sufficient for λ_j with ψ fixed. Thus

$$f_{Y_j}(y_j;\theta) = f_{S_j}(s_j;\theta)f_{Y_j|S_j}(y_j|s_j;\psi).$$

Then, in an obvious notation,

$$i^Y_{.00}(\theta) - \Sigma\{i^Y_{.jj}(\theta)\}^{-1}\{i^Y_{.0j}(\theta)\}^2 = i^{Y|S}_{.00} + i^S_{.00} - \Sigma(i^S_{.jj})^{-1}(i^S_{.0j})^2,$$

so that the conditional m.l.e. derived from Y given $S = s$ will be asymptotically efficient if

$$i^S_{.00}(\theta) - \Sigma\{i^S_{.jj}(\theta)\}^{-1}\{i^S_{.0j}(\theta)\}^2 = 0; \tag{1}$$

actually zero could be replaced by $o(i^{Y|S}_{.00})$ and under certain conditions on λ a more general result might then hold. Note that the condition (1) on $i^S(\theta)$ is equivalent to saying that $U^S_{.0}(\theta)$ is a linear function of $U^S_{.j}(\theta)$, so that under the assumption of independent S_j a sufficient and necessary condition is that $U^{S_j}_{j0}(\theta)$ is a linear function of $U^{S_j}_{jj}(\theta)$; i.e.

$$\frac{\partial}{\partial\psi}\log f_{S_j}(s_j;\theta) = \gamma_j(\theta)\frac{\partial}{\partial\lambda_j}\log f_{S_j}(s_j;\theta)(j = 1,\dots,n), \tag{2}$$

with $\gamma_j(\theta)$ independent of s_j. This result is the basis of Andersen's (1970) detailed analysis of the problem.

In the special case, $Y_{j1} + Y_{j2} = S_j$ is sufficient for λ_j given ψ. Of course the conditional likelihood given S_j is equivalent to the likelihood of $\{Y_{j2} - Y_{j1}, j = 1,\dots,n\}$, resulting in $\hat{\psi}^c = \bar{Y}_{.2} - \bar{Y}_{.1}$, which is actually equal to $\hat{\psi}$. Since S_j is $N(\psi + 2\lambda_j, 2)$ it follows quickly that (2) is satisfied with $\gamma_j(\theta) = \frac{1}{2}$, thus checking the asymptotic equivalence by the general method.

[*Theoretical Statistics*, Section 9.2; Rao, Section 5a; Silvey, Chapter 4]

9.6. Let $Y_1, \ldots, Y_n$ be successive variables in a two-state stationary Markov chain with transition probability $\text{pr}(Y_j = 1 \mid Y_{j-1} = 1) = \lambda$ and stationary probability $\psi = \text{pr}(Y_j = 1)$. Show that the variance of the limiting normal distribution of the m.l.e. $\hat{\psi}$ is $\psi(1 - \psi)(1 - 2\psi + \lambda)/\{n(1 - \lambda)\}$, which is also the variance of $\bar{Y}$. Hence verify that the explicit m.l.e. of λ with fixed ψ replaced by $\bar{Y}$ is asymptotically efficient.

Solution

The first step is to obtain the equilibrium distribution of the two-state Markov chain with $p_{st} = \text{pr}(Y_{j+1} = t \mid Y_j = s)$, and hence to show that in the new parameterization $p_{00} = (1 - 2\psi + \lambda\psi)/(1 - \psi)$ and $p_{01} = (1 - \lambda)\psi/(1 - \psi)$, with, of course, $p_{10} = 1 - \lambda$ and $p_{11} = \lambda$. For $0 < \lambda, \psi < 1$ the regularity conditions for consistency and asymptotic normality of $\hat{\theta} = (\hat{\psi}, \hat{\lambda})$ are satisfied.

Now

$$U_j^{\mathrm{T}}(\theta) = \left(\frac{\partial}{\partial \psi}, \frac{\partial}{\partial \lambda} \right) \log f(Y_j \mid Y_{j-1}; \theta)$$

$$i(\theta) = \sum_{j=2}^{n} \text{var}\{U_j(\theta); \theta\} + O(1) \sim n\,\text{var}\{U_2(\theta); \theta\}$$

and the four possible values of each component of $U_j(\theta)$ are given on differentiating the logs of the elements of the transition matrix. On taking variances, we calculate the information matrix for a single observation to be

$$
\begin{bmatrix}
\dfrac{(1-\lambda)^2}{(1-\psi)^4}\left(\dfrac{1}{p_{00}} + \dfrac{1}{p_{11}}\right) & \dfrac{(1-\lambda)\psi}{(1-\psi)^3}\left(\dfrac{1}{p_{00}} + \dfrac{1}{p_{01}}\right) \\[3ex]
\cdot & \dfrac{\psi^2}{(1-\psi)^2}\left(\dfrac{1}{p_{00}} + \dfrac{1}{p_{01}}\right) + \dfrac{1}{p_{10}} + \dfrac{1}{p_{11}}
\end{bmatrix}
$$

Inversion of n times this gives in particular for the leading element, the asymptotic variance of $\hat{\psi}$,

$$\psi(1-\psi)(1-2\psi+\lambda)(1-\lambda)^{-1}n^{-1}.$$

Now clearly $E(\bar{Y}) = \psi$ and a central limit theorem applies to $\bar{Y}$. We find its variance by an argument that applies to the mean of any stationary process:

$$\mathrm{var}(\bar{Y}) = \frac{1}{n^2}\Sigma\,\mathrm{var}(Y_j) + \frac{1}{n^2}\sum_{j\neq k}\mathrm{cov}(Y_j,Y_k)$$

$$= \frac{\sigma^2}{n} + \frac{2\sigma^2}{n^2}\sum_{h=1}^{n-1}(n-h)\gamma_h,$$

say, where $\gamma_h = \mathrm{cov}(Y_j, Y_{j+h})$. For our particular process

$$\sigma^2 = \psi(1-\psi), \gamma_h = \mathrm{pr}(Y_j = Y_{j+h} = 1) - \psi^2.$$

Further

$$\mathrm{pr}(Y_j = Y_{j+h} = 1) = \mathrm{pr}(Y_j = 1)\mathrm{pr}(Y_{j+h} = 1\,|\,Y_j = 1)$$
$$= \psi\{\psi + (1-\psi)(\lambda-\psi)^h/(1-\psi)^h\},$$

the last result following from a calculation of the h-step transition matrix of the chain. The form of $\mathrm{var}(\bar{Y})$ now follows.

So far, then, $\hat{\psi}$ and $\bar{Y}$ have been shown to be asymptotically normal with the same mean and variance. From this it can be established rigorously that $\bar{Y} = \hat{\psi} + o_p(n^{-1/2})$; this follows non-rigorously from the result of Problem 9.9, since $(\bar{Y}, \hat{\psi})$ have a singular limiting normal distribution with covariance $\mathbf{i}(\theta) \otimes \mathbf{I}$. We now show that the m.l.e. of λ with $\psi = \bar{Y}$, say $\tilde{\lambda}$, is asymptotically efficient.

Note that $\tilde{\lambda}$ is a solution of the likelihood equation

$$U_{.\lambda}(\lambda', \bar{Y}) = 0.$$

Expanding in Taylor series we have

$$U_{.\lambda}(\tilde{\lambda}, \bar{Y}) = U_{.\lambda}(\hat{\lambda}, \hat{\psi}) + (\tilde{\lambda} - \hat{\lambda})U_{.\lambda\lambda}(\lambda^*, \psi^*) + (\bar{Y} - \hat{\psi})U_{.\psi\lambda}(\lambda^*, \psi^*), \quad (1)$$

where

$$|\lambda^* - \hat{\lambda}| < |\tilde{\lambda} - \hat{\lambda}|, |\psi^* - \hat{\psi}| < |\bar{Y} - \hat{\psi}| \text{ and } U_{.\lambda}(\hat{\lambda}, \hat{\psi}) = 0.$$

By the consistency of (λ^*, ψ^*) and the law of large numbers,

$$n^{-1}U_{.\lambda\lambda}(\lambda^*, \psi^*) \to i_{\lambda\lambda}(\lambda, \psi) = \lim n^{-1}i_{.\lambda\lambda}(\lambda, \psi)$$
$$n^{-1}U_{.\lambda\psi}(\lambda^*, \psi^*) \to i_{\lambda\psi}(\lambda, \psi) = \lim n^{-1}i_{.\lambda\psi}(\lambda, \psi).$$

Therefore, because $\bar{Y} - \hat{\psi} = o_p(n^{-1/2})$, (1) gives

$$\tilde{\lambda} - \hat{\lambda} = o_p(n^{-1/2}).$$

It follows that $\sqrt{n}(\tilde{\lambda} - \lambda)$ and $\sqrt{n}(\hat{\lambda} - \lambda)$ have the same limiting normal distribution.

It is easy to verify that with $\psi = \bar{Y}, \tilde{\lambda}$ is the solution of a quadratic equation, whereas $\hat{\lambda}$ and $\hat{\psi}$ are the solutions to a fourth-order equation. Thus $(\bar{Y}_{.}, \tilde{\lambda})$ is easier to compute.

[*Theoretical Statistics*, Section 9.2; Rao, Section 5f; Silvey, Chapter 4; Klotz, 1973]

9.7. Let $Y_1, \ldots, Y_n$ be independent, each Y_j having a Poisson distribution with mean $\theta_1 + \theta_2 x_j$ for fixed x_j; the parameter (θ_1, θ_2) is restricted to make each mean positive. Show that the m.l.e. of (θ_1, θ_2) is asymptotically equivalent to a weighted least squares estimate. Make a comparison with the unweighted least squares estimate, including the special case $\theta_2 = 0$.

Solution

The log likelihood function is

$$\text{const} - \sum_{j=1}^{n} (\theta_1 + \theta_2 x_j) + \sum_{j=1}^{n} Y_j \log(\theta_1 + \theta_2 x_j)$$

and the score vector is

$$U_.(\theta) = \begin{bmatrix} -n + \Sigma Y_j(\theta_1 + \theta_2 x_j)^{-1} \\ -\Sigma x_j + \Sigma x_j Y_j(\theta_1 + \theta_2 x_j)^{-1} \end{bmatrix}.$$

Therefore the likelihood equation $U_.(\hat{\theta}) = 0$ is formally the same as the least-squares equations obtained by minimizing the weighted sum of squares $\Sigma w_j(Y_j - \theta_1 - \theta_2 x_j)^2$ with the substitution of $w_j = (\theta_1 + \theta_2 x_j)^{-1} = \{\text{var} (Y_j)\}^{-1}$ in the least squares equations. The maximum likelihood estimate will be a solution of the likelihood equation with high probability when the sample size is large, provided that the x_j and the parameter values are such that all the means $\theta_1 + \theta_2 x_j$ are bounded away from zero. Use of the 'empirical weight' $\tilde{w}_j = Y_j^{-1}$ with a modification for $Y_j = 0$ leads to estimates equivalent to maximum likelihood as $n \to \infty$ if all $E(Y_j)$ are large.

The likelihood equation must be solved iteratively, a possible starting point being the unweighted least squares estimates

$$\tilde{\theta}_1 = \bar{Y}_. - \tilde{\theta}_2 \bar{x}_. , \tilde{\theta}_2 = \Sigma Y_j(x_j - \bar{x}_.)/\Sigma(x_j - \bar{x}_.)^2.$$

One procedure for this and other similar problems for Poisson and binomial distributions is to use the method of weighted least squares, determining the weights via the estimated parameters in the previous stage of the iteration.

Computation of the information matrix from $\text{var}\{U_.(\theta)\}$ gives

$$i_.(\theta) = \begin{bmatrix} \Sigma(\theta_1 + \theta_2 x_j)^{-1} & \Sigma x_j(\theta_1 + \theta_2 x_j)^{-1} \\ . & \Sigma x_j^2(\theta_1 + \theta_2 x_j)^{-1} \end{bmatrix},$$

The inverse $\mathbf{i}^{-1}(\theta)$ can then be compared directly with the variance of the least squares estimates. For example, the approximate large-sample variance of $\hat{\theta}_2$ is the same as that for $\tilde{\theta}_2$ to $O(\theta_2)$.

[*Theoretical Statistics*, Section 9.2; Rao, Section 5f; Silvey, Chapter 4]

9.8. The asymptotic sufficiency of the m.l.e. $\hat{\theta}$ in regular problems implies only that the information lost summarizing Y by $\hat{\theta}$ is asymptotically negligible relative to $i(\theta)$. Show that, for one-dimensional θ, the loss of information is $E_{\hat{\theta}} \operatorname{var} \{U(\theta)|\hat{\theta};\theta\}$, which to first order can be derived from the variance of $U'(\theta)$ conditionally on $U(\hat{\theta}) = 0$. A similar calculation would be appropriate for a general consistent estimating equation.

Consider specifically the regular multinomial situation where $N_1, \ldots, N_m$ are cell frequencies in a sample of size n corresponding to cell probabilities $\pi_1(\theta), \ldots, \pi_m(\theta)$. Note that the N_j can be treated as independent variables with Poisson distributions of means $n\pi_j(\theta)$ constrained by $\Sigma N_j = n$, and that $U(\hat{\theta}) = 0$ is approximately equivalent to another linear restriction on the N_j. Hence derive an explicit expression for $i(\theta) - i_{\hat{\theta}}(\theta)$.

Use the same arguments to derive the information loss in using a general asymptotically efficient estimating equation. Discuss these results and their relation to second-order approximations for variances of the limiting normal distributions of efficient estimates.

Solution

The discussion here follows the non-rigorous treatment by Fisher (1925), which has subsequently been refined by Rao (1961) and Efron (1975).

By expressing the density of Y as the product of the density of Y given $\hat{\theta}$ and the density of $\hat{\theta}$, we have that

$$U(\theta;Y) = U(\theta;Y|\hat{\theta}) + U(\theta;\hat{\theta}).$$

The two components on the right are uncorrelated, so that the information loss in replacing Y by $\hat{\theta}$ is

$$\operatorname{var} \{U(\theta;Y|\hat{\theta});\theta\} = \operatorname{var} \{U(\theta;Y) - U(\theta;\hat{\theta});\theta\}$$

$$= E[\operatorname{var} \{U(\theta;Y)|\hat{\theta};\theta\}]. \tag{1}$$

In the discussion so far, $\hat{\theta}$ could be any estimate, but for maximum likelihood the condition $\hat{\theta} = t$ implies $U(t;Y) = 0$, and by Taylor expansion to first order

$$\operatorname{var} \{U(\theta;Y)|\hat{\theta} = t;\theta\} = (\theta - t)^2 \operatorname{var} \{U'(\theta;Y)|U(t;Y) = 0;\theta\}. \tag{2}$$

In general one would then use properties of the joint asymptotic normal distribution of $U_.(\theta;Y)$ and $U'(\theta;Y)$. The key result is that for scalar X_2

$$\operatorname{var}(X_2 \mid X_1 = x_1)$$
$$= \operatorname{var}(X_2) - \{\operatorname{cov}(X_1, X_2)\}^{\mathrm{T}}\{\operatorname{var}(X_1)\}^{-1}\operatorname{cov}(X_1, X_2), \qquad (3)$$

which we apply with $X_2 = U'(\theta), X_1 = U_.(\theta)$, the latter being a first-order approximation to $U_.(t)$ in (2).

For the multinomial problem, we use (3) in conjunction with the Poisson representation for N_j, according to which the N_j are independent Poisson variables with means $n\pi_j(\theta)$ restricted by $\Sigma N_j = n$. The approximate restriction $U_.(\theta) = 0$ implies $\Sigma N_j \pi_j'(\theta)/\pi_j(\theta) = 0$, and $U'(\theta) = \Sigma N_j \{\pi_j''(\theta)/\pi_j(\theta) - [\pi_j'(\theta)/\pi_j(\theta)]^2\}$. Therefore in applying (3), X_1 is a pair of linear combinations of the N_j, and X_2 is another linear combination. Detailed calculation gives that

$$i_.(\theta) - i_{\hat\theta}(\theta) \sim$$

$$\frac{\Sigma\{\pi_j''/\pi_j - (\pi_j'/\pi_j)^2\}}{\Sigma(\pi_j'/\pi_j)^2} - \Sigma\frac{(\pi_j')^2}{\pi_j} - \frac{[\Sigma\pi_j'\{\pi_j''/\pi_j - (\pi_j'/\pi_j)^2\}^2]}{\{\Sigma(\pi_j')^2/\pi_j\}^2}.$$

For a general estimating equation $g(T, n^{-1}N_1, \ldots, n^{-1}N_m) = 0$ a similar analysis is required to determine $i_.(\theta) - i_T(\theta)$; such an equation gives an efficient estimate, i.e. a first-order equivalent to $\hat\theta$, if $g(t, p_1, \ldots, p_m)$ satisfies

$$\left[\frac{\partial g}{\partial t} \middle/ \frac{\partial g}{\partial p_j}\right]_{t=\theta, p_j = \pi_j(\theta)} = -\frac{\pi_j'(\theta)}{\pi_j(\theta)}\{i(\theta)\}^{-1}.$$

Specific details are given by Rao (1961), where it is shown that information loss is least when $T = \hat\theta$.

When asymptotically equivalent estimates are compared by a more refined calculation, care is needed in relating, say, information loss to confidence interval and significance test properties. However, the results on information loss relate directly to large-sample variance properties, as Efron (1975) shows, in the sense that for bias-corrected efficient estimates T_n

$$\operatorname{var}(T_n;\theta) \sim i_{T_n}^{-1}(\theta) + n^{-2}c(\theta) + o(n^{-2}),$$

where $c(\theta)$ is independent of the method of estimation.

[*Theoretical Statistics*, Section 9.2; Rao, Sections 5f, 6e]

9.9.* Suppose that $Y_1, \ldots, Y_n$ are i.i.d. with continuous p.d.f.

$$f(y;\theta) = \begin{cases} c(\theta)d(y) & (a \leqslant y \leqslant b(\theta)), \\ 0 & \text{elsewhere}, \end{cases}$$

where $b(\theta)$ is a monotone function of the single parameter θ. Show that the

*Amended version.

m.l.e. of θ is $b^{-1}(Y_{(n)})$, and hence that the m.l. ratio criterion for testing $H_0 : \theta = \theta_0$ against the two-sided alternative $\theta \neq \theta_0$ is, under H_0, given by

$$W = -2n \log \int_a^{Y_{(n)}} c(\theta_0) d(y) dy,$$

which has exactly the chi-squared distribution with two degrees of freedom.

Solution

Suppose to be explicit that $b(\theta)$ is increasing. Then

$$\text{lik}(\theta; Y) = \left\{ \int_a^{b(\theta)} d(y) dy \right\}^{-n} \prod_{j=1}^n d(Y_j) \text{ for } Y_{(n)} \leqslant b(\theta),$$

whose maximum is obtained by minimizing the integral subject to $Y_{(n)} \leqslant b(\theta)$, i.e. by choosing $b(\hat{\theta}) = Y_{(n)}, \hat{\theta} = b^{-1}(Y_{(n)})$.
  The maximized likelihood is

$$\left\{ \int_a^{Y_{(n)}} d(y) dy \right\}^{-n} \prod d(Y_j).$$

The likelihood at θ_0 is zero if $Y_{(n)} > b(\theta_0)$, which is impossible under H_0, and is otherwise

$$\left\{ \int_a^{b(\theta_0)} d(y) dy \right\}^{-n} \prod d(Y_j) = \{c(\theta_0)\}^n \prod d(Y_j),$$

whence

$$W = -2n \log \int_a^{Y_{(n)}} c(\theta_0) d(y) dy.$$

  Now for any continuous random variable X with cumulative distribution function F, $V = F(X)$ has the uniform distribution on $(0, 1)$, so that, under H_0, W is minus twice the logarithm of $V_{(n)}^n$, where $V_{(n)}$ is the largest of n independent uniform variables. It follows that W is minus twice the logarithm of a uniform variable, and so has cumulative distribution function $1 - e^{-\frac{1}{2}z}$, which corresponds to the chi-squared distribution with two degrees of freedom.

[*Theoretical Statistics*, Section 9.3; Rao, Section 6e; Silvey, Chapter 7; Hogg, 1956]

9.10 Let $Y_1, \ldots, Y_n$ be i.i.d. with regular p.d.f. $f(y;\theta)$, where $\dim(\theta) > 1$. Suppose that θ is restricted to satisfy $\zeta(\theta) = 0$, where $\zeta(\cdot)$ is differentiable. Use the method of Lagrange multipliers to derive the constrained likelihood equation and derive the limiting normal distribution of the constrained m.l.e. $\tilde{\theta}$.

If the restriction $\zeta(\theta) = 0$ is a null hypothesis with alternative that $\zeta(\theta) \neq 0$, show that the m.l. ratio statistic is asymptotically equivalent to the standardized form of $\zeta^2(\hat{\theta})$, where $\hat{\theta}$ is the usual unconstrained m.l.e. Show that the corresponding version of the score statistic W_u is based on $U_.(\tilde{\theta})$.

Solution

For simplicity, suppose that the constraint $\zeta(\theta) = 0$ is scalar; the argument is easily extended to the vector case. There are a number of asymptotically equivalent ways of tackling the problem. One, simple in principle but often inconvenient in particular applications, is to reparameterize so that $\zeta(\theta)$ becomes one of the component parameters. Another is to work with the asymptotic normal form (1) of the Summary for the likelihood and with a local linearized form of the constraint, namely $(\theta - \theta_0)^T (\partial\zeta/\partial\theta_0) = 0$.

If, however, we treat the problem as one of constrained maximization, we consider $l(\theta') - \lambda\zeta(\theta')$ and solve

$$U_.(\tilde{\theta}) - \tilde{\lambda}\partial\zeta(\tilde{\theta})/\partial\tilde{\theta} = 0, \zeta(\tilde{\theta}) = 0$$

for θ and λ. Expanding about the true parameter value θ, we have

$$U_.(\theta) - \mathbf{i}_.(\theta)(\tilde{\theta} - \theta) - \tilde{\lambda}\partial\zeta(\theta)/\partial\theta = 0, (\tilde{\theta} - \theta)^T(\partial\zeta/\partial\theta) = 0,$$

so that, to this order,

$$\begin{bmatrix} U_.(\theta) \\ 0 \end{bmatrix} = \begin{bmatrix} \mathbf{i}_.(\theta) & -\partial\zeta/\partial\theta \\ (-\partial\zeta/\partial\theta)^T & 0 \end{bmatrix} \begin{bmatrix} \tilde{\theta} - \theta \\ \tilde{\lambda} \end{bmatrix} = \begin{bmatrix} \mathbf{P} & Q \\ Q^T & R \end{bmatrix}^{-1} \begin{bmatrix} \tilde{\theta} - \theta \\ \tilde{\lambda} \end{bmatrix},$$

say. The vector on the left-hand side is asymptotically $MN\{0, \mathbf{i}^{-1}(\theta)\}$, so that $\tilde{\theta} - \theta$ is $MN\{0, \mathbf{Pi}^{-1}(\theta)\mathbf{P}^T\}$, a singular normal distribution, subject to the locally linear constraint $\zeta(\tilde{\theta}) = 0$.

The likelihood ratio statistic for testing $H_0 : \zeta(\theta) = 0$ is

$$W = 2\{l(\hat{\theta}) - l(\tilde{\theta})\} \simeq (\hat{\theta} - \tilde{\theta})^T\mathbf{i}_.(\theta)(\hat{\theta} - \tilde{\theta}),$$

after expanding $l(\tilde{\theta})$ about $\hat{\theta}$. But also

$$\zeta(\hat{\theta}) = \zeta(\tilde{\theta}) + (\hat{\theta} - \tilde{\theta})^T\{\partial\zeta(\hat{\theta})/\partial\hat{\theta}\}$$

and $\zeta(\tilde{\theta}) = 0$, so that again asymptotically

$$W \simeq \{\zeta(\hat{\theta})\}^2 [\{\partial\zeta(\hat{\theta})/\partial\hat{\theta}\}^T\mathbf{i}^{-1}(\hat{\theta})\{\partial\zeta(\hat{\theta})/\partial\hat{\theta}\}]^{-1}$$

which has a limiting central chi-squared distribution with one degree of freedom under H_0.

An advantage of this latter form is that $\tilde{\theta}$ does not have to be calculated explicitly. Yet another form is

$$U^{\mathrm{T}}(\tilde{\theta})\mathbf{i}^{-1}(\tilde{\theta})U_{.}(\tilde{\theta}).$$

In general if ζ is q dimensional the analogous quadratic forms in $\zeta(\hat{\theta})$ and $U_{.}(\tilde{\theta})$ have limiting chi-squared distributions with q degrees of freedom.

[*Theoretical Statistics*, Section 9.2, 9.3; Rao, Section 6e; Silvey, Chapter 7; Aitchison and Silvey, 1958]

9.11. Consider a two-dimensional contingency table with cell frequencies $N_{jk}(j = 1, \ldots, r; k = 1, \ldots, c)$ and corresponding probabilities π_{jk}. For the null hypothesis of row-column independence with general alternative derive the forms of the W, W_u and W_e statistics.

Solution

There are several ways to approach this. One is to use the result of Problem 9.10 with $\theta = \{\pi_{jk}\}$, and with the constraints $\zeta(\theta) = 0$ equivalent to the constraints on π_{jk} dictated by row-column independence. Then the statistic based on $\zeta(\hat{\theta})$ is seen to be a quadratic form in the deviations observed frequency − fitted frequency $= N_{jk} - N_{j+}N_{+k}/n$, where N_{j+} and N_{+k} denote row and column sums respectively.

To proceed directly from the definitions of W_u and W_e given by (3) of the Summary is, in general, complicated. Therefore we limit the discussion to the special case $r = c = 2$. In this case we reparameterize to

$$\pi_{11} = K^{-1}e^{\lambda_1 + \lambda_2 + \psi}, \pi_{12} = K^{-1}e^{\lambda_1 - \lambda_2 - \psi}, \pi_{21} = K^{-1}e^{-\lambda_1 + \lambda_2 - \psi}$$
$$\pi_{22} = K^{-1}e^{-\lambda_1 - \lambda_2 + \psi},$$

where K is such the probabilities sum to one. The hypothesis of row-column independence is then equivalent to $\psi = 0$.

From the log likelihood function $\Sigma\Sigma N_{jk}\log\pi_{jk}$ we compute

$$U_{.\lambda_1} = -n\alpha_1 + (N_{1+} - N_{2+}), U_{.\lambda_2} = -n\alpha_2 + (N_{+1} - N_{+2}),$$
$$U_{.\psi} = -n\beta + (N_{11} + N_{22} - N_{12} - N_{21}),$$

where

$$\alpha_1 = \pi_{11} + \pi_{12} - \pi_{21} - \pi_{22}, \alpha_2 = \pi_{11} - \pi_{12} + \pi_{21} - \pi_{22},$$
$$\beta = \pi_{11} + \pi_{22} - \pi_{12} - \pi_{21}.$$

The information matrix is equal to minus the matrix of second derivatives of the log likelihood,

$$\mathbf{i} = n \begin{bmatrix} 1 - \alpha_1^2 & \beta - \alpha_1\alpha_2 & \alpha_2 - \alpha_1\beta \\ \cdot & 1 - \alpha_2^2 & \alpha_1 - \alpha_2\beta \\ \cdot & \cdot & 1 - \beta^2 \end{bmatrix}.$$

To compute the W_u statistic we note that under $H_0 : \psi = 0$ the m.l.e. of π_{jk} is $N_{j+} N_{+k}/n^2$, so that the fitted frequencies are

$$\tilde{N}_{jk} = N_{j+} N_{+k}/n,$$

and

$$U_{.\psi}(0, \hat{\lambda}_0) = (N_{11} - \tilde{N}_{11}) + (N_{22} - \tilde{N}_{22}) - (N_{12} - \tilde{N}_{12}) - (N_{21} - \tilde{N}_{21}).$$

It then follows readily that

$$W_u = \Sigma\Sigma(N_{jk} - \tilde{N}_{jk})^2/\tilde{N}_{jk},$$

which is the general result.

The W_e statistic is proportional to the square of

$$\hat{\psi} = \log\{(N_{11} N_{22})/(N_{12} N_{21})\},$$

and expansion under H_0 using $\log(1 + x) = x - \frac{1}{2}x^2 + \dots$ leads to the equivalent form

$$W_e \simeq \Sigma\Sigma(N_{jk} - \tilde{N}_{jk})^2/N_{jk}.$$

Both W_u and W_e have limiting chi-squared distributions with $(r-1)(c-1)$ degrees of freedom under H_0 for general r and c.

A more detailed analysis of likelihood ratio and equivalent chi-squared statistics for general contingency tables is given by Bishop *et al.* (1975). For similar problems, see Problems 9.15 and 9.17.

[*Theoretical Statistics*, Section 9.3; Rao, Sections 6b, 6e; Silvey, Chapter 7]

9.12. Suppose that $Y_1, \dots, Y_n$ are independent, Y_j being distributed in $N(\mu_j, \sigma^2)$, where either $\mu_j = \beta w_j$ or $\mu_j = \gamma z_j (j = 1, \dots, n)$, all parameters being unknown and the w_j's and z_j's being known constants. In order to test between the two models, consider the artificial exponential mixture density for Y of the form

$$f_Y(y; \psi, \beta, \gamma, \sigma^2 | w, z) \propto \{g(y; \beta w, \sigma^2)\}^\psi \{g(y; \gamma z, \sigma^2)\}^{1-\psi},$$

where $g(y; \mu, \sigma^2)$ is the $N(\mu, \sigma^2)$ density. Derive the score statistic W_u for testing $H_0 : \psi = 1$ versus $H_A : \psi < 1$. Compare the resulting test with that used in the usual exact analysis of this problem.

Solution

After normalizing the exponential mixture, the log likelihood for a single observation is, apart from a constant,

$$- \log \sigma - \frac{1}{2\sigma^2} \{ \psi(y - \beta w)^2 + (1 - \psi)(y - \gamma z)^2 - \psi(1 - \psi)(\beta w - \gamma z)^2 \}. \quad (1)$$

Notice that when $\psi = 1$, the parameter γ is not estimable. If we define $\lambda = (\beta, \gamma, \sigma^2)$, then the efficient score statistic for testing H_0 is the standardized form of $U_{.\psi}(1, \lambda) - b_{.\psi\lambda} U_{.\lambda}(1, \lambda)$, where $b_{.\psi\lambda}$ is the vector of coefficients of regression of $U_{.\psi}$ on $U_{.\lambda}$ evaluated at $(1, \lambda)$. In this particular case, the component of $U_{.\lambda}$ corresponding to γ is zero at $\psi = 1$, and the remaining components are zero if we substitute the m.l.e.'s for β and σ^2 under H_0. Therefore the score statistic corresponding to (3) of the Summary is the standardized form of $U_{.\psi}(1, \lambda)$ evaluated at $\beta = \hat{\beta}_0$ and $\sigma^2 = \hat{\sigma}_0^2$. Now with γ fixed, we find from (1) that

$$U_{.\psi}(1, \hat{\beta}_0, \gamma, \hat{\sigma}_0^2) = - \gamma(\Sigma z_j w_j - \hat{\beta}_0 \Sigma z_j w_j)/\hat{\sigma}_0^2.$$

But clearly γ cancels when we standardize this statistic, and we find that the standardized statistic is equal to

$$\sqrt{W_u} = \frac{\Sigma z_j y_j - \hat{\beta}_0 \Sigma z_j w_j}{\hat{\sigma}_0 \sqrt{\{ \Sigma(z_j - d w_j)^2 \}}},$$

where $d = \Sigma z_j w_j / \Sigma w_j^2$. This corresponds directly to the standard analysis for this problem, being equivalent to a test of the residual regression of y on z after adjusting for their regression on w. The only difference is that usually $\hat{\sigma}_0^2$ would be replaced by the mean square residual from regression on both w and z, in which case $\sqrt{W_u}$ would have an exact Student t distribution.

Atkinson (1970) gives a general discussion of the use of exponential mixtures in model comparisons, and relates this approach to the generalized likelihood ratio method used by Cox (1961, 1962).

[*Theoretical Statistics*, Section 9.3; Rao, Section 6e; Silvey, Chapter 7]

9.13. A bivariate random variable (X, Y) of the form $X = U + V, Y = U + W$, where U, V and W have independent Poisson distributions, is said to have a bivariate Poisson distribution. Note that the marginal distributions of X and Y are Poisson and that X and Y are independent if and only if $E(U) = 0$. Consider the construction of an asymptotic test of independence from independent pairs $(X_1, Y_1), \ldots, (X_n, Y_n)$. Show that the m.l. ratio statistic is computationally difficult to find, but that the efficient score statistic W_u, with the nuisance parameters $E(X)$ and $E(Y)$ estimated by $\bar{X}$ and $\bar{Y}$, leads to consideration of the test statistic $\Sigma(X_j - \bar{X})(Y_j - \bar{Y})/\sqrt{(\bar{X}\,\bar{Y}n)}$, having asymptotically a standard normal distribution under the null hypothesis.

Solution

Let U, V, W have Poisson means ψ, λ_v and λ_w respectively. Then by definition

$$\text{pr}(X = x, Y = y; \theta) = e^l = \sum_{u=0}^{\min(x,y)} \frac{\lambda_v^{x-u} \lambda_w^{y-u} \psi^u e^{-(\psi + \lambda_v + \lambda_w)}}{u!(x-u)!(y-u)!},$$

from which we calculate the components of the individual score vector at $\psi = 0$ to be

$$(\partial l/\partial \psi)_{\psi=0} = -1 + (xy)/(\lambda_v \lambda_w),$$

$$(\partial l/\partial \lambda_v)_{\psi=0} = -1 + x/\lambda_v, \quad (\partial l/\partial \lambda_w)_{\psi=0} = -1 + y/\lambda_w,$$

and thence the individual information matrix at $\psi = 0$ is

$$\mathbf{i}(0, \lambda) = \begin{bmatrix} \lambda_v^{-1} + \lambda_w^{-1} + (\lambda_v \lambda_w)^{-1} & \lambda_v^{-1} & \lambda_w^{-1} \\ \lambda_v^{-1} & \lambda_v^{-1} & 0 \\ \lambda_w^{-1} & 0 & \lambda_w^{-1} \end{bmatrix}.$$

Under H_0, X and Y are independent and the Poisson parameters are independently estimated by $\hat{\lambda}_{v0} = \bar{X}, \hat{\lambda}_{w0} = \bar{Y}$. Therefore

$$U_{\cdot\psi}(0, \hat{\lambda}_0) = -n + (\Sigma X_j Y_j)/(\bar{X}\,\bar{Y})$$

$$i^{\psi\psi}(0, \hat{\lambda}_0) = \hat{\lambda}_{v0} \hat{\lambda}_{w0}/n = \bar{X}\,\bar{Y}/n,$$

leading directly to the score statistic

$$W_u = \{U_{\cdot\psi}(0, \hat{\lambda}_0)\}^2 i^{\psi\psi}(0, \hat{\lambda}_0) = \{\Sigma(X_j - \bar{X})(Y_j - \bar{Y})\}^2/(n\bar{X}\,\bar{Y}).$$

Note that $\bar{X}$ and $\bar{Y}$ are minimal sufficient under H_0, so that W_u in principle defines a similar test using the conditional distribution of $\Sigma X_j Y_j$ given $\bar{X} = \bar{x}, \bar{Y} = \bar{y}$. The exact conditional variance of $\Sigma(X_j - \bar{X})(Y_j - \bar{Y})$ given $\bar{X} = \bar{x}$ and $\bar{Y} = \bar{y}$ is $(n-1)\bar{x}\,\bar{y}$.

[*Theoretical Statistics*, Section 9.3; Rao, Section 6e; Silvey, Chapter 7; Neyman, 1959]

9.14. Let $Y_1, \ldots, Y_n$ be i.i.d. in the density $f(y; \psi, \lambda)$ and let H_0 be the composite hypothesis that $(\psi, \lambda) \in \Omega_{\psi 0} \times \Omega_\lambda$ with alternative that $(\psi, \lambda) \in (\Omega_\psi - \Omega_{\psi 0}) \times \Omega_\lambda$. Show that the m.l. ratio criterion for testing H_0 is asymptotically equivalent to that for testing $H_{0\lambda}:(\psi,\lambda)\in\Omega_{\psi0}\times\{\lambda\}$ with the substitution $\lambda=\hat{\lambda}$ if and only if $\mathbf{i}_{.\psi\lambda}=0$. Comment on possible applications of this result.

Solution

It is implicitly understood that H_0 is a subspace hypothesis, i.e. that $\Omega_{\psi0}$ is a subspace of Ω_{ψ}. Suppose that ψ is isomorphic to (ξ,η) such that $\psi\in\Omega_{\psi0}$ implies $\xi=\xi_0$ and vice versa. Then write $\theta=(\xi,\eta,\lambda)$, and let $\phi=(\eta,\lambda)$, so that

$$\mathbf{i}_{.}(\theta)=\begin{bmatrix}\mathbf{i}_{.\xi\xi} & \mathbf{i}_{.\xi\phi}\\ \mathbf{i}_{.\xi\phi}^{T} & \mathbf{i}_{.\phi\phi}\end{bmatrix}.$$

We know that asymptotically the l.r. test statistic is equivalent to

$$W_e=(\hat{\xi}-\xi_0)^{T}\mathbf{i}_{.}(\hat{\xi}:\hat{\phi})(\hat{\xi}-\xi_0),$$

where

$$\mathbf{i}_{.}(\xi:\phi)=\mathbf{i}_{.\xi\xi}-\mathbf{i}_{.\xi\phi}\mathbf{i}_{.\phi\phi}^{-1}\mathbf{i}_{.\xi\phi}^{T}.$$

Also, the m.l.e. of $\psi=(\xi,\eta)$ when $\lambda=\hat{\lambda}$ is, of course, $\hat{\psi}$ so that the l.r. statistic with λ fixed at $\hat{\lambda}$ is

$$\tilde{W}_e=(\hat{\xi}-\xi_0)^{T}\mathbf{i}_{.}(\hat{\xi}:\hat{\eta})(\hat{\xi}-\xi_0),$$

where

$$\mathbf{i}_{.}(\xi:\eta)=\mathbf{i}_{.\xi\xi}-\mathbf{i}_{.\xi\eta}\mathbf{i}_{.\eta\eta}^{-1}\mathbf{i}_{.\xi\eta}^{T}.$$

The quadratic forms are equivalent if $\mathbf{i}_{.\xi\phi}\mathbf{i}_{.\phi\phi}^{-1}\mathbf{i}_{.\xi\phi}^{T}=\mathbf{i}_{.\xi\eta}\mathbf{i}_{.\eta\eta}^{-1}\mathbf{i}_{.\xi\eta}^{T}$, which implies that $\mathbf{i}_{.\psi\lambda}=0$. This is also a necessary condition as can be seen by expanding the left hand side, or by appeal to linear regression results. This result can be regarded as a substantial generalization of the result in regression theory that a partial regression coefficient has the variance of a total regression coefficient only under orthogonality.

Note that the condition $\mathbf{i}_{.\psi\lambda}=0$ implies a factorization of the asymptotically normal likelihood local to $\Omega_{\psi0}$ leading to cancellation of terms involving λ in the l.r.

The result is useful in situations where λ is easily estimated in Ω, as is often the case with scale parameters when ψ consists of location parameters.

A particular application in multivariate analysis is to the problem of testing that m mean vectors lie in q dimensions $(q<m)$, the special case $q=0$ corresponding to equality of the means. Treating the unrestricted m.l.e. of the covariance matrix as fixed leads to considerable simplification, and to the standard test based on canonical variates (Rao, Section 8c.6).

[*Theoretical Statistics*, Section 9.3; Rao, Section 6e; Silvey, Chapter 7]

9.15. Consider a discrete stationary stochastic process with r states, with M_{jk} the number of one-step transitions from state j to state k in a series of n consecutive observations. Show that the m.l. ratio statistic for testing the null hypothesis of serial independence against the alternative of first-order Markov dependence is asymptotically equivalent to the chi-squared statistic

$$T = \sum\sum \frac{(M_{jk} - \tilde{M}_{jk})^2}{\tilde{M}_{jk}},$$

where $\tilde{M}_{jk} = M_{j.}M_{.k}/(n-1)$. Derive the corresponding W_u statistic directly.

Solution

The transition counts M_{jk} correspond to Markov transition probabilities

$$\theta_{jk} = \operatorname{pr}(Y_i = k \mid Y_{i-1} = j)\,(j, k = 1, \ldots, r)$$

and the null hypothesis is $\theta_{jk} = \lambda_k$.
Let

$$M_{j.} = \sum_{k=1}^{r} M_{jk}, \quad M_{.k} = \sum_{j=1}^{r} M_{jk}$$

and let N_j be the frequency of state j in the sequence of the last $n-1$ observations. We suppose here that the first observation Y_1 is fixed, although this is irrelevant when n is very large. Then it is simple to show from

$$l(\theta) = \sum\sum M_{jk} \log \theta_{jk}$$

that $\hat{\theta}_{jk} = M_{jk}/M_{j.}$, whereas under the null hypothesis of independence $\hat{\theta}_{jk,0} = \hat{\lambda}_k = N_k/(n-1)$.

The likelihood ratio statistic is

$$\begin{aligned} W &= 2\{l(\hat{\theta}) - l(\hat{\theta}_0)\} \\ &= 2[\sum\sum M_{jk} \log(M_{jk}/M_{j.}) - \sum N_k \log\{N_k/(n-1)\}], \end{aligned}$$

and of course by our definition $N_k = M_{.k}$. Therefore

$$W = 2\sum\sum M_{jk} \log\left\{1 + \frac{(n-1)M_{jk} - M_{j.}M_{.k}}{M_{j.}M_{.k}}\right\}.$$

Expanding $\log(1+x) = x - \tfrac{1}{2}x^2 + O(x^3)$, using the equality $(n-1)\sum\sum M_{jk} = \sum M_{j.}\sum M_{.k}$ and the fact that under H_0

$$M_{jk}/M_{j.} = \lambda_k + o_p(1), \quad M_{.k}/(n-1) = \lambda_k + o_p(1)$$

imply $(n-1)M_{jk}/(M_{j.}M_{.k}) = 1 + o_p(1)$, we obtain

$$W = \sum\sum (M_{jk} - \tilde{M}_{jk})^2/\tilde{M}_{jk} + o_p(1) = T + o_p(1).$$

If the N_k were frequencies in the full sequence of length n, as is usual, another term $o_p(1)$ would appear and so leave the approximating chi-squared statistic unaltered. Standard theory for W shows that the limiting distribution of these equivalent statistics has $(r-1)^2$ degrees of freedom.

The statistic T is the score statistic W_u, whose direct derivation is very similar to that of the score statistic in Problem 9.11, making use of $U.(\hat{\theta}_0)$.

[*Theoretical Statistics*, Section 9.3; Rao, Section 6e; Silvey, Chapter 7; Anderson and Goodman, 1957]

9.16. In a regular parametric problem, a consistent estimate $T = t(Y)$ has a limiting $MN_q\{\theta, \mathbf{v}(\theta)\}$ distribution. Show that T and the m.l.e. $\hat{\theta}$ have a joint limiting normal distribution with cross-covariance matrix $\mathbf{i}^{-1}(\theta)$. Now for testing the null hypothesis $H_0 : \theta = \theta_0$ against the alternative $\theta \neq \theta_0$ consider the statistic W_T defined by

$$\exp(\tfrac{1}{2}W_T) = \text{lik}(T;Y)/\text{lik}(\theta_0;Y).$$

By comparing W_T with the m.l. ratio, show that the limiting distribution of W_T under H_0 is the same as that of

$$\sum_{j=1}^{q} Z_j^2 - \sum_{j=1}^{q} \alpha_j(\theta) Z_{q+j}^2,$$

where $Z_1, \ldots, Z_{2q}$ are i.i.d. in $N(0,1)$ and the $\alpha_j(\theta)$ are eigenvalues of $\mathbf{i}(\theta)\mathbf{v}(\theta) - \mathbf{I}$.

Suppose that $Y_1, \ldots, Y_n$ are i.i.d. with continuous density $f_Y(y;\theta)$, and that these continuous variables are grouped into m cells with corresponding probabilities $\pi_j(\theta)$ and frequencies $N_j, j = 1, \ldots, m$. Let $\hat{\theta}_Y$ be the m.l.e. obtained from the continuous data. Use arguments similar to those above to examine the limiting null distribution of the chi-squared goodness of fit statistic

$$\sum_{j=1}^{m} \frac{\{N_j - n\pi_j(\hat{\theta}_Y)\}^2}{n\pi_j(\hat{\theta}_Y)}.$$

Solution

We give only an outline solution omitting the mathematical details given in the references.

First suppose for simplicity that θ is a scalar. Then $aT + (1-a)\hat{\theta}$ has asymptotically, for any constant a, mean θ and variance $\{a^2 v(\theta) + 2a(1-a)\text{cov}(T,\hat{\theta}) + (1-a)^2/i.\}$. For this to have a minimum at $a = 0$ we must have $\text{cov}(T,\hat{\theta}) = 1/i$. Equivalently $T - \hat{\theta}$ and $\hat{\theta}$ are asymptotically uncorrelated.

To investigate W_T we have on expansion

$$W_T = 2[\{l_Y(T) - l_Y(\hat{\theta})\} + \{l_Y(\hat{\theta}) - l_Y(\theta_0)\}]$$
$$\sim (\hat{\theta} - \theta_0)^{\mathrm{T}} \mathbf{i}_.(\theta_0)(\hat{\theta} - \theta_0) - (T - \hat{\theta})^{\mathrm{T}} \mathbf{i}_.(\theta_0)(T - \hat{\theta}), \tag{1}$$

and by the argument in the first paragraph the second term is asymptotically independent of the first. We now apply the result (Rao, Section 8a) that if X is $MN(0, \mathbf{a})$, then $X^{\mathrm{T}} \mathbf{b} X = \Sigma \alpha_j Z_j^2$, where the Z_j are i.i.d. $N(0, 1)$ and the α_j are eigenvalues of $\mathbf{ba}$, taking $X^{\mathrm{T}} = (\hat{\theta}, T - \hat{\theta})^{\mathrm{T}}$ and $\mathbf{a} = \mathrm{diag}\{\mathbf{i}^{-1}(\theta), \mathbf{v}(\theta) - \mathbf{i}_.^{-1}(\theta)\}$.

This gives

$$W_T \sim \sum_{j=1}^{q} Z_j^2 - \sum_{k=1}^{q} \alpha_k Z_{q+k}^2, \tag{2}$$

with α_k the eigenvalues of $\mathbf{i}_.(\theta)\{\mathbf{v}(\theta) - \mathbf{i}_.^{-1}(\theta)\} = \mathbf{i}_.(\theta)\mathbf{v}(\theta) - \mathbf{I}$. Note that the eigenvalues α_k are non-negative, as is to be expected from the relation $W_T \leqslant W = Z_1^2 + \ldots + Z_q^2$.

To apply this approach to goodness of fit tests, suppose that we start from i.i.d. random variables $Y_1, \ldots, Y_n$ with p.d.f. $f(y; \theta)$. If we group these into m cells with probabilities $\pi_1(\theta), \ldots, \pi_m(\theta)$, a goodness of fit test can be based solely on the corresponding multinomial frequencies $N_1, \ldots, N_m$ and would use $\hat{\theta}_N$, the maximum likelihood estimate based solely on these frequencies.

The likelihood ratio statistic would then be, in an obvious notation,

$$W = 2[l_N(\hat{\pi}) - l_N\{\pi(\hat{\theta}_N)\}] = 2\Sigma N_j \log[N_j/\{n\pi_j(\hat{\theta}_N)\}],$$

with the asymptotically equivalent forms

$$W_u = \Sigma\{N_j - n\pi_j(\hat{\theta}_N)\}^2/\{n\pi_j(\hat{\theta}_N)\}$$
$$W_e \simeq \Sigma\{N_j - n\pi_j(\hat{\theta}_N)\}^2/N_j.$$

Each of these statistics has a limiting chi-squared distribution with $m - 1 - \dim(\theta)$ degrees of freedom.

It would often, however, be simpler and in principle better to estimate θ from the original Y's, for example to use the corresponding m.l.e. $\hat{\theta}_Y$. The apparent likelihood ratio statistic

$$\tilde{W} = 2[l_N(\hat{\pi}) - l_N\{\pi(\hat{\theta}_Y)\}],$$

or equivalent chi-squared statistics, have an asymptotic distribution not of the chi-squared form. By an expansion of $\tilde{W}$ similar to that in (1) we find that the limiting distribution of $\tilde{W}$ is of the form (2), depending on the eigenvalues of $\mathrm{var}(\hat{\theta}_Y)\{\mathrm{var}(\hat{\theta}_N)\}^{-1}$ and such that $\tilde{W} \geqslant W$. Watson (1958) discusses the situation where multinomial cell boundaries are estimated quantiles of the fitted distribution $f(y; \hat{\theta}_Y)$ and both he and Chernoff and Lehmann (1954) give detailed and rigorous discussions of the above points.

In general, the effect due to using $\hat{\theta}_N$ rather than $\hat{\theta}_Y$ is negligible, unless m is small, e.g. 3 or 4.

[*Theoretical Statistics*, Section 9.3; Rao, Sections 6b, 6e; Silvey, Chapter 7]

9.17*. Two random variables U and V taking non-negative integer values are called quasi-independent over a set $\mathscr{S}$ of values if for functions $\alpha(\cdot)$ and $\beta(\cdot)$

$$\mathrm{pr}(U = u, V = v) = \alpha(u)\beta(v) \quad (u, v \in \mathscr{S}).$$

A family of random variables $X^{(n)}$ and $Y^{(n)}$ taking values in $0 \leqslant x + y \leqslant n$ is called family (F)-independent if for fixed functions $\alpha'(\cdot), \beta'(\cdot), \gamma'(\cdot)$ and $\delta'(\cdot)$ not involving n

$$\mathrm{pr}(X^{(n)} = x, Y^{(n)} = y) = \alpha'(n)\beta'(x)\gamma'(y)\delta'(n - x - y)$$

for $n = 1, \ldots, N$. Discuss the relation between these definitions, giving examples where one is applicable and not the other.

Suggest how to test the null hypotheses of quasi-independence and F-independence.

Solution

Two discrete random variables Z and W are independent if for all z and w

$$\mathrm{pr}(Z = z, W = w) = \alpha''(z)\beta''(w);$$

the two definitions studied in this problem aim to generalize this notion. Quasi-independence is of most relevance in connexion with contingency tables (Goodman, 1968; Bishop *et al.*, 1975, Section 5.2), where the values u and v label the rows and columns of a two-dimensional table. Special cases arise when independence is expected to apply except for one cell, or for some small group of cells. Also if u represents an 'initial' state and v a 'final' state, independence may apply conditionally on movement having occurred; this leads to quasi-independence with $\mathscr{S}$ the set $\{u, v; u \neq v\}$.

F-independence is a more indirect notion, whose physical interpretation is less clear. Darroch (1971) has discussed in detail the derivation from requirements on the conditional distribution. Note that

$$\mathrm{pr}(X^{(n)} = x \mid Y^{(n)} = y) = \beta'(x)\delta'(n - x - y)\varepsilon'(n - y),$$

and so is a function only of x and $n - y$; there is a symmetrical property for the conditional distribution of $Y^{(n)}$ given $X^{(n)} = x$. In particular, for example, the definition implies that

$$\mathrm{pr}(X^{(10)} = 6 \mid Y^{(10)} = 2) = \mathrm{pr}(X^{(9)} = 6 \mid Y^{(9)} = 1) = \mathrm{pr}(X^{(8)} = 6 \mid Y^{(8)} = 0).$$

*Amended version

For example, let $X^{(n)}$ and $Y^{(n)}$ be the number of times out of n test periods in which the responses 'very good' and 'good' are observed, there being, perhaps, five distinct responses possible on each trial. The condition of F-independence is one special way in which the family of bivariate random variables might have interrelated distributions.

If $\delta'(\cdot) = 1$, then F-independence reduces to quasi-independence with $\mathcal{S} = \{(x,y); 0 \leqslant x + y \leqslant n\}$. In general, however, one kind of generalized independence does not imply the other.

To test consistency with these special models over some set of possible values, the maximum likelihood ratio can be found comparing a fit under the null hypothesis, maximized over the nuisance parameters, with that under an arbitrary multinomial distribution over the relevant lattice points.

To take a simple example, consider the null hypothesis of quasi-independence for the set $\{u, v; u \neq v\}$ in a $t \times t$ contingency table with cell frequencies N_{uv}. Under the null hypothesis the probabilities corresponding to diagonal cells are arbitrary, so that the m.l. estimates of expected frequencies for these cells are the observed frequencies. Because the same is true in general, we can disregard the diagonal cells. For the off-diagonal cells, the contribution to the total log likelihood is

$$\sum_{u} \sum_{v \neq u} N_{uv} \log \alpha(u) + \sum_{v} \sum_{u \neq v} N_{uv} \log \beta(v).$$

Thus the sufficient statistics are row and column sums omitting diagonal cells. The maximum likelihood estimates of expected cell frequencies are constrained to give the same sums, because the sufficient statistics are the m.l. estimates of their expectations for an exponential family distribution. The actual derivation of the m.l. estimates must proceed iteratively. If the resulting fitted frequencies are denoted $\tilde{N}_{uv}$, it follows that the m.l. ratio statistic is

$$W = 2 \sum_{u \neq v} N_{uv} \log(N_{uv}/\tilde{N}_{uv})$$

and the degrees of freedom are $(t - 1)(t - 1) - t = t^2 - 3t + 1$. This assumes that there are no other constraints on the table, such as fixed zeroes.

As in this example, iterative methods are usually necessary to obtain the m.l. estimates, and careful counting of degrees of freedom is called for. In the case of F-independence, the degrees of freedom are $\frac{1}{2}(n - 1)(n - 2)$ (Darroch and Ratcliff, 1973).

[*Theoretical Statistics*, Section 9.3(iii)]

9.18. Let $Z_1, \ldots, Z_n$ be i.i.d. in $N(\mu, \sigma^2)$, and let $Y_j = |Z_j|$. Show that using

Y the m.l. ratio test of $H_0 : \mu = 0$ against the alternatives $H_A : \mu \neq 0$, with σ^2 unknown, is asymptotically equivalent to that based on large values of $T = \Sigma Y_j^4 / (\Sigma Y_j^2)^2$. What is the limiting distribution of T?

Solution

The Y_j are i.i.d. with p.d.f. proportional to

$$\sigma^{-1} \exp\{ -\tfrac{1}{2}(y^2 + \mu^2)/\sigma^2 \} \cosh(y\mu/\sigma^2),$$

so that the log likelihood function is, apart from a constant,

$$l(\mu, \sigma^2) = -n\log\sigma - \frac{n\mu^2}{2\sigma^2} - \frac{\Sigma y_j^2}{2\sigma^2} + \Sigma\log\cosh(\mu y_j/\sigma^2).$$

It is easy to verify that for any μ, σ the maximum likelihood estimate is consistent for $|\mu|, \sigma$; of course $\pm|\mu|$ are equivalent in the likelihood function. The likelihood is not regular in the usual sense because the information matrix at $\mu = 0$ is not positive definite; in this parameterization $i_{.\mu\mu}(0, \sigma) = 0$. To obtain large-sample results requires expansion of the log likelihood to terms in $\mu^4, \mu^2\sigma^2$ and σ^4. This difficulty is avoided by reparameterizing to $\theta = (\xi, \tau) = (\mu^2, \sigma^2)$, for which the efficient scores are

$$U_{.\xi}(\theta) = -\frac{n}{2\tau} + \frac{1}{2\tau\sqrt{\xi}}\Sigma y_j \tanh(y_j\sqrt{\xi}/\tau),$$

$$U_{.\tau}(\theta) = -\frac{n}{2\tau} + \frac{n\xi}{2\tau^2} + \frac{\Sigma y_j^2}{2\tau^2} - \frac{\sqrt{\xi}}{\tau^2}\Sigma y_j \tanh(y_j\sqrt{\xi}/\tau).$$

One remaining difficulty is that under $H_0 : \xi = 0$, there is no open set in the parameter space surrounding the true parameter value; the information matrix is positive definite everywhere.

   Notice that at $\theta = (0, \tau)$

$$U_{.\xi} = U_{.\tau} = (\Sigma y_j^2 - n\tau)/(2\tau^2),$$

so that $(0, n^{-1}\Sigma y_j^2)$ is always a solution of the likelihood equation $U_{.} = 0$. However, this solution is only a local maximum if the second-derivative matrix for l is negative definite. Denoting second-order derivatives by $U_{.\xi\xi}$, etc., we find that at $\theta = (0, \tau)$

$$U_{.\xi\xi} = -\Sigma y_j^4/(3\tau^4), \; U_{.\xi\tau} = (n\tau - 2\Sigma y_j^2)/(2\tau^3),$$

$$U_{.\tau\tau} = (n\tau - 2\Sigma y_j^2)/(2\tau^3).$$

Clearly at $(0, \Sigma y_j^2/n)$ the second-derivative matrix for l is negative definite only if $3(\Sigma y_j^2)^2 < n\Sigma y_j^4$. In other cases there is a likelihood saddle-point at $(0, \Sigma y_j^2/n)$ and we must find the other local stationary point to obtain the m.l.e.

Further expansion of the likelihood equation gives, for small ξ,

$$0 = U_{.\xi}(\theta) = (\Sigma y_j^2 - n\tau)/(2\tau^2) - \xi\Sigma y_j^4/(6\tau^4) + O(\xi^2)$$

$$0 = U_{.\tau}(\theta) = -n/(2\tau) + n\xi/(2\tau^2) + \Sigma y_j^2/(2\tau^2)$$
$$- \xi\Sigma y_j^2/\tau^3 + \xi^2\Sigma y_j^4/(3\tau^5) + o(\xi^2),$$

the new solution being

$$\tilde{\xi} = (\Sigma y_j^2 - n\tilde{\tau})/n, \quad \tilde{\tau} = \Sigma y_j^4/(3n).$$

The log likelihood ratio statistic for testing $H_0 : \xi = 0$ is

$$W = 2\{l(\tilde{\xi}, \tilde{\tau}) - l(0, \hat{\tau}_0)\},$$

which is zero if $3(\Sigma y_j^2)^2 \leqslant n\Sigma y_j^4$. Expansion in the other case gives

$$W \simeq \tilde{\xi}^2 U_{.\xi\xi}(0, \hat{\tau}_0) + 2\tilde{\xi}(\hat{\tau} - \hat{\tau}_0)U_{.\xi\tau}(0, \hat{\tau}_0) + (\hat{\tau} - \hat{\tau}_0)^2 U_{.\tau\tau}(0, \hat{\tau}_0)$$

after some reduction, large values occurring for small values of $\hat{\tau}/\hat{\tau}_0 - 1$ $= [n\Sigma y_j^4/\{3(\Sigma y_j^2)^2\}]^{1/2} - 1$. The likelihood ratio test is, therefore, asymptotically equivalent to a test with critical region

$$w_\alpha = \{y : \frac{n\Sigma y_j^4}{3(\Sigma y_j^2)^2} < 1 - c_\alpha\}.$$

Note that the test statistic is the sample fourth cumulant, measuring kurtosis.

[*Theoretical Statistics*, Section 9.3; Rao, Section 6e; Silvey, Chapter 7; Hinkley, 1973]

9.20.* For the problem of testing $H_0 : \mu = 0$ versus $H_A : \mu \neq 0$ in the $N(\mu, \sigma^2)$ distribution with σ^2 unknown, compare numerically the exact distributional properties of the W_u and W_e statistics with the limiting chi-squared distribution. Derive second-order corrections for W_u and W_e based on first moments and determine numerically whether any improvement has been made over the first-order results.

Solution

The log likelihood function for $\theta = (\mu, \sigma^2)$ is

$$l(\theta) = \text{const} - \tfrac{1}{2}n \log \sigma^2 - \frac{1}{2\sigma^2}\Sigma(Y_j - \mu)^2,$$

*Problem 9.19 omitted.

from which standard calculations give

$$
U_{\cdot} = \begin{bmatrix} \dfrac{1}{\sigma^2}\Sigma(Y_j - \mu) \\[2em] -\dfrac{n}{\sigma^2} + \dfrac{1}{2\sigma^4}\Sigma(Y_j - \mu)^2 \end{bmatrix}, \quad \mathbf{i} = \mathrm{diag}(n/\sigma^2, \tfrac{1}{2}n/\sigma^4).
$$

The relevant estimators are $\hat{\mu} = \bar{Y}_{\cdot}, \hat{\sigma}^2 = \Sigma(Y_j - \bar{Y}_{\cdot})^2/n = \mathrm{ss}/n$, and, under $H_0 : \mu = 0, \hat{\sigma}_0^2 = (\mathrm{ss} + n\bar{Y}^2)/n$.

The general expressions for W_e and W_u may be written in this case

$$
W_e = n\hat{\mu}^2/\hat{\sigma}^2, \quad W_u = (n\bar{Y}_{\cdot}/\hat{\sigma}_0^2)^2 (\hat{\sigma}_0^2/n)
$$

so that if we define $T = \sqrt{\{n(n-1)/\mathrm{ss}\}}\,\bar{Y}_{\cdot}$, Student's t statistic, we have

$$
W_e = nT^2/(n-1), \quad W_u = nT^2\{1 + T^2/(n-1)\}^{-1}(n-1)^{-1}.
$$

For exact numerical comparisons with the limiting standard normal distributions of $\sqrt{W_e}$ and $\sqrt{W_u}$, take as an example the case $n = 10$ and $t = 2.262$, the two-sided 0.05 point of the Student t distribution on 9 degrees of freedom. The computed values of W_e and W_u are respectively 5.685 and 3.625, corresponding to chi-squared tail probabilities of 0.017 and 0.057. Clearly the asymptotic results are not very accurate especially for W_e. Note, incidentally, that W_u is not an increasing function of T^2.

To obtain corrections to W_e and W_u based on equating first moments to the mean of the limiting chi-squared distribution under H_0, we may use the facts that $E(T^2; H_0) = (n-1)/(n-3)$ and $E(T^4; H_0) = 3(n-1)^2/\{(n-3)(n-5)\}$. Then, clearly, $E(W_e; H_0) = n/(n-3)$, so that the mean-corrected version of W_e is $W_e^* = (n-3)W_e/n = (n-3)T^2/(n-1)$. For W_u, we expand first in a series in T^2, and find that

$$
E(W_u; H_0) = \frac{n}{n-1}E(T^2; H_0) - \frac{n}{(n-1)^2}E(T^4; H_0) + O(n^{-2})
$$

$$
= 1 + O(n^{-2}),
$$

so that $W_u^* = W_u$. These same results would appear without explicit use of the Student t distribution. For our single numerical example, the computed value of W_e^* is 3.98, corresponding to a chi-squared tail probability of 0.046. Thus $W_u^* = W_u$ and W_e^* would be reasonable for practical use in this case were the 'exact' solution not readily available, and provided that extreme tail probabilities are not required. A more extensive numerical study of this and other examples would be instructive.

In principle it is always desirable to examine the adequacy of approximations based on asymptotic theory, and consideration of second-order asymptotic theory is one valuable way of doing this.

[*Theoretical Statistics*, Section 9.3; Rao, Section 6e; Silvey, Chapter 7]

9.21. Use asymptotic methods to obtain confidence limits for both parameters in the model of Problem 4.13 and to test the adequacy of the model. Treat both parameters as unknown.

Solution

Apart from a constant, the log likelihood is

$$l(\mu, \rho) = T_1 \log \mu + T_2 \log \rho - \mu(1 - \rho^n)/(1 - \rho),$$

where $T_1 = \Sigma Y_j$ and $T_2 = \Sigma(j - 1) Y_j$. In principle, exact confidence limits for μ and ρ can be obtained respectively from the conditional distributions of T_1 given $T_2 = t_2$ and of T_2 given $T_1 = t_1$; see Chapters 5 and 7. For example, confidence limits for ρ consist of those extreme ρ_0 for which t_2 is not in the similar critical region for testing $H_0 : \rho = \rho_0$ against relevant alternatives.

Even so, consideration of asymptotic arguments might be required for simplicity, and in any case illustrates some instructive general points. The information matrix for the whole data is diagonal with leading element

$$E(-\partial^2 l/\partial \mu^2) = E(T_1)/\mu^2 = \sum_{r=0}^{n-1} \rho^r/\mu, \qquad (1)$$

there being a similar but slightly more complicated expression for the other diagonal element.

Note the following points.

(a) It is clear on general grounds, as well as from (1), that there is a difference between the cases $\rho \geqslant 1$ and $\rho < 1$, it being only in the former case that the total information is unbounded as $n \to \infty$.

(b) Equations for $\hat{\mu}$ and $\hat{\rho}$ are easily found, a non-linear equation for $\hat{\rho}$ resulting from elimination of $\hat{\mu}$. This equation simplifies considerably if one can recognise either $\rho^n \ll 1$ or $\rho^n \gg 1$.

(c) If $\rho \geqslant 1$, T_1 is asymptotically normal as $n \to \infty$. If $\rho < 1$, this does not follow directly from the central limit theorem applied to the non-identically distributed Y_j because $\text{var}(Y_n)/\text{var}(T_1)$ does not tend to zero; it does, however, follow immediately from the Poisson form of the distribution of T_1. Thus, with a consistent estimate of ρ available, confidence intervals for μ follow via (1).

(d) If $\rho < 1$, the total information is bounded as $n \to \infty$, the data ending with a long series of zeroes. Hence T_1 is not asymptotically normal as $n \to \infty$.

It may, however, be possible to justify a normal approximation via a notional series of problems in which $\mu \to \infty$ for fixed n; the crucial point is whether T_1 is large. Similar results apply to T_2. A detailed discussion for the similar models of the pure birth and pure death processes is given by Beyer *et al.* (1976).

To test goodness of fit, in principle we use the conditional distribution of the data given $T_1 = t_1$ and $T_2 = t_2$. One way of suggesting an appropriate test statistic, and of obtaining an approximate analysis useful when very few if any of the observations are zero, is to note that

$$E(\log Y_j) \sim \log \mu - (j-1)\log \rho, \text{var}(\log Y_j) \sim 1/E(Y_j) \sim 1/Y_j,$$

and hence to perform a weighted least squares analysis for linear regression of $\log Y_j$ on j. Linearity could be tested in the usual way by including a quadratic term, and the Poisson assumption could be tested via the residual weighted sum of squares.

[*Theoretical Statistics*, Section 9.3; Rao, Section 6e; Silvey, Chapter 7]

10 BAYESIAN METHODS

Summary

In previous chapters the unknown parameter θ is regarded as an unknown constant and methods are examined which are intended to perform well in repeated sampling whatever the true value of θ. In a Bayesian approach, on the other hand, θ is regarded as being the value of a random variable Θ having, in the absence of the data, a density $f_\Theta(\theta)$, the prior density, usually regarded as known. The model for the data specifies $f_{Y|\Theta}(y|\theta)$, the density of Y given $\Theta = \theta$.

Two advantages of the Bayesian approach are that the prior density provides a way of injecting further information into the analysis and that, given the above formulation, our final information about θ is summarized in the observed conditional density $f_{\Theta|Y}(\theta|y)$, called the posterior density. Since we are dealing with random variables, probability statements can be made and there is no need for special arguments and concepts. Difficulties with the Bayesian approach concern entirely the formulation; when is θ the value of a random variable with known prior density?

The mathematical problem of calculating $f_{\Theta|Y}(\theta|y)$ is solved by Bayes's theorem. For random variables, this is

$$f_{\Theta|Y}(\theta|y) = \frac{f_{Y|\Theta}(y|\theta)f_\Theta(\theta)}{f_Y(y)} = \frac{f_{Y|\Theta}(y|\theta)f_\Theta(\theta)}{\int f_{Y|\Theta}(y|t)f_\Theta(t)dt},$$

or simply

$$f_{\Theta|Y}(\theta|y) \propto f_{Y|\Theta}(y|\theta)f_\Theta(\theta).$$

Note that this depends on the data only through the observed likelihood function, so that inference does not depend on data that might have, but did not, occur, except in so far as these are needed implicitly to define the relevant densities.

When the model belongs to the exponential family, we can find a family of prior densities such that the posterior density is in the same family, with indexing constants modified in the light of the data. Such a family of priors is called conjugate, or closed under sampling, for the problem in question. Thus if $Y_1, \ldots, Y_n$ are i.i.d. with density $\exp\{a(\theta)b(y) + c(\theta) + d(y)\}$, we can take a prior density proportional to $\exp\{k_1 a(\theta) + k_2 c(\theta)\}$ and this covers many common problems.

The three main interpretations of prior density are (a) as frequency distributions, where there is a physical random mechanism generating the value θ; (b) as an objective measure of degree of rational belief, usually in an initial state of 'ignorance'; (c) as a subjective measure of what a particular individual, 'you', actually believes about θ. Possibility (a) is uncontroversial, but relatively rarely applicable. The other two approaches have extensive literatures. Approach (b) is attractive, but the idea of representing 'ignorance' raises formidable difficulties. It can be shown that for self-consistent manipulation of subjective probabilities, the usual laws of probability, including Bayes's theorem, are to be obeyed. The difficulties with this approach are partly that of assigning numerical probabilities especially in complex situations and partly that of dealing with vague subjective impressions and 'hard' information from data on an equal footing.

The Bayesian analogue of interval estimation involves specification of the posterior density of the unknown parameter, integrating out any nuisance parameters. Often this posterior density will be approximately normal.

One Bayesian analogue of significance testing involves attaching a non-zero prior probability that H_0 is exactly true and then computing the posterior odds in favour of H_0. This approach gives results quite different from those in sampling-theory significance tests.

In empirical Bayes problems, a prior frequency distribution is regarded as available and unknown, but to be estimated from relevant data.

Problems

10.1. Consider $n_1 + n_2$ experimental units, the jth being characterized by an unknown control value y_j and an unknown treatment value $z_j = y_j + \theta$. It is possible to observe either the control or the treatment value on a particular unit, but not both. Suppose that n_1 units are assigned to the control at random. Derive the likelihood function and describe its information content for θ. Now suppose that the y_j are a random sample from the p.d.f. $f(y)$, and that Θ has a prior density $g(\theta)$. Show that the posterior distribution of Θ is not the same as the prior distribution, even though no information about θ can be derived from the likelihood alone without appeal to ideas of repeated sampling.

Solution

Let $A_j = 1$ or 0 according as the jth individual is in the treatment or control group, and let X_j be the observed response. Then there are $\binom{n_1 + n_2}{n_1}$ possible vectors $(A_1, \ldots, A_{n_1 + n_2})$, which under the randomization assumption are all equally likely. The probability model is

$$\text{pr}(A = a, X = x \mid Y = y, \theta) = \begin{cases} \binom{n_1 + n_2}{n_1}^{-1} & (x_j = y_j + a_j\theta; j = 1, \ldots, n_1 + n_2), \\ 0 & \text{otherwise.} \end{cases}$$

Since the y_j are unknown, except for those directly observed, they have to be treated as parameters at this stage. The likelihood function is constant for all admissible θ values of $x - y$.

Note that the assumption above of a prior density on Θ provides no interaction with the likelihood unless a prior distribution is assumed also for Y. If the values of Y are assumed independent, with p.d.f. $f(y)$, often a physically unreasonable assumption, and if Θ independently has prior p.d.f. $g(\theta)$, then the joint p.d.f. of (A, X, Y) is

$$\binom{n_1 + n_2}{n_1}^{-1} \left\{ \prod_{j-1}^{n_1 + n_2} f(x_j - a_j\theta) \right\} g(\theta) \prod_{j:a_j = 1} \delta(y_j, x_j - \theta),$$

so that the posterior density of (Θ, Y) given $A = a, X = x$ is proportional to

$$g(\theta) \prod_{j:a_j = 1} f(x_j - \theta)\delta(y_j, x_j - \theta).$$

Integration over the y's gives the posterior density of Θ as proportional to

$$g(\theta) \prod_{j:a_j = 1} f(x_j - \theta),$$

which would be obtained directly from the assumption that treatment responses X are i.i.d. with p.d.f. $f(x - \theta)$. The posterior and prior distributions on Θ are different; an extra assumption about the observations has been included over and above the simple randomization model. Note that the randomization plays no part in the posterior distribution. If only the p.d.f. on Y is assumed, a 'marginal' likelihood for Θ is obtained as

$$\int \text{pr}(A = a, X = x \mid Y = y, \theta) \prod_{j=1}^{n} f(y_j)dy_j = \binom{n_1 + n_2}{n_1}^{-1} \prod_{j=1}^{n} f(x_j - a_j\theta),$$

proportional to $\prod_{j:a_j = 1} f(x_j - \theta)$, the conventional form of the likelihood.

A more realistic analysis of this problem would require the Y_j to have p.d.f. $f(y - \gamma)$ with γ unknown, or would treat the density as unknown.

The example illustrates some of the difficulties of accommodating the important practical device of randomization within some kinds of statistical formalism. The point is partly that approaches, such as the Bayesian one, which require a rather full specification of the problem, tend not to need randomization; rather randomization is concerned with making reasonable those assumptions that are made automatically in the Bayesian formulation. For discussion of randomization in a Bayesian setting, see also Stone (1969). The role of randomization is seen more clearly in the sampling theory approach, in particular in connexion with tests of significance. It is necessary in the sampling approach that the design actually used is not distinguishable in an important respect from the reference set of designs used in calculating probabilities.

[*Theoretical Statistics*, Section 10.2; Rao, Section 5b.1; Silvey, Section 9.6; Lindley, p.21, 35 et seq.]

10.2.* Let Y be the number of 'ones' in n observations corresponding to random sampling without replacement from a finite population of size m containing θ 'ones'. Thus Y has a hypergeometric distribution. Suppose further that the prior distribution of Θ is itself hypergeometric. Obtain the posterior distribution of $\Theta - y$, the number of 'ones' remaining in the population, given $Y = y$. Show that in a special limiting case the resulting posterior does not depend on y. Explain the physical basis of this last result and comment on its implications for acceptance sampling.

Solution

The hypergeometric distribution of Y given $\Theta = \theta$ is

$$\text{pr}(Y = y | \Theta = \theta) = \binom{\theta}{y}\binom{m-\theta}{n-y} \Big/ \binom{m}{n} \quad (0 \leqslant y \leqslant \theta; 0 \leqslant n - y \leqslant m - \theta).$$

Take the hypergeometric prior distribution to be of the form

$$\text{pr}(\Theta = \theta) = \binom{m}{\theta}\binom{A-m}{B-\theta} \Big/ \binom{A}{B} \quad (0 \leqslant \theta \leqslant m).$$

Then by Bayes's theorem

$$\text{pr}(\Theta = \alpha + y | Y = y) \propto \binom{\alpha+y}{y}\binom{m-\alpha-y}{n-y}\binom{m}{\alpha+y}\binom{A-m}{B-\alpha-y}$$

*Amended version.

$$= \frac{m!(A-m)!}{\alpha!y!(n-y)!(m-n-\alpha)!(B-\alpha-y)!(A-m-B+\alpha+y)!}.$$

This will be independent of y only when $A, B \to \infty$ with $A/B = \gamma$, in which case Θ has a binomial prior distribution.

In the context of acceptance sampling, if a lot of size m is a random selection from an effectively infinite population with known proportion of 'ones', then sampling without replacement from the lot gives no additional information about the unsampled units in that particular lot; the 'ones' occur totally randomly.

[*Theoretical Statistics*, Section 10.2; Rao, Section 5b.1; Silvey, Chapter 10; Lindley, p. 24; Mood, 1943]

10.4*. Let $Y_{jk}(j = 1,\dots,m; k = 1,\dots,r)$ follow a normal-theory components of variance model, i.e. $Y_{jk} = \mu + \eta_j + \varepsilon_{jk}$, where the η_j's and ε_{jk}'s are independently normally distributed with zero means and variances respectively σ_b^2 and σ_w^2. Define $\sigma^2 = r\sigma_b^2 + \sigma_w^2$. The minimal sufficient statistic is, in the usual notation, $(\bar{Y}_{..}, \mathrm{ss}_b, \mathrm{ss}_w)$. Two Bayesian analyses are contemplated for μ, in the first of which only $(\bar{Y}_{..}, \mathrm{ss}_b)$ is to be used. Explain why the exclusion of ss_w might be thought to be sensible, and why this is incorrect.

In the first analysis using $(\bar{Y}_{..}, \mathrm{ss}_b)$, the prior density is taken to be proportional to $d\mu d\sigma/\sigma, \sigma_w$ not being involved. Deduce that the posterior distribution of μ is proportional to the Student t distribution with $m-1$ degrees of freedom. The second analysis uses the full minimal sufficient statistic with prior density proportional to $d\mu d\sigma_w d\sigma/(\sigma_w \sigma)$ over the region $\sigma \geqslant \sigma_w$. Prove that this leads to a more dispersed posterior distribution for μ than the first analysis.

Comment on the surprising aspects of this last result and its implications for the consistent choice of improper distributions.

Solution

We have $Y_{jk} = \mu + \eta_j + \varepsilon_{jk}(j = 1,\dots,m; k = 1,\dots,r)$, where the η_j are independently $N(0,\sigma_b^2)$ and the ε_{jk} are independently $N(0,\sigma_w^2)$; this is the random effects model of analysis of variance. For the derivation of the minimal sufficient static $(\bar{Y}_{..}, \mathrm{ss}_b, \mathrm{ss}_w)$, see Problem 2.4.

With the definition $\sigma^2 = r\sigma_b^2 + \sigma_w^2$, we have that

$$f_{\bar{Y}_{..}, \mathrm{ss}_b, \mathrm{ss}_w}(\bar{y}_{..}, \mathrm{ss}_b, \mathrm{ss}_w; \mu, \sigma_b^2, \sigma_w^2) = f_{\bar{Y}_{..}, \mathrm{ss}_b}(\bar{y}_{..}, \mathrm{ss}_b; \mu, \sigma^2) f_{\mathrm{ss}_w}(\mathrm{ss}_w; \sigma_w^2). \quad (1)$$

In fact $(\bar{Y}_{..}, \mathrm{ss}_b, \mathrm{ss}_w)$ are independent, $\bar{Y}_{..}$ being $N\{\mu, \sigma^2/(rm)\}, \mathrm{ss}_b = \sigma^2 \chi_{m-1}^2$

---

* Problem 10.3 omitted.

and $ss_w = \sigma_w^2 \chi^2_{mr-m.}$. These results form the basis of classical analysis of variance, in which in particular confidence intervals for μ are based on the Student t distribution of

$$T = \sqrt{(rm)}(\bar{Y}_{..} - \mu)/\{ss_b/(m-1)\}^{1/2}. \tag{2}$$

Now the factorization (1) would make ss_w ancillary in the extended sense for μ were the parameter space unconstrained. However, $\sigma^2 \geqslant \sigma_w^2$. It is therefore plausible that the information about σ_w^2 contained in ss_w can be used in inference about σ^2.

In the first analysis, $d\mu d\sigma/\sigma$ is the conventional, but improper, invariant prior. A standard calculation shows that

$$f_{M|\bar{Y}_{..},SS_b}(\mu|\bar{y}_{..}, ss_b) \propto g_{m-1}(t), \tag{3}$$

where $g_d(\cdot)$ is the Student t density on d degrees of freedom, and t is given by (2) above.

In the second analysis, with prior density $d\mu d\sigma_w d\sigma/(\sigma_w \sigma)$ restricted to $\sigma \geqslant \sigma_w$, information from ss_w enters through the inequality. The complete likelihood function gives the posterior density proportional to

$$\sigma^{-m-1}\sigma_w^{-(r-1)m-1}\exp\left\{-\frac{rm(\bar{y}_{..}-\mu)^2}{2\sigma^2} - \frac{ss_w}{2\sigma_w^2} - \frac{ss_b}{2\sigma^2}\right\}.$$

We now have to integrate out σ and σ_w, and it is convenient to change variables to

$$u = \frac{rm(\bar{y}_{..}-\mu)^2 + ss_b}{2\sigma^2}, \quad v = \frac{ss_w}{2\sigma_w^2}.$$

The Jacobian is

$$\left|\frac{\partial(u,v)}{\partial(\sigma,\sigma_w)}\right| = \frac{\partial u}{\partial \sigma}\frac{\partial v}{\partial \sigma_w} = \frac{4uv}{\sigma\sigma_w},$$

so that, for $v/u \geqslant ss_w\{rm(\bar{y}-\mu)^2 + ss_b\}^{-1}$, $f_{M,U,V}(\mu,u,v|\bar{y}_{..}, ss_b, ss_w)$ is proportional to

$$\{rm(\bar{y}_{..}-\mu)^2 + ss_b\}^{-\frac{1}{2}m}ss_w^{-\frac{1}{2}m(r-1)}u^{-\frac{1}{2}m-1}v^{-\frac{1}{2}m(r-1)-1}e^{-u-v}$$
$$= ss_b^{-\frac{1}{2}m}ss_w^{-\frac{1}{2}m(r-1)}\{1 + t^2/(m-1)\}^{-\frac{1}{2}m}u^{-\frac{1}{2}m-1}v^{-\frac{1}{2}m(r-1)}e^{-u-v}.$$

The integral with respect to u and v is proportional to

$$h[(ss_b/ss_w)\{1 + t^2/(m-1)\}],$$

where

$$h(x) = \int_0^x z^{\frac{1}{2}(m-1)}(1+z)^{-\frac{1}{2}rm}dz$$

is an increasing function of x. Therefore

$$f_{M|\bar{Y}_{..},SS_b,SS_w}(\mu \,|\, \bar{y}_{..}, SS_b, SS_w) \propto g_{m-1}(t)h[(SS_b/SS_w)\{1 + t^2/(m-1)\}].$$

This last result is surprising in the sense that it is a more dispersed density than (3), both being centred at $\bar{y}_{..}$. One's feeling is that inclusion of SS_w in the analysis should produce a sharper inference about μ, e.g. shorter confidence intervals, but the reverse has occurred. Two points are relevant here (Stone and Springer, 1965). First, the choice of prior in the second analysis effectively makes SS_b/SS_w equal to zero with unconditional probability 1. Secondly, a more 'natural' prior for σ_w given σ and μ is uniform on $[0, \sigma]$, and this removes the paradox. The central point is that choice of objective prior distributions is non-trivial if inconsistency is to be avoided. For further important results on this, see Stone and Dawid (1972) and Dawid *et al.* (1973).

[*Theoretical Statistics*, Sections 10.3 and 10.4; Rao, Section 5b.1; Silvey, Chapter 10; Lindley, p. 55]

10.5. Let Y be a $N(\mu, \sigma_0^2)$ variable. Contrast the posterior expected values of μ given $Y = y$ for large y when the priors are the standard normal and standard Student t distributions.

Solution

If the prior distribution of M is $N(\xi_0, v_0)$, then the posterior distribution of M given y has mean $(y/\sigma_0^2 + \xi_0/v_0)/(1/\sigma_0^2 + 1/v_0)$. Hence

$$E(M \,|\, Y = y) - y = -\sigma_0^2(y - \xi_0)/(\sigma_0^2 + v_0),$$

which is unbounded as a function of y. This fact is sometimes regarded as an argument against the normal prior; in particular erroneous specification of ξ_0 can lead to very substantial deviations from μ in the posterior mean.

If the prior density of M is $f(\mu)$, say of mean zero, and Y is $N(\mu, 1)$ with density $\phi(y - \mu)$, we have

$$E(M \,|\, Y = y) - y = -\int wf(y - w)\phi(w)dw \Big/ \int f(y - w)\phi(w)dw. \qquad (1)$$

It can now be shown that under suitable conditions on the prior density $f(\cdot)$ the right-hand side of (1) tends to zero as $|y|$ increases.

The following outlines the proof in the special case $f(w) \propto (1 + w^2)^{-a}$.

To evaluate the numerator of (1), consider

$$\int w f(y-w)\phi(w)dw - f(y)\int w\phi(w)dw$$

$$= f(y)\int w\phi(w)\left[\frac{(1+y^2)^a}{\{1+(y-w)^2\}^a} - 1\right]dw. \qquad (2)$$

It is not too difficult to show that the integral on the right-hand side of (2) tends to zero as $y \to \infty$. For this, suppose that $y > 0$ and note that:

(i) for $|w| \leqslant B$ the term in square brackets is arbitrarily small by choice of y;

(ii) for $w < -B$ this term is between -1 and 0 and the integral therefore small by choice of B;

(iii) for $w > B$ the term has a maximum of order w^{2a}, and therefore the integral is arbitrarily small by a suitable choice of B.

A similar result holds for the denominator of (1) and it follows that $E(M|Y=y) - y$ tends to zero as $y \to \infty$.

The results of Dawid (1973) are far more general, and include the following interesting conclusions:

(a) for the situation considered here the whole posterior distribution of M tends to $f(\mu - y)$, f being the Student t density;

(b) if $Y - \mu$ has a Student t distribution and M has prior p.d.f. $\phi(\mu - \xi_0)$, then for large y, $E(M|Y=y) \sim E(M) = \xi_0$.

[*Theoretical Statistics*, Section 10.4; Rao, Section 5b.1]

10.6. Comment critically on the following discussion of the connexion between the subjective and the frequency interpretations of probability. Let $A_1, \ldots, A_n$ be uncertain events from a large number n of quite separate situations, e.g. from separate fields of study. Suppose that they all have for 'you' approximately the same subjective probability p. Further let F be the event that the proportion of $A_1, \ldots, A_n$ that are true is between $p - \varepsilon$ and $p + \varepsilon$, for some fixed small ε, e.g. $\varepsilon = 10^{-2}$. Then

(i) because the A_j refer to different situations, it is reasonable for 'you' to treat them as independent;

(ii) because subjective probability obeys the ordinary laws of probability, the weak law of large numbers implies that for large enough n the subjective probability of F is close to one;

(iii) therefore 'you' should, to be consistent, be prepared to bet heavily that F is true, i.e. that your subjective probabilities have a hypothetical frequency interpretation.

Solution

(i) That there is a connexion between subjective probability and frequency is part of the theory of subjective probability as given, for example, by de Finetti (1972). In one sense the argument, as stated, is a version of this.

(ii) The conventional treatment of subjective probability puts emphasis on measuring how 'you' feel about the occurrence of an event A, without asking 'why'. A more nearly normative theory of subjective probability suggests that one should find a number of events thought for some rational reason to have about the same probability as A and then find what proportion of these events in fact occur, in order to measure the subjective probability of A. This is the reverse of de Finetti's approach.

(iii) There remains something paradoxical in the idea that just because a series of unrelated events are thought by 'you' to have about the same subjective probability, this implies a strong belief about a rather strange empirical event in the real world, namely F.

[*Theoretical Statistics*, Section 10.4; Lindley, Section 2]

10.7*. An observation y is associated with a constant θ such that y is represented by a random variable Y with density $f(y;\theta)$. In repeated experimentation, the successive values of θ have a known frequency distribution, so that a particular θ may be represented by the random variable Θ with this distribution. A $1-\alpha$ confidence region $\mathcal{R}_\alpha(y)$ for the value θ associated with y is to be such that the doubly unconditional probability $\mathrm{pr}\{\Theta\in\mathcal{R}_\alpha(Y)\}$ is equal to $1-\alpha$. The optimal confidence region is said to be that with smallest expected area. Apply the general Neyman-Pearson lemma of Problem 4.2 to show that the optimal confidence region is

$$\{\theta : f_{\Theta|Y}(\theta|y) \geq k_\alpha\},$$

where k_α corresponds to the confidence level $1-\alpha$.

Solution

Let the marginal p.d.f. of Y be $g(y)$, so that the joint p.d.f. of (Y,θ) is $g(y)f(\theta|y)$. Let w be the region in $\Omega\times\mathcal{Y}$ obtained by associating with each possible $y\in\mathcal{Y}$ the relevant confidence region $\mathcal{R}_\alpha(y)$. Then we aim to minimize $\int_w g(y)d\theta dy$ subject to $\int_w g(y)f(\theta|y)d\theta dy = 1-\alpha$. In terms of the generalized Neyman-Pearson lemma of Problem 4.2 we wish to maximize $\int_{\bar{w}} g(y)d\theta dy$ subject to $\int_{\bar{w}} g(y)f(\theta|y)d\theta dy = \alpha$ and the solution is

$$\bar{w} = \{(y,\theta):g(y) \geq k_\alpha^{-1}g(y)f(\theta|y)\}.$$
$$w = \{(y,\theta):f(\theta|y) \geq k_\alpha\}.$$

*Amended version.

It is important that k_α is a constant, independent of y. The confidence region for fixed y is thus a so-called Highest Posterior Density region, but its size is a function of y, say $1 - \alpha(y)$, where $\int \alpha(y)g(y)dy = \alpha$. For observations y that are relatively uninformative about θ the confidence region may be very large, even the whole parameter space. The assignment of the unconditional level α to such a procedure violates the likelihood principle.

Further details together with some examples may be found in Neyman (1952).

[*Theoretical Statistics*, Section 10.5; Silvey, Section 10.3; Lindley, p. 18]

10.8. A Poisson process of known rate ρ is observed in continuous time. The prior p.d.f. of P is

$$\frac{t_0(t_0\rho)^{n_0-1}e^{-t_0\rho}}{\Gamma(n_0)}.$$

It is observed that the nth event occurs at time t. Obtain the posterior p.d.f. of P. Prove that the probability that the subsequent interval $(t, t + h)$ contains no events is $(t_0 + t)^{n_0+n}/(t_0 + t + h)^{n_0+n}$. For what values of (t_0, n_0) does the posterior distribution of P give answers agreeing formally with those obtained by confidence interval arguments?

Solution

Bayes's theorem gives

$$f_{P|Y}(\rho|y) \propto f_P(\rho)f_{Y|P}(y|\rho) = \frac{t_0(t_0\rho)^{n_0-1}e^{-\rho t_0}}{\Gamma(n_0)} \cdot \frac{\rho(\rho t)^{n-1}e^{-\rho t}}{\Gamma(n)}.$$

Thus, after normalization, we have

$$f_{P|Y}(\rho|y) = (t_0 + t)^{n+n_0}\rho^{n+n_0-1}e^{-\rho(t+t_0)}/\Gamma(n_0 + n),$$

again a gamma distribution. For the event $\mathscr{E}_0$ of zero events in the interval $(t, t + h)$ we then obtain

$$\text{pr}(\mathscr{E}_0|y) = \int_0^\infty \text{pr}(\mathscr{E}_0|\rho, y)f_{P|Y}(\rho|y)d\rho = \int_0^\infty e^{-\rho h}f_{P|Y}(\rho|y)d\rho$$

$$= \{(t + t_0)/(t + t_0 + h)\}^{n+n_0},$$

this following, for example, from the formula for the moment generating function of the gamma distribution.

Because the observations are specified in terms of the random interval, T_n, to the nth event, the confidence interval approach to prediction is in terms of the interval $X\dagger$, say, to the next event after t. Thus $T_n = X_1 + \ldots + X_n$ and is sufficient, where $X_1, \ldots, X_n, X\dagger$ are i.i.d. and exponentially distributed with parameter ρ. The simplest approach is now to note that $R = X\dagger/T_n$ has a distribution not involving ρ and it now follows from first principles, or from the relation with the variance ratio distribution, that

$$\operatorname{pr}(R > r) = \int_0^\infty e^{-ru} \frac{u^{n-1}e^{-u}}{\Gamma(n)} \, du = (1+r)^{-n}.$$

Thus a lower limit for $X\dagger$ at level α is $h = r_\alpha^* t$, where $(1 + r_\alpha^*)^{-n} = 1 - \alpha$; i.e. $\alpha = 1 - (1 + h/t)^{-n}$. This agrees formally with the Bayesian solution with $t_0 = n_0 = 0$, i.e. for the improper prior $f_P(\rho) \propto \rho^{-1}$. Such agreement is a common feature of scale parameter problems.

[*Theoretical Statistics*, Sections 10.5, 7.5; Rao, Sections 5b.1, 2; Lindley, Section 9]

10.10. Let y_1 and y_2 be the numbers of successes in sets of n_1 and n_2 Bernoulli trials, the corresponding probabilities of success being θ_1 and θ_2. Suppose that the sharp hypothesis $H_0 : \theta_1 = \theta_2$ has positive prior probability and that if H_0 is not true then Θ_1 and Θ_2 have independent beta prior distributions. Using a suitable prior distribution for the nuisance parameter when H_0 is true, calculate the ratio of the posterior and prior odds of H_0.

Solution

The general theory relevant to this problem may be summarized as follows. Suppose that θ is expressed as (ψ, λ) such that H_0 specifies that $\psi = \psi_0$. Let the free parameter Λ have prior density $p_0(\lambda)$ under H_0, and suppose that under the alternative hypothesis, $H_A, (\Psi, \Lambda)$ has prior density $p_A(\psi, \lambda)$. Then application of Bayes's theorem gives

$$\frac{\operatorname{pr}(H_0 \mid Y = y)}{\operatorname{pr}(H_A \mid Y = y)} = \frac{\operatorname{pr}(H_0)}{\operatorname{pr}(H_A)} \times \frac{\int p_0(\lambda) f_{Y\mid\Psi,\Lambda}(y \mid \psi_0, \lambda) d\lambda}{\iint_{\psi \neq \psi_0} p_A(\psi, \lambda) f_{Y\mid\Psi,\Lambda}(y \mid \psi, \lambda) d\psi d\lambda}. \tag{1}$$

Under the reasonable assumption that the prior density of Λ is continuous at $\psi = \psi_0$, in particular that $p_0(\lambda) \propto p_A(\psi_0, \lambda)$, (1) simplifies to

$$\text{posterior odds} = \text{prior odds} \times \frac{f_{\Psi|Y,H_A}(\psi_0|y, H_A)}{f_{\Psi|H_A}(\psi_0|H_A)}, \qquad (2)$$

where the posterior densities are limits as $\psi \to \psi_0$.

In this particular case, under the alternative hypothesis we take a conjugate prior density on (Θ_1, Θ_2) of the form

$$p_A(\theta_1, \theta_2) \propto \theta_1^{a_{11}-1}(1-\theta_1)^{a_{12}-1}\theta_2^{a_{21}-1}(1-\theta_2)^{a_{22}-1},$$

the particular choice of a_{ij} depending on the application. For n_{i1} 'successes' in sample i and n_{i2} 'failures' in sample $i (i = 1, 2)$, the analysis involves the posterior p.d.f.

$$f_{\Theta|Y,H_A}(\theta|n, H_A) = \frac{\prod_{i=1}^{2} \theta_i^{m_{i1}-1}(1-\theta_i)^{m_{i2}-1}}{B(m_{11}, m_{12})B(m_{21}, m_{22})},$$

where $m_{ij} = a_{ij} + n_{ij}$ and $B(.,.)$ is the beta function.

It turns out that the exact form of the test depends on the choice of parametrization (ψ, λ). Two possible choices will illustrate this phenomenon, namely (i) $\psi = \theta_1 - \theta_2, \lambda = \frac{1}{2}(\theta_1 + \theta_2)$ and (ii) $\theta_1 = (1 + \psi\lambda)^{-1}, \theta_2 = (1 + \lambda)^{-1}$, the latter corresponding to an analysis on the log odds (natural parameter) scale.

For case (i), the Jacobian of the transformation is unity, so that the joint posterior of (Ψ, Λ) under H_A at $\psi = 0$ is

$$f_{\Psi\Lambda|Y,H_A}(0, \lambda|y, H_A) = \frac{\lambda^{m_{.1}-2}(1-\lambda)^{m_{.2}-2}}{B(m_{11}, m_{12})B(m_{21}, m_{22})},$$

where $m_{.i} = m_{1i} + m_{2i}$.

Consequently, by integrating with respect to λ over $0 \leqslant \lambda \leqslant 1$,

$$f_{\Psi|Y,H_A}(0|y, H_A) = \frac{B(m_{.1} - 1, m_{.2} - 1)}{B(m_{11}, m_{12})B(m_{21}, m_{22})}.$$

It follows from (2) that the posterior odds of H_0 versus H_A are

$$\frac{p_0}{1-p_0} \times \frac{B(m_{.1} - 1, m_{.2} - 1)}{B(m_{11}, m_{12})B(m_{21}, m_{22})} \times \frac{B(a_{11}, a_{12})B(a_{21}, a_{22})}{B(a_{.1} - 1, a_{.2} - 1)}.$$

In case (ii), the Jacobian of the transformation is

$$|J| = \left|\frac{\partial(\theta_1, \theta_2)}{\partial(\psi, \lambda)}\right| = \lambda(1 + \psi\lambda)^{-2}(1 + \lambda)^{-2},$$

so that

$$f_{\Psi,\Lambda|Y,H_A}(0,\lambda\,|\,y,H_A) = \frac{(1+\lambda)^{-m_{..}}\lambda^{m_{.2}-1}}{B(m_{11},m_{12})B(m_{21},m_{22})}.$$

Integration with respect to λ over $(0,\infty)$ gives

$$f_{\Psi|Y,H_A}(0\,|\,y,H_A) = \frac{B(m_{.1},m_{.2})}{B(m_{11},m_{12})B(m_{21},m_{22})},$$

which differs from the result in case (i), and consequently gives different posterior odds for H_0.

In some ways the second analysis is preferable, at least in the sense that the log odds ratio is a natural parameterization. But it is conceptually disturbing that the answer is not unique, and that in the present case substantial numerical disagreement between the solutions is possible. A similar phenomenon occurs in the Student problem, where tests of $H_0 : \mu = 0$ and $H_0' : \mu/\sigma = 0$ yield different solutions. The phenomenon is discussed by Dickey (1971).

[*Theoretical Statistics*, Section 10.5; Lindley, p. 30 et seq.]

10.11. Suppose that there are two alternative models for the vector random variable Y, both models containing nuisance parameters. Denote the corresponding p.d.f.'s by $g(y\,;\phi)$ and $h(y\,;\chi)$. Let the prior probabilities of the models be π_g and π_h and, conditionally on the correctness of the relevant model, let the prior p.d.f.'s of Φ and X be $p_g(\phi)$ and $p_h(\chi)$. Adopt an asymptotic Bayesian argument to show that the ratio of the posterior probabilities of the two models is approximately

$$\frac{\pi_g}{\pi_h} \times \frac{g(y\,;\hat{\phi})}{h(y\,;\hat{\chi})} \times \frac{(2\pi)^{\frac{1}{2}q_g}}{(2\pi)^{\frac{1}{2}q_h}} \times \frac{p_g(\hat{\phi})}{p_h(\hat{\chi})} \times \frac{\Delta_\phi^{-\frac{1}{2}}}{\Delta_\chi^{-\frac{1}{2}}},$$

where Δ_ϕ and Δ_χ are the information determinants associated with the estimation of ϕ and χ, and q_g and q_h are the dimensions of the parameters.

Examine, in particular, the special case where both models are normal-theory linear models with known variance.

Comment on the difficulties of assigning a numerical value to $p_g(\hat{\phi})/p_h(\hat{\chi})$. Produce some justification for this ratio being approximately proportional to $(\Delta_\phi/\Delta_\chi)^{1/2}$, at least when the degrees of freedom in the two models are equal.

Solution

The ratio of the posterior probabilities of the two models is

$$\frac{\pi_g \int\limits_{-\infty}^{\infty} g(y;\phi)p_g(\phi)d\phi}{\pi_h \int\limits_{-\infty}^{\infty} h(y;\chi)p_h(\chi)d\chi}. \tag{1}$$

A central result of asymptotic theory is that when the number n of component observations is large the log likelihood is quadratic in the neighbourhood of the maximum and in fact

$$\log g(y;\phi) = \log g(y;\hat{\phi}) - \tfrac{1}{2}(\phi - \hat{\phi})^{\mathrm{T}}\mathscr{I}_g(\phi - \hat{\phi}) + o(\|\phi - \hat{\phi}\|^2),$$

$$\log h(y;\chi) = \log h(y;\hat{\chi}) - \tfrac{1}{2}(\chi - \hat{\chi})^{\mathrm{T}}\mathscr{I}_h(\chi - \hat{\chi}) + o(\|\chi - \hat{\chi}\|^2),$$

and $\mathscr{I}_g$ and $\mathscr{I}_h$ are the matrices of minus the second derivatives evaluated at the maximum, and are typically of order n. We can treat $p_g(\phi)$ and $p_h(\chi)$ as approximately constant if (i) they are continuous and non-zero at the true value and (ii) they satisfy a weak condition on their behaviour where the other factor in the integrands in (1) are small. Thus the numerator, for example, is approximately

$$\pi_g p_g(\hat{\phi}) \int\limits_{-\infty}^{\infty} \exp\{-\tfrac{1}{2}(\phi - \hat{\phi})^{\mathrm{T}}\mathscr{I}_g(\phi - \hat{\phi})\}d\phi = \pi_g p_g(\hat{\phi})(2\pi)^{\frac{1}{2}q_g}\Delta_\phi^{-\frac{1}{2}}.$$

Thus the approximate ratio of posterior probabilities is the value given.

In particular, if the two models are linear with known variances σ_g^2 and σ_h^2 and with design matrices $\mathbf{x}_g$ and $\mathbf{x}_h$, then, for example,

$$g(y;\hat{\phi}) = \frac{1}{(2\pi)^{\frac{1}{2}n}\sigma_g^n}\exp\left(-\frac{\mathrm{SS}_g}{2\sigma_g^2}\right), \Delta_\phi = |\mathbf{x}_g^{\mathrm{T}}\mathbf{x}_g|/\sigma_g^{2q_g},$$

where SS_g is the residual sum of squares under the first model. Thus the approximate ratio of posterior probabilities is

$$\frac{\pi_g}{\pi_h} \times \left(\frac{\sigma_h}{\sigma_g}\right)^n \exp\left(-\frac{\mathrm{SS}_g}{2\sigma_g^2} + \frac{\mathrm{SS}_h}{2\sigma_h^2}\right) \times \frac{(2\pi)^{\frac{1}{2}q_g}}{(2\pi)^{\frac{1}{2}q_h}} \times \frac{p_g(\hat{\phi})}{p_h(\hat{\chi})} \times \frac{|\mathbf{x}_g^{\mathrm{T}}\mathbf{x}_g|^{-\frac{1}{2}}\sigma_g^{q_g}}{|\mathbf{x}_h^{\mathrm{T}}\mathbf{x}_h|^{-\frac{1}{2}}\sigma_h^{q_h}}. \tag{2}$$

If both variances are unknown, the second and last factors have σ_g and σ_h replaced by maximum likelihood estimates, and the conditional prior densities in the penultimate factor include a contribution for the variances.

There is no difficulty in principle with (2), but note that with the approximately uniform prior densities, $p_g(\hat{\phi})$ and $p_h(\hat{\chi})$ do not cancel, as they would in any calculation 'within' an individual model. There is usually no reason to expect the factor $p_g(\hat{\phi})/p_h(\hat{\chi})$ to be near unity; indeed the parameter spaces over which these densities are defined are in general quite different. From a subjectivist viewpoint it is in principle possible in any particular application to determine 'your' numerical value for this ratio. Sometimes, however, the following argument is useful in deducing an approximate numerical value.

Often, although not necessarily, the two models will give roughly similar results; otherwise 'careful' comparison of them will hardly be necessary. Consider then the case where $q_g = q_h$ and the linear models are in some rough sense nearly equivalent. Further if the prior for, say, ϕ is normal with wide dispersion, then $p_g(\hat{\phi}) \simeq (2\pi)^{-\frac{1}{2}q_g}|\Sigma_\phi|^{-\frac{1}{2}}$, where Σ_ϕ is the prior covariance matrix. Then the numerator of the last three factors in (2) is essentially the ratio of the square roots of the prior generalized variance of ϕ to the posterior generalized variance. This ratio can be expected to be approximately the same for both models; if the models were exactly equivalent the ratio would be exactly one. Since quite general models are locally linear, the general conclusion is that when $q_g = q_h$,

$$p_g(\hat{\phi})/p_h(\hat{\chi}) \simeq (\Delta_\phi/\Delta_\chi)^{1/2}.$$

If $q_g \neq q_h$, say $q_g > q_h$, the argument is even more tentative. Suppose that the first model is reparameterized so that the first q_h parameters are roughly equivalent to those in the second model and that the remaining $q_g - q_h$ parameters are orthogonal to the first set, and specify the additional richness of the first model. Then the previous argument applies to the first parameters. For the remaining $q_g - q_h$ parameters suppose that the prior information is equivalent to that from n_0 data values of the structure under consideration. Then the contribution to the final factor is $(n_0/n)^{q_g-q_h}$. To summarize with this special and approximate choice of priors, the ratio of posterior probabilities is

$$\frac{\pi_g}{\pi_h} \times \frac{g(y;\hat{\phi})}{h(y;\hat{\chi})} \times \left(\frac{n_0}{n}\right)^{q_g-q_h};$$

often it would be reasonable to suppose n_0 in the range $\frac{1}{2}$ to 2. Note that as n increases there is a loading against the model with more parameters.

For further details on this difficult and important problem, see, for example, Cox (1961) and Box and Hill (1967).

[*Theoretical Statistics*, Sections 10.5 and 10.6]

10.12. Obtain an empirical Bayes solution to the problem of estimating a normal mean from m sets of data with different variances. As in Problem

9.2, suppose that the number m of sets is large and that the variances $\sigma_1^2, \ldots, \sigma_m^2$ have a prior density of the conjugate inverse gamma form. Show that the mode of the m.l.e. of the posterior distribution of the mean μ is given by a statistic of the same general form as $\tilde{\mu}_a$ in Problem 9.2.

Solution

Suppose first that the variance τ has the known prior density

$$p_0(\tau) = (\tfrac{1}{2}f_0\tau_0')^{\frac{1}{2}f_0}\tau^{-\frac{1}{2}f_0-1}\exp\left(-\tfrac{1}{2}f_0\tau_0'/\tau\right)/\Gamma(\tfrac{1}{2}f_0),$$

where f_0 is an effective degrees of freedom and the mean is $\tau_0 = \tau_0'f_0/(f_0-2)$. Now consider a single set of random variables $Y_1, \ldots, Y_n$ which given τ are i.i.d. in $N(\mu, \tau)$. The marginal p.d.f. of $Y_1, \ldots, Y_n$ is

$$\int\limits_0^\infty (2\pi)^{-\frac{1}{2}n}\tau^{-\frac{1}{2}n}\exp\left\{-\frac{\Sigma(y_j-\mu)^2}{2\tau}\right\}p_0(\tau)d\tau\,;$$

thus $(\bar{Y}, \text{MS})$ form a minimal sufficient statistic. Given several independent such samples, the full likelihood can be obtained as a product.

Omitting factors not involving μ, we thus obtain the full log likelihood as

$$-\tfrac{1}{2}\Sigma(f_j+f_0+1)\log\left\{1+\frac{n_j(\bar{y}_j-\mu)^2}{f_j\text{MS}_j+f_0\tau_0'}\right\}, \tag{1}$$

where for the jth set of data, $f_j = n_j - 1$. One way of understanding the form of this is to note that for a single set of data MS is ancillary, having a distribution not depending on μ, and that conditionally on MS, $\bar{Y}$ has the form

$$\mu+\left\{\frac{(f\text{MS}+f_0\tau_0')}{n(f+f_0)}\right\}T_{f+f_0},$$

where T_a denotes a Student t random variable with a degrees of freedom. The form (1) derives essentially from this being a product of Student t densities.

On maximizing (1) we have the estimating equation

$$\Sigma\frac{n_j(f_j+f_0+1)(\bar{y}_j-\tilde{\mu})}{f_j\text{MS}_j+f_0\tau_0'+n_j(\bar{y}_j-\tilde{\mu})^2}=0.$$

If, as would usually be the case, f_0 and τ_0' are unknown, they can be estimated, for instance, by maximum likelihood from the joint density of the mean squares within samples.

[*Theoretical Statistics*, Section 10.7; Rao, Section 5b.4; Cox, 1975]

Problem 10.13 omitted.

11 DECISION THEORY

Summary

In the formulation of Chapter 10, the assumption of a probability model for the observed random variable Y is supplemented by a prior density over the possible parameter values. In statistical decision theory there is specified also a set $\mathscr{D}$ of possible decisions, d, one of which is to be chosen in the light of the data. Further a utility function, $u(\theta,d)$, is known giving the gain arising from decision d when θ is the true parameter value. The objective is to maximize the expected utility. A decision function, $\delta(y)$, is a rule specifying for any given $Y = y$ the decision to be taken.

In principle, the solution is to compute the posterior distribution of Θ given $Y = y$ and hence to find the conditional expected utility corresponding to any decision d,

$$E\{u(\Theta, d)|Y = y\} ;$$

the decision d maximizing this is chosen. This is called the Bayes decision rule.

In some problems, utility can be taken as approximately equivalent to money. Under some reasonable assumptions of self-consistency, a utility exists for any individual; the reconciliation of conflicting utility functions raises difficult issues.

Although calculation of the Bayes decision rule requires all the elements specified above, it is possible to consider incompletely specified decision problems. The most important case is when a utility function is available, but no prior distribution. The utility function is modified to the regret function, or decision loss,

$$w(\theta, d) = \sup_{d^* \in \mathscr{D}} u(\theta, d^*) - u(\theta, d).$$

The risk function for any decision rule is the expected regret as a function of θ:

$$r(\theta, \delta) = E_Y[w\{\theta, \delta(Y)\};\theta].$$

Decision rules have now to be compared on the basis of functions of θ and in general a simple choice is not possible. If, however, a decision rule has a risk function dominated by that of some other rule, the first rule is called inadmissible. Otherwise the rule is called admissible; a Bayes rule with respect to a proper prior distribution is admissible.

One rather artificial way of choosing between risk functions is to characterize each risk function by its maximum,

$$m(\delta) = \sup_{\theta \in \Omega} r(\theta, \delta),$$

and to take that rule, the minimax rule, with minimum $m(\delta)$. The risk function of the minimax rule is (usually) constant.

The above discussion refers to a single decision problem. Often in applications a sequence of interrelated decision problems is involved. Solution is normally by recursion using dynamic programming.

Problems

11.1. From data y, the posterior p.d.f. of a scalar parameter θ is found. The possible decisions d_t are indexed by a real number t. Three possible utility functions are contemplated, namely

(i) $a - b_1(t - \theta)^2$,
(ii) $a - b_2|t - \theta|$,
(iii) $a - b_3(t - \theta)^4$,

where $b_k > 0 \, (k = 1, 2, 3)$.

Show that the Bayes decision rules for (i) and (ii) are, respectively, the mean and median of the posterior distribution, and that for (iii) it is $\mu_\theta + \kappa_\theta \sigma_\theta$, where $\kappa_\theta^3 + 3\kappa_\theta - \gamma_{1\theta} = 0$ and $\mu_\theta, \sigma_\theta$ and $\gamma_{1\theta}$ are respectively the mean, standard deviation and skewness of the posterior distribution.

Explain qualitatively the reason for the difference between the answers for (i) and (ii).

Solution

Given y, θ is the value of a random variable Θ having a known distribution, the posterior distribution. For utility function (i) we choose t to minimize $E\{(\Theta - t)^2\} = E(\Theta^2) - 2tE(\Theta) + t^2$. Differentiation shows that maximum expected utility is achieved at $t = E(\Theta) = \mu_\theta$, the mean of the posterior distribution.

A similar calculation for utility function (ii) gives the median of Θ; minimization is by a direct calculation. For utility function (iii) we have to minimize

$$E\{(\Theta - t)^4\} = E[\{(\Theta - t) + (t - \mu_\theta)\}^4]$$
$$= E\{(\Theta - \mu_\theta)^4\} + 4\gamma_{1\theta}\sigma_\theta^3(\mu_\theta - t) + 6\sigma_\theta^2(\mu_\theta - t)^2 + (\mu_\theta - t)^4.$$

The minimizing t satisfies

$$- 4\gamma_{1\theta}\sigma_\theta^3 - 12\sigma_\theta^2(\mu_\theta - t) - 4(\mu_\theta - t)^3 = 0,$$

so that if $t = \mu_\theta + \kappa_\theta\sigma_\theta$ we have $\kappa_\theta^3 + 3\kappa_\theta - \gamma_{1\theta} = 0$, care being necessary to take the correct root; note that if $\gamma_{1\theta} = 0$, then $\kappa_\theta = 0$ so that the posterior mean is recovered.

The difference between the answers is explained qualitatively by the relative dependence on the tails of the distribution of Θ.

[*Theoretical Statistics*, Section 11.3; Rao, Section 5b; Silvey, Section 11.6]

11.2. Suppose that Y is $N(\mu, 1)$, where μ is 1 with prior probability π and -1 with prior probability $1 - \pi$. Find the Bayes rule for discriminating between the two possible values of μ when the zero-one regret function is used.

Now suppose that $Y_1, \ldots, Y_n$ are conditionally independent in $N(\mu_1, 1), \ldots, N(\mu_n, 1)$, where the μ_j are independently distributed in the above two-point prior distribution. Construct an empirical Bayes discrimination rule, estimating π from the data. Examine critically the qualitative and quantitative properties of this rule.

Solution

Given $Y = y$ the random variable M representing μ is such that

$$\frac{\text{pr}(M = 1 \mid Y = y)}{\text{pr}(M = -1 \mid Y = y)} = \left(\frac{\pi}{1 - \pi}\right)\exp\{-\tfrac{1}{2}(y - 1)^2 + \tfrac{1}{2}(y + 1)^2\} = \frac{\pi e^{2y}}{1 - \pi}.$$

That is, the decision d_1, corresponding to $M = 1$, is taken if and only if $y > \tfrac{1}{2}\log\{(1 - \pi)/\pi\}$.

The marginal p.d.f. of Y is

$$\frac{1}{\sqrt{(2\pi)}}\exp(-\tfrac{1}{2}y^2 - \tfrac{1}{2})\{\pi e^y + (1 - \pi)e^{-y}\}$$

and from observations $y_1, \ldots, y_n$ the parameter π can be estimated by $\hat\pi$, the maximum likelihood estimate. The difference between π and $\hat\pi$ is $O(1/\sqrt{n})$ in probability and the difference in the expected utilities of the decision rules using π and $\hat\pi$ will tend to zero as $n \to \infty$. A simpler estimate than $\hat\pi$ is the unbiased estimate $\tilde\pi = \tfrac{1}{2}(1 + \bar{Y})$ restricted to the interval $(0, 1)$.

If forced to reach a decision from a single value y in isolation, one would presumably take decision d_1 if and only if $y > 0$. Clearly substantial improvement is possible by considering the problems collectively, at least provided the proportion of $+1$'s is not too near $\tfrac{1}{2}$.

In an alternative version of the problem there are past data $y_1, \dots, y_n$ and a decision has to be reached on the basis of a future observation y_{n+1} about the corresponding population mean μ_{n+1}.

An extreme example of the rule using $\tilde{\pi}$ is that if $y_1 = 0$ this, on its own, suggests that $\mu_1 = -1$ is not unreasonable, but combined with $y_2 > 0$ it points toward both means being positive.

Such empirical Bayes problems were first studied by Robbins (1951); see also more recent work by Maritz (1970) and Copas (1969).

[*Theoretical Statistics*, Sections 11.3 and 10.6; Rao, Section 5b; Lindley, p. 64]

11.3. To represent an interval estimation problem in decision-theoretic terms, it is assumed that for a scalar parameter θ the regret function corresponding to the interval $[t_1, t_2]$ is

$$w(\theta; t_1, t_2) = \begin{cases} a(t_1 - \theta) + (t_2 - t_1) & (\theta < t_1), \\ (t_2 - t_1) & (t_1 \leqslant \theta \leqslant t_2), \\ b(\theta - t_2) + (t_2 - t_1) & (t_2 < \theta), \end{cases}$$

where $a, b > 0$. Taking for simplicity the situation where the posterior distribution of Θ is $N(\bar{y}, \sigma_0^2/n)$, explore the connexion between the effective confidence interval and a and b.

Generalize the discussion to the construction of an interval estimate for the mean of a normal distribution with unknown variance, using the conjugate prior distributions, and a scale invariant regret function.

Solution

The proposed regret function expresses the double idea that:
(i) the longer the interval, the less useful it is;
(ii) there is a loss if the true parameter value is outside the interval and the further outside it is, the greater the loss.

The expected regret is

$$(t_2 - t_1) + a \int_{-\infty}^{t_1} (t_1 - \theta) f_\Theta(\theta \mid y) d\theta + b \int_{t_1}^{\infty} (\theta - t_2) f_\Theta(\theta \mid y) d\theta,$$

where $f_\Theta(\theta \mid y)$ is the posterior density of Θ. We have to choose t_1 and t_2 to minimize this, and on differentiating this leads to the equations for the stationary value

$$-1 + a \int_{-\infty}^{t_1} f_\Theta(\theta|y)d\theta = 0, \; 1 - b \int_{t_2}^{\infty} f_\Theta(\theta|y)d\theta = 0.$$

Thus t_1 and t_2 are the lower and upper $1/a$ and $1/b$ points of the posterior distribution. This requires that $a, b > 1$ and $1/a + 1/b \leqslant 1$; indeed without these conditions it will be best to take an interval of zero length at a value $t_1 = t_2$ corresponding to the lower $b/(a + b)$ point and to accept the resulting loss.

Note that the above argument applies to the normal-theory problem whether or not σ is known, provided that the regret function remains as specified independently of σ. It may, however, often be a better approximation to take the regret as σ^{-1} times the function specified; for example, the penalty of taking a long interval then depends on length relative to σ. There is then a fairly direct generalization of the earlier result. The posterior distribution of the mean θ and standard deviation σ is now involved and the expected regret for minimization is

$$(t_2 - t_1)E(\Sigma^{-1}|Y = y) + a \int_0^\infty d\sigma \int_{-\infty}^{t_1} \left(\frac{t_1 - \theta}{\sigma}\right) f(\theta, \sigma|y)d\theta$$

$$+ b \int_0^\infty d\sigma \int_{t_2}^{\infty} \left(\frac{\theta - t_2}{\sigma}\right) f(\theta, \sigma|y)d\theta$$

and the equation for t_1, for example, becomes

$$-E(\Sigma^{-1}|Y = y) + a \int_{-\infty}^{t_1} d\theta \int_0^\infty \frac{d\sigma}{\sigma} f(\theta, \sigma|y) = 0.$$

There are a number of special cases, for example when Σ is independent of Θ, when the posterior density has a scale and location form. Explicit details for the normal-theory case are given by Aitchison and Dunsmore (1968).

[*Theoretical Statistics*, Section 11.3 and 11.7; Rao, Section 5b; Silvey, Chapters 10 and 11; Lindley, p. 57]

11.4. There are m normal distributions of variance σ^2 whose means $\mu_1, \ldots, \mu_m$ have independently the prior distribution $N(\xi_0, v_0)$. A number r of observations are available independently from each distribution and the one with largest observed mean is selected as 'best'. The utility achieved by selecting a population of mean μ is $a\mu$. Show, for example by first finding the conditional expected utility given the largest observed mean, that the expected utility of the procedure is

$$a\xi_0 + \frac{ag_{mm}v_0}{(v_0 + \sigma_0^2/r)^{1/2}},$$

where g_{mm} is the expected value of the largest of m observations from the standard normal distribution.

Solution

If a sample has mean $\bar{y}$, the corresponding population mean has a posterior distribution of mean

$$\frac{\xi/v_0 + \bar{y}/(\sigma_0^2/r)}{1/v_0 + 1/(\sigma_0^2/r)}$$

and therefore if this distribution is selected the expected utility is a times this. Now the sample means $\bar{Y}_1, \ldots, \bar{Y}_m$ have marginal distributions that are independently normal with mean ξ_0 and variance $v_0 + \sigma_0^2/r$. Thus the expected value of the sample mean actually chosen is $\xi_0 + g_{mm}(v_0 + \sigma_0^2/r)^{1/2}$, and therefore the expected utility of the procedure is

$$a\frac{\xi_0/v_0 + \{\xi_0 + g_{mm}(v_0 + \sigma_0^2/r)^{1/2}\}/(\sigma_0^2/r)}{1/v_0 + 1/(\sigma_0^2/r)},$$

which reduces to the required form.

[*Theoretical Statistics*, Section 11.3; Rao, Section 5b; Silvey, Chapters 10 and 11]

11.5. Let $S = \Sigma b(Y_j)/n$ be the sufficient statistic for the one-dimensional parameter exponential family, with $\mu(\theta) = E(S;\theta)$. Using the Cramér–Rao lower bound of Chapter 8, show that any estimate $T = t(Y)$ which has uniformly lower risk than S for estimating $\mu(\theta)$ with regret function $\{t - \mu(\theta)\}^2$ must be unbiased. Hence deduce the admissibility of S.

Solution

The statistic S achieves the Cramér–Rao lower bound for unbiased estimates, so that if T has bias $b(\theta)$

$$\mathrm{var}\,(T\,;\theta) \geqslant \{1 + b'(\theta)\}^2\,\mathrm{var}\,(S\,;\theta).$$

Therefore, since the mean squared error of T is

$$\mathrm{var}\,(T\,;\theta) + \{b(\theta)\}^2,$$

T's having uniformly lower mean squared error than S implies at least that

$$\{1 + b'(\theta)\}^2\,\mathrm{var}\,(S\,;\theta) + \{b(\theta)\}^2 \leqslant \mathrm{var}\,(S\,;\theta), \tag{1}$$

with strict inequality for some θ. Therefore $-1 \leqslant 1 + b'(\theta) \leqslant 1$, with strict inequality for some θ, i.e. $-2 \leqslant b'(\theta) \leqslant 0$. But the same result must hold for any reparametrization $\psi(\theta)$ which implies that for all $\psi(\theta)$, $-2 \leqslant b'(\theta)d\theta/d\psi \leqslant 0$. This is clearly impossible unless $b'(\theta) = 0$ everywhere, in which case only strict equality holds in (1) and $b(\theta) = 0$ everywhere.

[*Theoretical Statistics*, Section 11.6; Rao, Section 5b; Silvey, Section 2.10; Girshick and Savage, 1951]

11.6. Suppose that Y is distributed in $N(\mu, \sigma_0^2)$ and that μ has the $N(0, v_0)$ prior distribution, σ_0^2 and v_0 both being known. If risk is proportional to mean squared error, then the Bayes estimate $\delta_B(Y)$ for μ has minimal Bayes risk, but its risk function is unbounded, whereas the m.l.e. $\delta_{ML}(Y)$ has minimax risk. A compromise estimate is

$$\delta_C(Y) = \begin{cases} \delta_{ML}(Y) + a & (Y < -k), \\ \delta_B(Y) & (-k \leqslant Y \leqslant k), \\ \delta_{ML}(Y) - a & (Y > k), \end{cases}$$

where a and k are chosen to make $\delta_C(\cdot)$ a continuous function, but are otherwise arbitrary. Compare the Bayes risk and risk function of $\delta_C(Y)$ with those of the m.l. and Bayes estimates, and comment on the applicability of such a compromise.

Describe and investigate a corresponding compromise between the m.l.e. and the James-Stein estimate for a vector of normal means.

Solution

The maximum likelihood estimate and the Bayes estimate are respectively

$$\delta_{ML} = Y, \delta_B = Y\{1 - (1 + \gamma_0)^{-1}\}, \gamma_0 = v_0/\sigma_0^2,$$

with risk functions, assuming squared error loss,

$$r(\mu\,;\delta_{ML}) = \sigma_0^2, r(\mu\,;\delta_B) = \mu^2(1 + \gamma_0)^{-2} + \gamma_0^2(1 + \gamma_0)^{-2}\sigma_0^2\,;$$

note that $\qquad r(\mu;\delta_B) \leqslant r(\mu;\delta_{ML})$ for $\mu^2 \leqslant \sigma_0^2 + 2v_0$,

which suggests that the rule $\delta_C(Y)$ might have good risk properties. The corresponding Bayes risks of δ_{ML} and δ_B are

$$r_B(\delta_{ML}) = \sigma_0^2, r_B(\delta_B) = \sigma_0^2 (1 + \gamma_0)^{-1} \gamma_0.$$

For the compromise estimator $\delta_C(Y)$ note that $\delta_{ML}(k) - a = \delta_B(k)$ implies the relationship $k = a(\gamma_0 + 1)$. Define $a = c\sigma_0$ and then suppose in the calculations that $\sigma_0 = 1$; this simply removes a factor σ_0^2 from risks. First we compute the Bayes risk of $\delta_C(Y)$, for which it is convenient to write

$$\delta_C(Y) = \left\{ 1 - \psi\left(\frac{Y^2}{1 + \gamma_0}\right) \right\} Y, \psi(u) = \begin{cases} (1 + \gamma_0)^{-1} & (0 \leqslant u \leqslant c^2(1 + \gamma_0)), \\ (c\sqrt{\gamma_0} + 1)/\sqrt{u} & (c^2(1 + \gamma_0) < u). \end{cases}$$

Then

$$r_B(\delta_C) = E\{M - \delta_C(Y)\}^2 = E\{M - \delta_B(Y) + \delta_B(Y) - \delta_C(Y)\}^2$$

$$= \frac{\gamma_0}{\gamma_0 + 1} + \frac{1}{\gamma_0 + 1} E\left[\left(\frac{Y^2}{\gamma_0 + 1}\right) \left\{ 1 - (\gamma_0 + 1)^2 \psi\left(\frac{Y^2}{\gamma_0 + 1}\right) \right\}^2 \right].$$

Now $Y^2(\gamma_0 + 1)^{-1}$ has the chi-squared distribution with one degree of freedom and for any function $h(\cdot)$ $E\{\chi_1^2 h(\chi_1^2)\} = E\{h(\chi_3^2)\}$, so that

$$r_B(\delta_C) = \frac{\gamma_0}{\gamma_0 + 1} + \frac{1}{\gamma_0 + 1} E[\{1 - (\gamma_0 + 1)^2 \psi(\chi_3^2)\}^2].$$

Direct calculation of the expectation gives the result

$$r_B(\delta_C) = \frac{\gamma_0}{\gamma_0 + 1} + \frac{2}{\gamma_0 + 1} \{(b^2 + 1)\Phi(-b) - b\phi(b)\}, b = c(\gamma_0 + 1)^{1/2}.$$

This is halfway between $r_B(\delta_{ML})$ and $r_B(\delta_B)$ when $b \simeq 0.4$.

The risk function $r(\mu;\delta_C)$ is obtained directly by integration of $\{\delta_C(Y) - \mu\}^2$ with respect to the $N(\mu, 1)$ density, and after some straightforward algebra

$$r(\mu, \delta_C) = 1 + c^2 + g(\mu^2),$$

where $g(\mu^2)$ is negative with maximum value zero as $\mu^2 \to \infty$. Thus the risk is bounded and, naturally, is a maximum when $\delta_C(Y) = \delta_{ML}(Y) - a$.

This discussion can be extended to the case where the vector Y is $MN_p(\mu, I)$ and hence by canonical reduction to the general linear model with known variance. Here the Bayes rule when $\mu_1, \ldots, \mu_p$ are i.i.d. $N(0, v_0)$ is again

$$\delta_B = \{1 - (\gamma_0 + 1)^{-1}\} Y$$

and an empirical Bayes analogue is the James–Stein estimator

$$\delta_{ST} = \{1 - (p - 2)/\Sigma Y_j^2\} Y,$$

whose risk function for sum of squared error loss is always smaller than that for δ_{ML} when $p \geqslant 3$. The analogue of $\delta_C(Y)$ would now apply separately to each co-ordinate; the object would be to limit co-ordinate-wise mean squared error, which may be as large as $\Sigma \mu_j^2$. One such 'compromise' estimate,

$$\delta_{CST}(Y) = \left[1 - \frac{p-2}{\Sigma Y_j^2} \psi \left\{ \frac{(p-2)Y_i^2}{\Sigma Y_j^2} \right\} \right] Y_i \ (i = 1, \ldots, p)$$

with $\psi(u) = \min(1, d/\sqrt{u})$, is investigated in detail by Efron and Morris (1972); they also discuss the case with unknown sampling variance σ^2. The qualitative conclusion from their numerical work is that a fairly effective bound can be put on the risk of a single component while retaining much of the ensemble advantage of the James–Stein estimate.

[*Theoretical Statistics*, Sections 11.6 and 11.8; Rao, Section 5b; Lindley, p. 49]

11.7. Let $Y_1, \ldots, Y_n$ be i.i.d. in $N(\mu, \sigma^2)$ with both μ and σ^2 unknown. Location invariant estimates of σ^2 are necessarily functions of the maximal invariant $ss = \Sigma(Y_j - \bar{Y})^2$. Prove that any such invariant estimate is inadmissible for regret function $w(\sigma^2, d) \propto (d - \sigma^2)^2$, by showing that

$$T = \min\left(\frac{ss}{n+1}, \frac{ss + n\bar{Y}^2}{n+2} \right)^2$$

has uniformly lower risk than $ss/(n+1)$. Explain qualitatively why T might be a good estimate.

Solution

The estimate $ss/(n+1)$ may be shown to minimize expected regret among all estimates based solely on ss.

The quantities ss and $n\bar{Y}^2$ are, respectively, distributed as $\sigma^2 \chi_{n-1}^2(0)$ and $\sigma^2 \chi_1^2(\lambda)$ random variables, where $\lambda = n\mu^2/\sigma^2$ and $\chi_m^2(\lambda)$ denotes a chi-squared random variable with m degrees of freedom and non-centrality λ, i.e. expectation $m + \lambda$. Stein (1964) considers a more general situation including estimators

$$T^* = \min\left\{ \frac{\sigma^2 \chi_{v_1}^2(0)}{v_1 + 2}, \frac{\sigma^2 \chi_{v_1}^2(0) + \sigma^2 \chi_{v_2}^2(\lambda)}{v_1 + v_2 + 2} \right\},$$

which are uniformly superior to $T^\dagger = \sigma^2 \chi_{v_1}^2(0)/(v+2)$. The solution below extends immediately to this case.

We denote ss and $n\bar{Y}^2$ by W and Z and without loss of generality suppose $\sigma^2 = 1$, thus removing a factor σ^4 from the risk functions. Then, with $v = n - 1$, we may write

$$T = \min\left(\frac{W}{W + Z}, \frac{v + 2}{v + 3}\right)\left(\frac{W + Z}{v + 2}\right).$$

Now we use the representation $Z = E\{\chi_{1+2J}^2(0)\} = E(Z_J)$, say, where J has a Poisson distribution with mean $\frac{1}{2}\lambda$. The risk function of the usual estimator $W/(v + 2)$ can then be expressed as

$$E\left\{\left(\frac{W}{W + Z}\right)\left(\frac{W + Z}{v + 2}\right) - 1\right\}^2$$

$$= EE\left[\left\{\left(\frac{W}{W + Z}\right)\left(\frac{W + Z}{v + 2}\right) - 1\right\}^2 \middle| J, \frac{W}{W + Z}\right].$$

But since $W + Z_J$ and $W/(W + Z_J)$ are independent, the conditional expectation is

$$\left(\frac{W}{W + Z_J}\right)^2 \frac{(v + 3 + 2J)(v + 5 + 2J)}{(v + 2)^2} - 2\left(\frac{W}{W + Z_J}\right)\frac{(v + 3 + 2J)}{(v + 2)} + 1$$

$$= \frac{(v + 3 + 2J)(v + 5 + 2J)}{(v + 2)^2}\left\{\left(\frac{W}{W + Z_J}\right) - \left(\frac{v + 2}{v + 5 + 2J}\right)\right\}^2 + \frac{2}{v + 5 + 2J}.$$

But now

$$\left|\min\left(\frac{W}{W + Z_J}, \frac{v + 2}{v + 3}\right) - \left(\frac{v + 2}{v + 5 + 2J}\right)\right| \leqslant \left|\frac{W}{W + Z_J} - \frac{v + 2}{v + 5 + 2J}\right|$$

for all values of $W/(W + Z_J)$ and J, so that the corresponding conditional, and hence unconditional, risk of T is at least as small.

The exact risk function may be expressed in terms of non-central F probabilities. Note that if n and/or μ/σ is very large, so that λ is very large, then J is large with high probability and consequently T will usually be the estimator $\mathrm{ss}/(n + 1)$; one can show directly that the risk function of T is an increasing function of λ with maximum

$$\left\{1 - \left(\frac{n - 1}{n + 1}\right)^2\right\}\sigma^4.$$

There are several comments to be made concerning the inadmissibility of the invariant estimate, and the superiority of T. First, recall that ss is not sufficient for σ^2 and the explicit use of information from $\bar{Y}$ should not be surprising. The qualitative form of T seems quite reasonable, in that if the Student t test makes $\mu = 0$ a plausible hypothesis, then we might conclude that $n\bar{Y}^2$ is close to unbiased for σ^2; if we know $\mu = 0$ then $(\text{ss} + n\bar{Y}^2)/(n+2)$ is the minimum mean squared error estimate for σ^2. If μ/σ is very different from zero, then T will nearly always be the invariant estimate. Note that $\bar{Y}$ should be replaced by $\bar{Y} - m$ if μ is known to be close to m, in order to get most of the advantage from T. In other words, in complete absence of knowledge about μ/σ there may be little reduction in mean squared error using an estimate such as T and in such a case invariance may be a reasonable requirement. It would be unwise to believe that the theoretical result has no practical relevance, since analogues of T are frequently used in connection with analysis of variance and multiple regression analysis.

[*Theoretical Statistics*, Sections 11.6 and 11.8; Rao, Section 5b]

11.8. To compare two treatments, n_0 paired observations are available, leading to a normal posterior distribution for the difference in treatment means, the usual normal-theory assumptions having been made. There is the possibility of taking further observations and the number of such observations is to be determined, the cost of n_1 further observations being $k_0 + k_1 n_1$ ($n_1 = 1, 2, \ldots$). For the problem of choosing between the two treatments, derive an expression for determining the optimum n_1 assuming that the utilities are linear in the treatment means.

Solution

If the two treatment means are μ_1 and μ_2, and if the prior distributions of $M_1 + M_2$ and $\Delta = M_2 - M_1$ are independent, and if the difference of the utilities of d_2 and of d_1 is $a + b\delta$, then the analysis can be based on the differences of the responses under the two treatments. If the observed mean treatment difference is x, based on n pairs of observations, the posterior distribution of Δ is normal with mean and variance

$$\left(\frac{x}{\sigma_0^2/n} + \frac{\xi_0}{v_0}\right)\bigg/\left(\frac{1}{\sigma_0^2/n} + \frac{1}{v_0}\right) \text{ and } \left(\frac{1}{\sigma_0^2/n} + \frac{1}{v_0}\right)^{-1},$$

in an obvious notation and assuming the prior distribution of Δ to be normal.

To determine an optimum n_1 we argue in reverse. Let n be fixed. Then the optimum decision depends on $a + bE(\Delta|x)$ and the conditional expected utility, given $X = x$, is

$$\max\left\{a + b\left(\frac{x}{\sigma_0^2/n} + \frac{\xi_0}{v_0}\right)\bigg/\left(\frac{1}{\sigma_0^2/n} + \frac{1}{v_0}\right), 0\right\}.$$

The marginal distribution of X is normal with mean ξ_0 and variance v_0

$+ \sigma_0^2/n$, so that the unconditional expected utility is obtained on taking expectations. After simplification, we get

$$(a + b\xi_0)\Phi\left\{\frac{a + b\xi_0}{bv_0(v_0 + \sigma_0^2/n)^{1/2}}\right\} + \left(a + \frac{b\xi_0\sigma_0^2/n}{v_0 + \sigma_0^2/n}\right)\phi\left\{\frac{a + b\xi_0}{bv_0(v_0 + \sigma_0^2/n)^{1/2}}\right\}.$$

If $n = n_0$ this is the 'total' expected utility. If $n = n_0 + n_1$, then the cost $k_0 + k_1 n_1$ has to be subtracted. The optimum can now be found numerically. Specific details are given by Grundy et al. (1956).

[*Theoretical Statistics*, Section 11.9; Rao, Section 5b; Silvey, Chapter 11; Lindley, p. 29]

REFERENCES

For a general account of the topic involved in each Problem we have referred where relevant to the five books below. The remaining references concern the sources and specialized details of individual Problems.

Cox, D.R. and Hinkley, D.V. (1974). *Theoretical Statistics.* London, Chapman and Hall. (Referred to by its title.)

Lehmann, E.L. (1959). *Testing Statistical Hypotheses.* New York, Wiley.

Lindley, D.V. (1971). *Bayesian Statistics, a Review.* Philadelphia, S.I.A.M.

Rao, C.R. (1973). *Linear Statistical Inference and its Applications.* 2nd edition. New York, Wiley.

Silvey, S.D. (1975). *Statistical Inference.* London, Chapman and Hall.

Abramowitz, M. and Stegun, I.A. (1965). *Handbook of mathematical functions.* New York, Dover.

Aitchison, J. and Dunsmore, I.R. (1968). Linear-loss interval estimation of location and scale parameters. *Biometrika* **55**, 141–8.

Aitchison, J. and Silvey, S.D. (1958). Maximum-likelihood estimation of parameters subject to restraints. *Ann. Math. Statist.* **29**, 813–28.

Andersen, E.B. (1970). Asymptotic properties of conditional maximum-likelihood estimators. *J.R. Statist. Soc.*, B, **32**, 283–301.

Anderson, T.W. (1958). *An Introduction to Multivariate Statistical Analysis.* New York, Wiley.

Anderson, T.W. and Goodman, L.A. (1957). Statistical inference about Markov chains. *Ann. Math. Statist.* **28**, 89–110.

Andrews, D.F., Gnanadesikan, R. and Warner, J.L. (1971). Transformations of multivariate data. *Biometrics* **27**, 825–40.

Andrews, D.F., Gnanadesikan, R. and Warner, J.L. (1973). Methods for assessing multivariate normality. In *Multivariate Analysis*, III, pp. 95–116, ed. Krishnaiah, P.R. New York, Academic Press.

Atiqullah, M. (1962). The estimation of residual variance in quadratically balanced least-squares problems and the robustness of the *F*-test. *Biometrika* **9**, 83–91.

Atkinson, A.C. (1970). A method for discriminating between models (with discussion). *J.R. Statist. Soc.* B, **32**, 323–53.

Bahadur, R.R. (1954). Sufficiency and statistical decision functions. *Ann. Math. Statist.* **25**, 423–62.

Barnard, G.A. (1947). Review of book *Sequential analysis* by Wald, A. *J. Amer. Statist. Assoc.* **42**, 658–64.

Barnard, G.A. (1963). The logic of least squares. *J.R. Statist. Soc.*, B. **25** 124–7.

Barnard, G.A. and Sprott, D.A. (1971). A note on Basu's examples of anomalous ancillary statistics (with discussion). In *Foundations of Statistical Inference*, pp. 163–76, eds. Godambe, V.P. and Sprott, D.A. Toronto, Holt, Rinehart and Winston.

Bartlett, M.S. (1936). The information available in small samples. *Proc. Camb. Phil. Soc.* **32**, 560–6.

Bartlett, M.S. (1966). *An Introduction to Stochastic Processes.* 2nd edition. Cambridge University Press.

Basu, D. (1955). On statistics independent of sufficient statistics. *Sankhyā* **20**, 223–6.

Basu, D. (1964). Recovery of ancillary information. *Sankhyā*, A, **26**, 3–16.

Beyer, J. E., Keiding, N. and Simonsen, W. (1976). The exact behaviour of the maximum likelihood estimator in the pure birth process and the pure death process. *Scand. J. Statist.* **3**, 61–72.

Billingsley, P. (1961a). Statistical methods in Markov chains. *Ann. Math. Statist.* **32**, 12–40.

Billingsley, P. (1961b). *Statistical Inference for Markov Processes.* University of Chicago Press.

Billingsley, P. (1968). *Convergence of Probability Measures.* New York, Wiley.

Bishop, Y.M.M., Fienberg, S.E. and Holland, P.W. (1975). *Discrete Multivariate Analysis.* Cambridge, Mass, M.I.T. Press.

Box, G.E.P. and Hill, W.J. (1967). Discrimination among mechanistic models. *Technometrics* **9**, 57–71.

Buehler, R.J. (1971). Measuring information and uncertainty (with discussion). In *Foundations of Statistical Inference*, pp. 330–41, eds. Godambe, V.P. and Sprott, D.A. Toronto, Holt, Rinehart and Winston.

Chernoff, H. and Lehmann, E.L. (1954). The use of maximum likelihood estimates in χ^2 tests for goodness of fit. *Ann. Math. Statist.* 25, 579–86.

Cohen, L. (1958). On mixed single sample experiments. *Ann. Math. Statist.*, **29**, 947–71.

Copas, J.B. (1969). Compound decisions and empirical Bayes (with discussion). *J.R. Statist. Soc.*, B, **31**, 397–425.

Cormack, R.M. (1968). The statistics of capture-recapture methods.

Oceanogr. Mar. Biol. Ann. Rev. **6**, 455–506.

Cox, D.R. (1961). Tests of separate families of hypotheses. *Proc. 4th Berkeley Symp.* **1**, 105–23.

Cox, D.R. (1962). Further results on tests of separate families of hypotheses. *J.R. Statist. Soc.*, B, **24**, 406–24.

Cox, D.R. (1964a). Some problems of statistical analysis connected with congestion (with discussion). In *Congestion Theory*, pp. 289–316, eds. Smith, W.L. and Wilkinson, W.E. Univ. of North Carolina Press.

Cox, D.R. (1964b). Some applications of exponential ordered scores. *J.R. Statist. Soc.*, B, **26**, 103–10.

Cox, D.R. (1968). Notes on some aspects of regression analysis. *J.R. Statist. Soc.* A, **131**, 265–79.

Cox, D.R. (1970). *The Analysis of Binary Data*. London, Methuen.

Cox, D.R. (1971). The choice between alternative ancillary statistics. *J.R. Statist. Soc.*, B, **33**, 251–5.

Cox, D.R. (1975). A note on partially Bayes inference and the linear model. *Biometrika* **62**, 651–4.

Cox, D.R. (1978). Some remarks on the role in statistics of graphical methods. *Appl. Statistics* to appear.

Cox D.R. and Lewis, P.A.W. (1966). *The Statistical Analysis of Series of Events*. London, Methuen.

Cramér, H. (1946). *Mathematical Methods of Statistics*. Princeton University Press.

Dar, S.N. (1962). On the comparison of the sensitivities of experiments. *J.R. Statist. Soc.*, B, 24, 447–53.

Darroch, J.N. (1971). A definition of independence for bounded-sum, non-negative, integer-valued variables. *Biometrika* **58**, 357–68.

Darroch, J.N. and Ratcliff, D. (1973). Tests of *F*-independence with reference to quasi-independence and Waite's fingerprint data. *Biometrika* **60**, 395–401.

Dawid, A.P. (1973). Posterior expectations for large observations. *Biometrika* **60**, 664–7.

Dawid, A.P., Stone, M. and Zidek, J. (1973). Marginalization paradoxes in Bayesian and structural inference (with discussion). *J.R. Statist. Soc.*, B, **35**, 189–233.

de Finetti, B. (1972). *Probability, Induction and Statistics*. London, Wiley.

Dickey, J.M. (1971). The weighted likelihood ratio, linear hypotheses on normal location parameters. *Ann. Math. Statist.* **42**, 204–23.

Durbin, J. (1960). Estimation of parameters in time-series regression models. *J.R. Statist. Soc.*, B, **22**, 139–53.

Durbin, J. (1973). *Distribution Theory for Tests based on the Sample Distribution Function*. Philadelphia, S.I.A.M.

Efron, B. (1971). Does an observed sequence of numbers follow a simple rule? (with discussion). *J. Amer. Statist. Assoc.* **66**, 552–68.

Efron, B. (1975). Defining the curvature of a statistical problem (with discussion). *Ann. Statist.* **3**, 1189–242.

Efron, B. and Hinkley, D.V. (1978). Assessing the accuracy of the maximum likelihood estimator: observed versus expected Fisher information. (To be published.)

Efron, B. and Morris, C. (1972). Limiting the risk of Bayes and empirical Bayes estimators-Part II: the empirical Bayes case. *J. Amer. Statist. Assoc.* **67**, 130–9.

Feller, W. (1968). *An Introduction to Probability Theory and its Applications*, Vol. **1**. 3rd edition. New York, Wiley.

Ferguson, T.S. (1961). On the rejection of outliers. *Proc. 4th Berkeley Symp.* **1**, 253–87.

Fisher, R.A. (1925). Theory of statistical estimation. *Proc. Camb. Phil. Soc.* **22**, 700–25.

Fisher, R.A. (1934). Two new properties of mathematical likelihood. *Proc. R. Soc.* A, **144**, 285–307.

Fraser, D.A.S. (1961). The fiducial method and invariance. *Biometrika* **48**, 261–80.

Fraser, D.A.S. (1968). *The Structure of Inference*. New York, Wiley.

Gaver, D.P. and Hoel, D.G. (1970). Comparison of certain small-sample Poisson probability estimates. *Technometrics* **12**, 835–50.

Girshick, M.A. and Savage, L.J. (1951). Bayes and minimax estimates for quadratic loss functions. *Proc. 2nd Berkeley Symp.*, 53–73.

Gnanadesikan, R. (1977). *Methods for Statistical Data Analysis of Multivariate Observations*. New York, Wiley.

Godambe, V.P. (1960). An optimum property of regular maximum likelihood estimation. *Ann. Math. Statist.* **31**, 1208–11.

Godambe, V.P. and Thompson, M.E. (1971). The specification of prior knowledge by classes of prior distributions in survey sampling estimation (with discussion). In *Foundations of Statistical Inference*, pp. 243–58, eds. Godambe, V.P. and Sprott, D.A. Toronto, Holt, Rinehart and Winston.

Goodman, L.A. (1953). Sequential sampling tagging for population size problems. *Ann. Math. Statist.* **24**, 56–69.

Goodman, L.A. (1968). The analysis of cross-classified data: independence, quasi-independence and interactions in contingency tables with or without missing entries. *J. Amer. Statist. Assoc.* **63**, 1091–131.

Grundy, P.M. and Healy, M.J.R. (1950). Restricted randomization and quasi-Latin squares. *J.R. Statist. Soc.* B, **12**, 286–91.

Grundy, P.M., Healy, M.J.R. and Rees, D.H. (1956). Economic choice of the amount of experimentation (with discussion). *J.R. Statist. Soc.*, B, **18**, 32–55.

Healy, M.J.R. (1968). Multivariate normal plotting. *Appl. Statistics* **17**, 157–61.

Hinkley, D.V. (1973). Two-sample tests with unordered pairs. *J.R. Statist. Soc.*, B, **35**, 337–46.

Hinkley, D.V. (1977). Conditional inference about a normal mean with known coefficient of variation. *Biometrika* **64**, 105–8.

Hoeffding, W. (1948). A class of statistics with asymptotically normal distribution. *Ann. Math. Statist.* **19**, 293–325.

Hoeffding, W. (1965). Asymptotically optimal tests for multinomial distributions (with discussion). *Ann. Math. Statist.* **36**, 369–408.

Hogg, R.V. (1956). On the distribution of the likelihood ratio. *Ann. Math. Statist.* **27**, 529–32.

Kalbfleisch, J.D. (1975). Sufficiency and conditionality. *Biometrika* **62**, 251–9.

Kempthorne, O. (1952). *The design and analysis of experiments.* New York, Wiley.

Kempthorne, O. (1966). Some aspects of experimental inference. *J. Amer. Statist. Assoc.* **61**, 11–34.

Kempthorne, O. and Doerfler, T.E. (1969). The behaviour of some significance tests under experimental randomization. *Biometrika* **56**, 231–48.

Kendall, M.G. (1962). *Rank Correlation Methods.* 3rd edition. London, Griffin.

Kendall, M.G. (1973). Entropy, probability and information. *Rev. Int. Inst. Statist.* **41**, 59–68.

Kendall, M.G. and Stuart, A. (1967–69). *Advanced Theory of Statistics,* Vols. 1–3, (3rd, 2nd and 2nd editions). London, Griffin.

Klotz, J. (1973). Statistical inference in Bernoulli trials with dependence. *Ann. Statist.* **1**, 373–9.

Koopman, B.O. (1936). On distribution admitting a sufficient statistic. *Trans. Amer. Math. Soc.* **39**, 399–409.

Kullback, S. (1968). *Information Theory and Statistics.* New York, Dover.

Lauritzen, S. (1974). Sufficiency prediction and extreme models. *Scand. J. Statist.* **1**, 128–34.

Lindley, D.V., East, D.A. and Hamilton, P.A. (1960). Tables for making inferences about the variance of a normal distribution. *Biometrika* **47**, 433–7.

Littell, R.C. and Folks, J.L. (1971). Asymptotic optimality of Fisher's method of combining independent tests. *J.Amer. Statist. Assoc.* **66**, 802–6.

Mandel, J. (1971). A new analysis of variance model for non-additive data. *Technometrics* **13**, 1–18.

Mardia, K.V. (1971). The effect of nonnormality on some multivariate tests and robustness to nonnormality in the linear model. *Biometrika* **58**, 105–21.

Mardia, K.V. (1972). *Statistics of Directional Data*. London, Academic Press.

Maritz, J.S. (1970). *Empirical Bayes Methods*. London, Methuen.

Martin-Löf, P. (1974). The notion of redundancy and its use as a qualitative measure of the discrepancy between a statistical hypothesis and a set of observed data. *Scand. J. Statist.* **1**, 3–18.

Mood, A.M. (1943). On the dependence of sampling inspection plans upon population distribution. *Ann. Math. Statist.* **14**, 415–25.

Nelder, J.A. and Wedderburn, R.W.M. (1972). Generalized linear models. *J.R. Statist. Soc.*, A, **135**, 370–84.

Neyman, J. (1952). *Lectures and Conferences on Mathematical Statistics*. 2nd edition. Washington, U.S. Dept. Agric. Grad. School.

Neyman, J. (1959). Optimal asymptotic tests of composite statistical hypotheses. In *Probability and statistics*, pp. 213–34, ed. Grenander, U. Stockholm, Almqvist and Wiksell.

Neyman, J. and Pearson, E.S. (1933). On the problem of the most efficient tests of statistical hypotheses. *Phil. Trans. R. Soc.*, A, **231**, 289–337.

Neyman, J. and Pearson, E.S. (1936). Contributions to the theory of testing statistical hypotheses. I. Unbiased critical regions of type A and type A_1. *Stat. Res. Mem.* **1**, 1–37.

Neyman, J. and Pearson, E.S. (1967). *Joint Statistical Papers*. Cambridge University Press.

Neyman, J. and Scott, E.L. (1948). Consistent estimates based on partially consistent observations. *Econometrica* **16**, 1–32.

Neyman, J. and Scott, E.L. (1960). Correction for bias introduced by a transformation of variables. *Ann. Math. Statist.* **31**, 643–61.

Pearson, E.S. and Hartley, H.O. (1970). *Biometrika Tables for Statisticians*. Vol. **1**, 3rd edition. Cambridge University Press.

Pearson, E.S. and Hartley, H.O. (1972). *Biometrika Tables for Statisticians*, Vol. **2**, Cambridge University Press.

Pearson, K. (1900). On the criterion that a given system of deviations from the probable in the case of a correlated system of variables is such that it can reasonably be supposed to have arisen from random sampling. *Phil. Mag. Series 5*, **50**, 157–75.

Pierce, D.A. (1973). On some difficulties in a frequency theory of inference. *Ann. Statist.* **1**, 241–50.

Pitman, E.J.G. (1936). Sufficient statistics and intrinsic accuracy. *Proc. Camb. Phil. Soc.* **32**, 567–79.

Quenouille, M.H. (1949). Approximate tests of correlation in time-series. *J.R. Statist. Soc.*, B, **11**, 68–84.

Quenouille, M.H. (1956). Notes on bias in estimation. *Biometrika* **43**, 353–60.

Raiffa, H. and Schlaifer, R. (1961). *Applied Statistical Decision Theory.* Boston, Harvard Business School.

Rao, C.R. (1961). Asymptotic efficiency and limiting information. *Proc. 4th Berkeley Symp.* **1**, 531–45.

Robbins, H. (1951). Asymptotically subminimax solutions of compound statistical decision problems. *Proc. 2nd Berkeley Symp.*, 131–148.

Royall, R.M. (1976). Likelihood functions in finite population sampling theory. *Biometrika* **63**, 605–14.

Scheffé, H. (1959). *The Analysis of Variance.* New York, Wiley.

Seber, G.A.F. (1973). *The Estimation of Animal Abundance and Related Parameters.* London, Griffin.

Shapiro, S.S. and Wilk, M.B. (1965). An analysis of variance test for normality (complete samples). *Biometrika* **52**, 591–611.

Shapiro, S.S., Wilk, M.B. and Chen, H.J. (1968). A comparative study of various tests for normality. *J. Amer. Statist. Assoc.* **63**, 1343–72.

Stein, C. (1945). A two-sample test for a linear hypothesis whose power is independent of the variance. *Ann. Math. Statist.* **16**, 243–58.

Stein, C. (1964). Inadmissibility of the usual estimator for the variance of a normal distribution with unknown mean. *Ann. Inst. Statist. Math.* **16**, 155–60.

Stone, M. (1969). The role of experimental randomization in Bayesian statistics: finite sampling and two Bayesians. *Biometrika* **56**, 681–3.

Stone, M. (1974). Cross-validatory choice and assessment of statistical predictions (with discussion). *J.R. Statist. Soc.*, B, **36**, 111–47.

Stone, M. (1977). Asymptotics for and against cross-validation. *Biometrika* **64**, 29–35.

Stone, M. and Dawid, A.P. (1972). UnBayesian implications of improper Bayes inference in routine statistical problems. *Biometrika* **59**, 369–75.

Stone, M. and Springer, B.G.F. (1965). A paradox involving quasi prior distributions. *Biometrika* **52**, 623–7.

Sukhatme, P.V. (1936). On the analysis of k samples from exponential populations with especial reference to the problem of random intervals. *Statist. Res. Mem.* **1**, 94–112.

Sverdrup, E. (1975). Tests without power. *Scand. J. Statist.* **2**, 158–60.

Tallis, G.M. (1969). Note on a calibration problem. *Biometrika* **56**, 505–8.

Uthoff, V.A. (1970). An optimum test property of two well-known statistics. *J. Amer. Statist. Assoc.* **65**, 1597–600.

Wald, A. (1947). *Sequential Analysis*. New York, Wiley.

Watson, G.S. (1958). On chi-squared goodness-of-fit tests for continuous distributions (with discussion). *J.R. Statist. Soc.*, B, **20**, 44–72.

Wetherill, G.B. (1975). *Sequential Methods in Statistics*. 2nd edition. London, Chapman and Hall.

White, L.V. (1973). An extension of the general equivalence theorem to nonlinear models. *Biometrika* **60**, 345–8.

Wilk, M.B., Gnanadesikan, R. and Freeny, A.E. (1963). Estimation of error variance from smallest ordered contrasts. *J. Amer. Statist. Assoc.* **58**, 152–60.

Williams, E.J. (1962). Exact fiducial limits in nonlinear estimation. *J.R. Statist. Soc.*, B, **24**, 125–39.

AUTHOR INDEX

References to *Theoretical Statistics* and to the books by Lehmann, Lindley, Rao and Silvey are not recorded here.

Abramowitz, M. 104, 176
Aitchison, J. 133, 168, 176
Andersen, E.B. 125, 176
Anderson, T.W. 24, 64, 139, 176
Andrews, D.F. 26, 176
Atiqullah, M. 113, 176
Atkinson, A.C. 135, 177

Bahadur, R.R. 10, 177
Barnard, G.A. 13, 41, 89, 114, 177
Bartlett, M.S. 6, 79, 122, 177
Basu, D. 16, 48, 177
Beyer, J.E. 147, 177
Billingsley, P. 7, 21, 58, 79, 177
Bishop, Y.M.M. 134, 141, 177
Box, G.E.P. 162, 177
Buehler, R.J. 91, 177

Chen, H.J. 26, 182
Chernoff, H. 140, 177
Cohen, L. 43, 178
Copas, J.B. 167, 178
Cormack, R.M. 12, 178
Cox, D.R. 7, 8, 26, 31, 48, 56, 58, 75, 135, 162, 163, 178
Cramér, H. 120, 178

Dar, S.N. 62, 178
Darroch, J.N. 141, 142, 178
Dawid, A.P. 154, 155, 178, 182
de Finetti, B. 156, 178
Dickey, J.M. 160, 178
Doerfler, T.E. 85, 180

Dunsmore, I.R. 168, 176
Durbin, J. 24, 101, 102, 179

East, D.A. 45, 181
Efron, B. 41, 47, 89, 129, 130, 172, 179

Feller, W. 33, 179
Ferguson, T.S. 60, 179
Fienberg, S.E. 134, 141, 177
Fisher, R.A. 10, 16, 129, 179
Folks, J.L. 34, 181
Fraser, D.A.S. 90, 179
Freeny, A.E. 27, 183

Gaver, D.P. 11, 179
Girshick, M.A. 170, 179
Gnanadesikan, R. 26, 27, 176, 179, 183
Godambe, V.P. 18, 100, 179
Goodman, L.A. 12, 24, 139, 141, 179
Grundy, P.M. 78, 175, 180

Hamilton, P.A. 45, 181
Hartley, H.O. 20, 28, 63, 181, 182
Healy, M.J.R. 26, 78, 175, 180
Hill, W.J. 162, 177
Hinkley, D.V. 42, 89, 144, 180
Hoeffding, W. 81, 180
Hoel, D.G. 111, 179
Hogg, R.V. 131, 180
Holland, P.W. 134, 141, 177

Kalbfleisch, J.D. 32, 180
Keiding, N. 147, 177

Kempthorne, O. 78, 85, 180
Kendall, M.G. 22, 28, 52, 73, 180
Klotz, J. 128, 180
Koopman, B.O. 13, 180
Kullback, S. 52, 180

Lauritzen, S. 10, 180
Lehmann, E.L. 140, 177
Lewis, P.A.W. 56, 178
Lindley, D.V. 45, 181
Littell, R.C. 34, 181

Mandel, J. 4, 181
Mardia, K.V. 20, 26, 181
Maritz, J.S. 167, 181
Martin-Löf, P. 22, 181
Mood, A.M. 152, 181
Morris, C. 172, 179

Nelder, J.A. 15, 181
Neyman, J. 33, 39, 107, 122, 136, 157, 181

Pearson, E.S. 20, 28, 39, 63, 181, 182
Pearson, K. 21, 182
Pierce, D.A. 88, 182
Pitman, E.J.G. 13, 182

Quenouille, M.H. 112, 182

Raiffa, H. 18, 182
Rao, C.R. 129, 130, 182
Ratcliff, D. 142, 178
Rees, D.H. 175, 180
Robbins, H. 167, 182

Royall, R.M. 18, 182

Savage, L.J. 170, 179
Scheffé, H. 4, 182
Schlaifer, R. 18, 182
Scott, E.L. 107, 122, 181
Seber, G.A.F. 12, 182
Shapiro, S.S. 26, 182
Silvey, S.D. 133, 176
Simonsen, W. 147, 177
Springer, B.G.F. 154, 183
Sprott, D.A. 89, 177
Stegun, I.A. 104, 176
Stein, C. 92, 172, 182
Stone, M. 110, 151, 154, 178, 182, 183
Stuart, A. 28, 180
Sukhatme, P.V. 27, 183
Sverdrup, E. 22, 183

Tallis, G.M. 116, 183
Thompson, M.E. 18, 179

Uthoff, V.A. 63, 183

Wald, A. 41, 183
Warner, J.L. 26, 176
Watson, G.S. 140, 183
Wedderburn, R.W.M. 15, 181
Wetherill, G.B. 41, 183
White, L.V. 50, 124, 183
Wilk, M.B. 26, 27, 182, 183
Williams, E.J. 93, 183

Zidek, J. 154, 178

SUBJECT INDEX

References to topics in a particular Problem are to the page on which the statement of the Problem begins. Readers of *Theoretical Statistics* may wish to consult corresponding entries in the index to that book.

Absolute test of significance 21
Acceptance sampling 151
Adequacy of fit, *see* Goodness of fit test
Admissibility, definition of 165
Analysis of variance 3, 7, 75, 120, 170, 172
  see also Linear model
Ancillary statistic 3, 9, 16, 35, 41, 47, 83, 86, 88, 162
Asymptotic normality, *see* Maximum likelihood estimate; Maximum likelihood ratio test; Order statistics; Rank test, linear; U statistic
Asymptotic relative efficiency, *see* Efficiency
Autoregressive process 4, 9, 101

Bayes's theorem 3, 148
Bayesian decision theory 156, 164–175
Bayesian inference
  general 3, 18, 90, 148–163
  hypothesis tests in 149, 158, 160
  ignorance in 149, 152
  interval estimation in 149, 156
  prediction in 157
  subjective degrees of belief in 155
  see also Bayesian decision theory; Empirical Bayes methods
Bernoulli trials 8, 28, 31, 54, 158
  see also Binary data; Binomial distribution

Bias, *see* Point estimate
Binary data 8, 20, 24, 31, 57, 93, 158
  see also Binomial distribution
Binomial distribution 14, 28, 31, 42, 57, 84, 85, 93, 151
  see also Bernoulli trials; Binary data; Negative binomial distribution
Bivariate distribution
  normal 72, 114, 124
  Poisson 135
Bonferroni bound 33
Brownian motion 78

Capture-recapture sampling 10
Cauchy distribution 88
Chi-squared statistic 21, 22, 25, 118, 138, 139
Choice between models, *see* Discrimination; Separate families
Closed under sampling, *see* Conjugate prior distribution
Coherency 90
Completeness 2, 54, 96
Components of variance 7, 61, 152
Conditional inference 3, 35, 47, 83, 86, 88
  see also Conditional likelihood
Conditional information 88
Conditional likelihood 118, 124
Conditionality principle, *see* Conditional inference
Confidence limit, interval and region

Bayesian 156, 157, 167
conditional 88
conservative 82
decision theory approach to 167
definitions of 82, 83
difficulties with 83
discrete data, with 82
fixed length (interval) 91
future observations, for 83, 93, 157
interpretation of 83, 89, 90
invariant 83
large samples, in 118
likelihood based (region) 83, 86, 97
nesting of 83
optimality of 82, 86, 156
pivotal quantity, from 107
point estimate, relation with 95, 97, 107
probability statement, as 89, 90
score, using 92
similar 83
vector parameter, for 83
Conjugate prior distribution 148
Consistent estimate
definition of 117
see also Maximum likelihood estimate
Contingency table 21, 133, 138, 141
Continuity correction 70, 84, 85
Correlation coefficient 63, 72, 105
Cost, *see* Utility
Covariance matrices, comparison of 65
Cramér-Rao lower bound 95, 96, 98, 99, 113, 124, 169
Cramér-von Mises statistic 23
Critical region, *see* Significance test
Cumulants 15, 24, 27, 44, 69, 118, 165

Decision theory 3, 39, 156, 164–175
Dependence
nonparametric measure of 72
see also Autoregressive process;
Binary data; Independence; Markov
process; Regression, linear
Design of experiments 49
Directions on a circle 20
Discrimination 158, 160, 166
see also Significance test
Distance test 23, 25, 68, 78

see also Chi-squared statistic; Distribution-free test; Separate families
Distribution-free test 67–81
see also Distance test; Permutation
test; Randomization test; Rank test
Double exponential distribution 120
Dynamic programming 165, 174

Edgeworth series 70, 97
Efficiency
point estimate, of 119
test, of 34
see also Maximum likelihood estimate
Efficient score
asymptotic sufficiency of 117, 129
definition and properties of 36
information, and 36, 50, 129
interval estimation, in 92
locally most powerful test statistic,
as 36, 45, 49, 59, 73
m.l. estimation, role in 117, 119, 124, 126, 129
point estimation, in 96, 102
transformation, under 36, 49, 50
vector 36, 50
see also Locally most powerful test;
Score test statistic
Empirical Bayes methods 120, 149, 162, 166, 170
Entropy 122
Estimate, *see* Point estimate; Interval
estimate
Estimating equation 99, 101, 117, 119, 120, 132
see also Likelihood equation
Estimator, *see* Point estimate
Exponential distribution 14, 27, 43, 58, 74, 102, 103
see also Double exponential
distribution; Poisson distribution
Exponential family 3, 13, 14, 15, 28, 35, 39, 54, 98, 124, 133, 134, 148
Exponential regression 49, 92

F-independence 141
Factorization theorem, *see* Sufficiency
Fiducial probability 89, 90
Finite population 10, 16, 69

see also Permutation test;
    Randomization test
Fisher information, *see* Information,
    Fisher
Fisher's exact test for 2×2 table 93
Fisher-Cornish series expansion 70, 97
Fixed width confidence interval 91
Future observations, *see* Prediction

Gamma distribution 14, 27, 59, 157
Gauss's theorem 113
Geometric distribution 28, 31, 54
Goodness of fit test
    chi-squared 21, 22, 25, 118, 133, 138,
        139
    Cramér-von Mises test 23
    distance, based on 23, 25
    graphical 25, 27, 30
    Kolmogorov 23, 78
    nuisance parameters, with 118, 133,
        138, 139, 146
    parametric models, of 2, 24, 25, 27, 30,
        44
see also special distributions
Graphical analysis 25, 27, 30
Group of transformations, *see* Invariance
    methods
Grouped data, *see* Chi-squared statistic

Highest posterior density region,
    definition of 156
Hypergeometric distribution 151
Hypothesis, *see* Significance test
Hypothesis test, *see* Bayesian inference;
    Significance test

Ignorance, *see* Bayesian inference
Improper prior distribution, *see* Bayesian
    inference, ignorance
Inadmissibility, definition of 165
Independence
    F-, definition of 141
    quasi-, definition of 141
    tests of 21, 79, 135, 138, 141
    see also Regression, linear
Index of dispersion 28
Information, Fisher
    asymptotic sufficiency and 118, 129

conditional 47, 88
Cramér-Rao lower bound, in 96, 98,
    99
definition of 36, 49, 102
dependent data, for 48
estimation of 117
loss of 118, 129
maximum likelihood, in 117, 129, 136,
    139, 146
transformation, after 36, 50, 102
Information theory, general 51, 122
Interval estimate, *see* Bayesian inference;
    Confidence limit, interval and region;
    Fiducial probability
Invariance methods 16, 54, 58, 59
Inverse estimation 114

Jackknife 96, 106–11
James-Stein estimate 170

Kendall's tau 72
Kolmogorov distance statistic 23, 78

Lagrange multiplier test 132
Large-sample theory
    see Maximum likelihood; Order
        statistics; Rank test, linear; Score
        test statistic; U statistic
Least squares estimate, *see* Linear
    model; Regression, linear
Level of significance, *see* Significance
    test
Likelihood
    approach 3
    asymptotic form for 117, 132, 160
    conditional 118
    definition of 2
    finite population, for 16, 149
    multimodal 88
    posterior 162
    principle 16, 31, 156
    see also Likelihood equation; Likeli-
        hood ratio; Maximum likelihood
Likelihood equation 117, 119, 120,
    126, 132, 142
    see also Estimating equation;
        Maximum likelihood estimate
Likelihood ratio

level of significance and 41
minimal sufficiency and 2
sequential test, in 39
see also Maximum likelihood ratio test,
    Neyman-Pearson lemma
Likelihood-based confidence region, *see*
    Confidence limit, interval and region
Linear model 3, 7, 8, 12, 14, 50, 54, 56,
    74, 75, 109, 112, 113, 120, 122, 134,
    136, 160, 170, 172
    see also Analysis of variance;
        Exponential family; Normal means;
        Regression, linear
Linear rank statistic, *see* Rank test,
    linear
Linear regression, *see* Regression,
    linear; Linear model
Locally most powerful test 36, 37, 45,
    68, 92
    see also Score test statistic
Location family 16, 68, 73, 84, 88, 149
    see also Scale family; and special
        distributions
Log normal distribution 27, 106
Logistic model 8, 57

Mann-Whitney test, *see* Wilcoxon test
Markov process 4, 6, 9, 10, 20, 24, 48,
    55, 57, 101, 110, 126, 138, 157
Matched pairs experiment 70, 174
Maximal invariant 54, 58, 59
Maximum likelihood estimate
    asymptotic efficiency of 124
    asymptotic normality of 117, 120, 146
    asymptotic sufficiency of 117, 129, 136
    asymptotic variance of 117
    Bayesian inference, and 150, 162, 170
    computation of 103, 128, 142
    conditional 124
    confidence intervals, in 97
    consistency of 117, 119
    definition of 117
    efficient alternatives 118, 126, 128, 129
    higher-order properties of 118, 129
    incidental parameters, with 118, 120
    information content of 118, 129, 139
    invariance of 119
    regularity conditions for 117, 119

see also Maximum likelihood test
Maximum likelihood ratio test
    asymptotic distribution of 118, 130,
        139
    boundary, on 142
    composite hypotheses, for 118, 132, 133
    conditional 118
    consistency of 118
    correction to 144
    definition of 54, 64, 118
    equivalent forms of 118, 132, 133, 136,
        138
    incidental parameters, with 118
    inefficient statistic, using 139
    nuisance parameters, with 118, 132,
        133, 141
    power of 119
    separate families, for 119, 134
    similar 119
    see also Likelihood ratio; Maximum
        likelihood test; Score test statistic
Maximum likelihood test 118, 132, 133,
    136, 144
    see also Maximum likelihood estimate;
        Maximum likelihood ratio test; Score
        test statistic
Median unbiased estimate 97
Minimax decision rule 164
Minimum chi-squared estimate 118, 129
Minimum mean squared error estimate,
    see Point estimate
Minimum variance unbiased estimate,
    see Point estimate
Multinomial distribution 21, 22, 47,
    129, 133, 139
    see also Binomial distribution;
        Contingency table
Multivariate analysis, *see* Multivariate
    analysis of variance; Multivariate
    normal distribution
Multivariate analysis of variance 63, 65
Multivariate normal distribution 7, 12,
    25, 63, 65, 136
    see also Bivariate distribution,
        normal; Multivariate analysis of
        variance

Natural parameter 3, 14, 15

Negative binomial distribution 14
Neyman structure, definition of 53
Neyman-Pearson lemma 35, 36, 37, 156
Non-linear regression, *see* Regression, non-linear
Nonparametric test, *see* Distribution-free test
Normal distribution 12, 24, 30, 44, 45, 49, 56, 62, 106
  see also Bivariate distribution, normal; Multivariate normal distribution; Normal mean; Normal mean and variance; Normal means; Normal variance
Normal mean 32, 41, 89, 91, 99, 120, 142, 144, 152, 154, 158, 162, 166, 167, 170
  see also Normal mean and variance; Normal means
Normal mean and variance 41, 89
Normal means
  several 168, 170
  two 174
  see also Analysis of variance; Linear model; Multivariate normal distribution; Normal mean
Normal-theory linear model, *see* Linear model
Normal variance 45, 56, 61, 65, 97, 104, 105, 108, 172
  see also Normal distribution
Notation 1

Odds ratio 8, 12, 57
Orbit 54
Order statistics 9, 16, 25, 27, 43, 74, 79, 86, 130, 168
Outliers 43

Parameters
  choice of 12, 55, 97, 158
  incidental 118, 120, 124
  nuisance 53
  transformation of 36, 108
Permutation test 67, 84
  see also Rank test, linear
Pitman efficiency 119

Point estimate
  Bayesian 154, 165, 169
  bias of 95, 96, 99
  bias reduction for 96, 104–111
  combination of 101, 120
  confidence interval and 95, 97
  consistency of 117, 119
  Cramér-Rao lower bound for 95, 96, 98, 99, 113, 124, 169
  cross-validation and 109
  decision theory, in 164, 165, 168, 169, 170, 172
  empirical Bayes 120
  estimating equation for 99, 101, 120
  invariant 95, 172
  jackknifed 96, 106, 107, 108
  mean squared error of 95, 170, 172
  median unbiased 97
  minimum mean squared error 96
  minimum variance unbiased 96, 98, 103, 106, 112, 113, 169
  m.l. 103
  Rao-Blackwell theorem for 96, 103
  robust 97
  sample splitting and 96, 106–9
  variance lower bound 95, 96, 98, 99
  see also Maximum likelihood estimate; and special distributions
Poisson distribution 28, 49, 55, 110, 128, 129, 135, 146, 157
  see also Exponential distribution
Poisson process
  see Exponential distribution; Poisson distribution
Posterior distribution, *see* Bayesian inference
Power of test 35
Prediction 9, 85, 93, 109, 114, 122, 157
  see also Inverse estimation
Predictive sufficiency 9
Prior distribution, *see* Bayesian decision theory; Bayesian inference
Probability statements about parameters
  non-Bayesian 89, 90
  see also Bayesian inference
Pseudo-values 96
Pure likelihood approach 3
Pure significance test, definition of 19

Quadratic forms, estimating variance, in 108, 112
Quadratically balanced design 112
Quantile 85
Quasi-independence 141
Queue, likelihood for 6

Random effects model 7, 61, 152
Randomization model 75, 149
Randomization test 67, 68, 70, 75
Randomized critical region 42
Randomized decision function 42
Rank correlation 21, 72
Rank test, linear 67, 73, 74
Rao-Blackwell theorem 68, 79, 96, 103
Rational degree of belief, *see* Bayesian inference
Rectangular distribution, *see* Uniform distribution
Regression, linear 3, 12, 136, 146, 172
   see also Linear model; Logistic model; Poisson distribution
Regression, non-linear 3, 49, 92, 128
Regret, definition of 164
Repeated sampling 3
Risk function, definition of 164
Robustness 97

Sample distribution function 23, 78
Sample size
   choice of 174
Sample splitting methods, *see* Jackknife
Sampling finite population 10, 16, 69
Sampling theory approach 3, 149
Scale family 16, 27
   see also Location family; and special distributions
Score test statistic 36, 45, 49, 59, 73, 118, 119, 132, 133, 134, 135, 144
Second-order large-sample properties, *see* Maximum likelihood; Score test statistic
Selection effect, significance test, in 33
Separate families 119, 134
Sequential decision problems 165, 174
Sequential estimation 91
Sequential likelihood ratio test 39
Sequential sampling 10, 31, 39, 41, 91, 174

Several normal means, *see* Normal means, several
Sharp hypothesis 158
Shrinking 109, 170, 172
Sign test 68, 97
Significance test
   absolute 21
   Bayesian analogues of 149, 158, 160
   combination of 19, 33, 34
   composite hypotheses for 19, 27, 53–66
   confidence limits, defining 82, 84
   critical region for 35
   difficulties with 19, 21, 42
   discrete problems, in 35, 41
   distribution-free 67–81
   invariant 19, 54, 58, 59, 61, 62, 63, 64
   large-sample 117–147
   level of 19
   likelihood ratio 41
   locally most powerful 36, 37, 49, 68
   Neyman structure for 53
   nonparametric 67–81
   nuisance parameters, with 53–66
   optimal 35
   permutation 67, 79, 84
   power of 35
   prediction, in 83, 93
   pure 19–34
   randomization 67, 70, 149
   randomized 42
   sequential 39
   similar 27, 28, 53, 119, 135
   simple hypotheses, for 19, 35–52
   simultaneous 33
   two-sided 35, 37
   unbiased 35, 37, 45
   uniformly most powerful 35, 53
Stein estimate 170, 172
Stochastic process 4, 6, 9, 10, 20, 24, 28, 55, 57, 78, 104, 110, 126, 138, 157
   see also Markov process
Stopping rule 10, 31, 39, 41, 91
Structural probability 90
Student's *t* test, *see* Normal mean
Subjective probability, *see* Bayesian inference
Sufficiency

asymptotic 117, 129, 136
Bayesian 18
complete 2
composite hypotheses and 53–66
definition of 2
estimation, use in 68, 79, 96, 103
factorization theorem 2, 13
interpretation of 2
invariance and 16
likelihood, relation to 2
linear 12
minimal 2, 3
predictive 9
principle 2
reduction by 3–12, 152

Tagging 10

Time series 4, 20, 101
Transformation
    parameters, of 36, 108
    variance, to stabilize 105
Transition count 20, 24, 48, 57, 138
Two-sample problem 67–70, 174

U statistic 79
Uniform distribution 9, 20, 62, 86, 107, 130
Union-intersection method 65
Utility 164

Weibull distribution 27
Weighted means problem 120
Wilcoxon test 67, 68, 69